B A S I C
SCHOOL LAW

BY
SHEILA DOW FORD, ESQ.
MICHAEL F. KAELBER, ESQ.
DONNA M. KAYE, ESQ.
KIM CHAPMAN-BELIN, ESQ.
and
CHRISTINA E. WEAVER, ESQ.

A PUBLICATION OF THE NEW JERSEY SCHOOL BOARDS ASSOCIATION
TRENTON, NEW JERSEY

ISBN 0-912337-10-9
New Jersey School Boards Association
School Board Library Series Volume 1
BASIC SCHOOL LAW
By: Dow Ford • Kaelber • Kaye • Chapman-Belin • Weaver
Foreword by: Dr. Robert E. Boose

Interior Design by: Christine Gadekar
Cover Design by: Adriana DiGiacomantonio

© 1992 New Jersey School Boards Association
P.O. Box 909, Trenton, New Jersey 08605-0909
Printed in the United States of America.

Library of Congress No. 92-080246

TABLE OF CONTENTS

1 THE LEGAL STRUCTURE OF NEW JERSEY PUBLIC EDUCATION   1

2 THE LEGAL STRUCTURE OF LOCAL SCHOOL DISTRICTS   19

3 THE LOCAL BOARD OF EDUCATION   26

4 THOROUGH AND EFFICIENT—SCHOOL FINANCE AND EDUCATION QUALITY   34

5 THE EDUCATIONAL ENVIRONMENT   47

FOREWORD

Since the 1984 revisions to the *Basic School Law* publication, many aspects of education law in New Jersey have undergone dramatic changes. This, the 1992 revised edition, details important information on the most significant of these changes.

It is an expanded publication with an emphasis on providing, in a concise and forthright fashion, analyses of the legal roles, responsibilities and relationships of the various public and private entities engaged in education. As such, it helps to clarify the sometimes confusing laws and regulations under which our public schools are governed.

As was the case with earlier editions, this updated and expanded *Basic School Law* will serve as an important resource tool in imparting the essentials on the myriad of laws and regulations which form the foundation for the structure of our public schools.

The NJSBA is hopeful that *Basic School Law* will become a much used and often cited document for all involved in public school education in New Jersey.

Robert E. Boose, Ed.D.
Executive Director
New Jersey School Boards Association

Trenton, New Jersey
January 1992

PREFACE TO THE FOURTH EDITION

It is with great pride that the Legal Department of the New Jersey School Boards Association presents the fourth edition of *Basic School Law*. Although in some respects this revised edition is similar to its predecessor, this volume builds upon the foundation laid by the previous edition in explaining clearly and concisely the major reforms in education since the last edition was published in 1984.

Most significant among these changes was the demise in 1990 of Chapter 212, *P.L.* 1975, the guaranteed tax base formula under which public schools were funded for 15 years. Concomitant with the repeal of Chapter 212 was the advent of The Quality Education Act of 1990, Chapter 52., *P.L.* 1990, ushering in the foundation aid school funding formula and its various amendments, under which public schools in New Jersey currently are funded. Significant reform also occurred in the area of special education. Chapter five, a large portion of which is devoted to special education, provides valuable information on the complex of both federal and state laws and regulations governing this area.

I acknowledge with sincere gratitude the diligent work of the Legal Department Attorneys, Michael F. Kaelber, Donna M. Kaye, Kim Chapman-Belin and Christina Weaver, whose steady, time-on-task approach to the drafting and revisions of the various chapters has resulted in an informative manuscript that is not only knowledgeable, but also readable.

Donna Kaye deserves special recognition for employing her unique blend of assertiveness and humor to bring focus to the goals and deadlines attendant to completion of this book.

I also wish to thank legal secretaries Cindy Stanhope and Barbara Deveney, as well as Judy Jeronis of the Word Processing Department. Together they spearheaded the typing of the manuscript with their nimble fingers, sharp eyes, and quick wit, all of which were in abundance as they worked their way through the project. Typographer Cynthia Miller and Graphics Associate Adriana DiGiacomantonio were also a tremendous help in expediting the publication of this document.

Sheila Dow Ford
Director, Legal Department

THE LEGAL STRUCTURE OF NEW JERSEY PUBLIC EDUCATION

1

"The powers not delegated to the United States by the Constitution...are reserved to the States respectively, or to the people."

— *Tenth Amendment, U.S. Constitution.*

THE FLOW OF AUTHORITY TO EDUCATE

The Source Provisions

By virtue of the tenth amendment to the United States Constitution, the authority to provide public education is reserved to the individual states. The people of New Jersey have specifically made education a concern of state government since 1875, and the language of that mandate has not changed since then:

The Legislature shall provide for the maintenance and support of a thorough and efficient system of free public schools for the instruction of all children in the State between the ages of five and eighteen years.[1]

This provision, however, does not prevent the Legislature from providing education to persons younger than five and older than 18 years of age.[2] The Supreme Court has said that the area within which the Legislature may act to advance the public welfare is vast, and the Legislature must have leeway in deciding whether to act, and if so, how far to go.[3]

On the other hand, the "thorough and efficient" provision of the state constitution does impose upon the Legislature an affirmative duty of providing a system of free schools for persons within the specified age group; the thorough and efficent system must afford "that educational opportunity which is needed in the contemporary setting to equip a child for

---

[1]N.J. Const. 1947, art. 8, sec. 4, par. 1. Same provision appears in N.J. Const. 1844, art. 4, sec. 7, par. 6, by amendment of 1875.

[2]*Trustees of Rutgers College v. Morgan*, 70 *N.J.L.* 460 (Sup. Ct. 1904), aff'd 71 *N.J.L.* 663 (E. & A. 1904) See also F. Op. Atty. Gen., July 22, 1949, No. 82.

[3]*West Morris Regional Bd. of Ed. v. Sills* 58 *N.J.* 464, 480 (1971).

his role as a citizen and as a competitor in the labor market."[4]

In addition to this specific school mandate, the New Jersey Constitution contains other provisions which define certain boundaries of the public education enterprise. These include, most notably, a section which provides that no person shall be segregated in the public schools because of religious principles, race, color, ancestry or national origin.[5] The constitution also guarantees that public employees shall have the right to organize and to present their grievances and proposals through representatives of their own choosing.[6]

Finally, the constitution specifically permits the Legislature to provide for the transportation of children within the ages of five and 18 years "to and from any school," so long as there are "reasonable limitations as to the distance to be prescribed."[7]

The Sharing of Authority

Under New Jersey's consititiuional form of government, it is clear that the authority and the power to educate are shared among several agencies. "Local control" has been taken to mean that the educational function of government is controlled exclusively at the local level. This notion of home rule is, however, an unwarranted myth. In fact, New Jersey's educational system is based on a concept of lay control, not local control, and the exercise of that power is shared among officials at all levels of government.

Local political subdivisions, including school districts, are not sovereign entities.[8] They may readily be bridged when necessary to vindicate federal or state constitutional rights and policies.[9] In fact, this alignment of power does not entail any general departure from the historic home rule principles and practices in New Jersey, but insures that constitutional mandates will be carried out.[10]

The New Jersey Constitution clearly and unequivocally places prime and absolute responsibility for education upon the state Legislature.[11] The Legislature may not delegate or abdicate to others its exclusive function to make the law, but it may delegate to governmental agencies or public officials the power and function to make subordinate rules, orders and

---

[4]*Robinson v. Cahill*, 62 *N.J.* 473, 515 (1973).

[5]N.J. Const. 1947, art. 1, par. 5.

[6]N.J. Const. 1947, art. 1, par. 19.

[7]N.J. Const. 1947, art. 8, sec. 4, par. 3.

[8]*Jenkins v. Morris Twp. School District*, 58 *N.J.* 483, 500 (1971).

[9]*Id.* at 500.

[10]*Id.* at 500.

[11]See *Robinson v. Cahill, supra*, 62 *N.J.* at 508-09.

findings of fact, within standards and policies prescribed legislatively.[12] It is through such delegation of authority that the Supreme Court has often approved the administrative handling of educational controversies.[13]

The power which the Legislature does delegate may be altered or withdrawn at almost any time. For example, the Legislature in New Jersey may alter the power of local school boards to abide by contracts they have previously entered, provided that any private parties involved assent to the change.[14]

Thus, the flow of educational authority in New Jersey is voluntarily delegated by the Legislature to local, county and state officials. In some areas of responsibility, the lawmakers have set mandatory standards by express statutory provision. In other areas, the Legislature has delegated such authority to state level officials. And, in still other areas, local boards are vested with broad discretion to set their own standards. Although some have been critical of the concentration of power in state level officials,[15] the touchstone of that structure is a concept of delegated and shared legislative authority.

The Doctrine of Implied Powers

As an assurance that governmental authority properly flows to those who are to exercise it, the state constitution confers on local governing bodies not only express powers, but also those powers which are necessary or can fairly be implied as incidental to those expressly conferred.[16] This is known as the doctrine of implied powers, and embodies a concept which has been applied by the courts to school districts as well.[17]

In applying the doctrine of implied powers to actions taken by school authorities, courts must resolve the conflict between the need to adhere strictly to what the Legislature articulates as law and the desire to allow school officials reasonable latitude in governing by inferring what the Legislature actually means. Thus, the courts have found that a board has implied authority to expend public funds for printing a booklet explaining

---

12*Pascucci v. Vagott*, 71 *N.J.* 40 (1976); *Burton v. Sills*, 53 *N.J.* 86 (1968), appeal dismissed 394 *U.S.* 812; *Veix v. Senace Bldg. and Loan Assn.*, 126 *N.J.L.* 314 (E. & A. 1941).

13*Abbott v. Burke*, 100 *N.J.* 269, 300 (1985).

14*Lenahan v. Bd. of Ed. of Lakeland Regional High School District*, 1972 *S.L.D.* 577; citing *City of Worcester v. Worcester R.R. Co.*, 196 *U.S.* 539 (1905) and *City of Trenton v. State of New Jersey*, 292 *U.S.* 182 (1923).

15Note, "Schools and School Districts—The Subtle Move Toward Total State Control," 2 Seton Hall L. Rev. 174 (1970).

16*N.J. Const.* 1947, art. 4, sec. 7, par. 11.

17*Resnick v. East Brunswick Twp. Bd. of Ed.*, 77 *N.J.* 88 (1978); *Bd. of Ed. of Union County Vocational School v. Finne*, 88 *N.J. Super.* 91, 106 (Law Div. 1965); *Merry v. Bd. of Ed. of Paterson*, 100 *N.J.L.* 273 (Sup. Ct. 1924).

school building projects,[18] as well as the authority to compensate teaching staff members for unused sick leave.[19] On the other hand, the Appellate Division of Superior Court has held that a county educational services commission lacks the implied authority to contract with a private firm to provide special education services to member boards.[20] Similarly, the state board of education has declined to find an implied authority in a local board of education to form a self-insurance fund for employee health benefits.[21]

The Legislature has itself utilized a form of the doctrine of implied powers. Under a special validating provision, the Legislature has assured that state, county and local education officials will have the power to implement the actions called for by the education laws. In this regard, whenever an education statute makes the action of an official dependent upon the approval of another official or body, the latter has the power to approve such action even though that power is not specifically set forth.[22]

In addition to the foregoing, each major type of educational organization in New Jersey is expressly given a broad grant of authority from which to imply further powers: the State Board of Higher Education,[23] the State Board of Education,[24] and local boards of education.[25]

STATE EDUCATIONAL INSTITUTIONS

Introduction

Under the state constitution, all the executive and administrative offices, departments and instrumentalities of state government must be allocated by law among not more than twenty principal departments of government, according to the major purposes they serve.[26] Until 1966, the entire education function was exercised by one department. At that time, however, the administration of the state educational enterprise had become so complex and specialized that these functions were divided into two separate areas, higher education and elementary-secondary education. Thus, the modern state educational structure takes up two of the 20 principal departments of state government.

---

[18]*Citizens to Protect Public Funds v. Parsippany-Troy Hills Bd. of Ed.*, 13 *N.J.* 172 (1953).

[19]*Maywood Ed. Assn. v. Maywood Bd. of Ed.*, 131 *N.J. Super.* 551 (Ch. Div. 1974).

[20]*NJEA v. Essex County Educational Services Commission*, unpublished, App. Div. Docket No. A-3986-80T2 (October 15, 1981).

[21]*Irvington Ed. Assn. v. Irvington Bd. of Ed.*, Unpublished Appellate Division decision, Docket No. A-4805-82T5, decided February 9, 1984.

[22]*N.J.S.A.* 18A:2-1.

[23]*N.J.S.A.* 18A:3-16.

[24]*N.J.S.A.* 18A:4-16.

[25]*N.J.S.A.* 18A:11-1.

[26]N.J. Const. 1947, art. 5, sec. 4, par. 1.

The Department of Higher Education

The public institutions of higher education in New Jersey include the six state colleges, the county colleges, the public junior colleges, the University of Medicine and Dentistry of New Jersey, industrial schools, New Jersey Institute of Technology (formerly Newark College of Engineering), Rutgers University and any other such institutions as authorized by law.[27] Jurisdiction over these institutions is vested in a Department of Higher Education, which consists of a board of higher education, a chancellor of higher education, and several bureaus and administrative divisions.[28] The department's general charge is to assist in the coordination of state and federal activities relating to higher education, to advise the governor on the affairs and problems of higher education, to stimulate new programs in higher education through public relations and technical assistance, to encourage cooperative programs by existing institutions, and to act as a clearinghouse for information in this field.[29]

The State Board of Higher Education is composed of the chairperson of the board of governors of Rutgers, the chairperson of the board of trustees of The New Jersey Institute of Technology, the chairperson of the New Jersey State College Governing Boards Association, the chairperson of the board of trustees of the College of Medicine & Dentistry of New Jersey, the chairperson of the council of county colleges, the president of the state board of education, a representative of the private colleges and universities of New Jersey who is designated by the Association of Independent Colleges and Universities with the approval of the governor, and nine citizens, all residents of the state, of whom at least two must be women.[30] The Chancellor of Higher Education and the state Commissioner of Education are *ex officio* members without vote.[31] The citizen members of the board are appointed by the governor with the advice and consent of the senate and are selected as far as practicable on the basis of their knowledge of, or experience in, problems of higher education, and without regard to their political beliefs or affiliations.[32] Their terms run for six years.[33]

It is the duty of the board of higher education to advance long-range planning for the system of higher education as a whole in this state, and to establish general policies for the governance of the separate institutions.[34] However, the State Board of Higher Education does not actually

---

[27]*N.J.S.A.* 18A:62-1.

[28]*N.J.S.A.* 18A:3-1; 1-1.

[29]*N.J.S.A.* 18A:3-3.

[30]*N.J.S.A.* 18A:3-6.

[31]*N.J.S.A.* 18A:3-6.

[32]*N.J.S.A.* 18A:3-8.

[33]*N.J.S.A.* 18A:3-8.

[34]*N.J.S.A.* 18A:3-13.

administer the individual institutions of higher education, which have reserved to themselves specifically the right to administer their programs.[35] The overall thrust of the State Board of Higher Education is to coordinate the activities of these individual institutions, and to maintain general financial oversight of the entire state system.[36] To this end, the Legislature has mandated that the board of higher education carry out a number of specific tasks, which include reviewing the development of a master plan, establishing admission standards and minimum course standards, reviewing budget requests, and setting other specific policies.[37]

The chancellor of higher education serves as the chief executive officer and administrator of the department and is charged with carrying out the policies and regulations promulgated by the State Board of Higher Education.[38]

The State Department of Education

The general supervision and control of public education in this state, except for higher education as defined in the preceding section, is vested in the State Department of Education, a principal department in the executive branch of state government.[39] The State Department of Education consists of the State Board of Education, the Commissioner of Education, and other bureaus and administrative divisions, including the division of the state library, archives and history, and the division of the state museum.[40]

The New Jersey Constitution requires that each principal department of government be headed by a single executive unless otherwise provided by law.[41] Unlike the department of higher education, of which the chancellor is specifically deemed the head of the department, the State Department of Education has as its head, under express provisions of law, the State Board of Education.[42]

The State Board of Education

The State Board of Education consists of the chairperson of the Board of Higher Education or his designee, who shall be a citizen member of the Board of Higher Education, and the Chancellor of Higher Education,

---

[35]*N.J.S.A.* 18A:3-13.

[36]*N.J.S.A.* 18A:3-13.

[37]*N.J.S.A.* 18A:3-14.

[38]*N.J.S.A.* 18A:3-20, 21.

[39]*N.J.S.A.* 18A:4-10, 4-1.

[40]*N.J.S.A.* 18A:4-1, 73-1 *et seq.*

[41]N.J. Const. 1947, art. 5, sec. 4, par. 2.

[42]*N.J.S.A.* 18A:4-1.

who is an *ex officio* member without vote, and 12 additional members who are citizens of the state, having resided here for not less than five years immediately preceding their appointment, not less than three of whom are women, and not more than one of whom is appointed from among the residents of any one county.[43] Members of the state board are appointed by the governor with the advice and consent of the senate for overlapping terms of six years, and they serve without compensation.[44]

The state board must meet publicly at least once each month at such time and in such places within the state as it may prescribe, and none of its meetings may commence later than 8:00 p.m.[45] The state board organizes at its first regular meeting following June 30 of each year by the election of a president and a vice president from its own members who serve for one year and until their respective successors are elected and qualified.[46] The Commissioner of Education serves as the secretary of the state board.[47]

The state board is required to formulate plans and make recommendations for the unified, continuous and efficient development of public education, other than higher education, of people of all ages within the state.[48] To accomplish this, the state board is given the power to make and enforce, and to alter and repeal rules for its own governance, and for implementing and carrying out the school laws of this state.[49]

The board's rule-making authority is subject to the provisions of the Administrative Procedure Act.[50] Before a rule is adopted, the state board must provide at least 30 days' notice of its intended action. Such notice must be published in the *New Jersey Register*, mailed to all persons who have made a timely request to the state board for advance notice of its rule-making proceedings, filed with the President of the Senate and Speaker of the General Assembly and publicized in such a manner that those persons most likely to be affected will be informed. There must be included with the proposed rule a statement setting forth a summary of the rule, an explanation of its purpose and effect, the specific legal authority for its adoption, a description of its projected socio-economic impact, and a regulatory flexibility analysis, or, a statement that such an analysis is not needed.[51] The state board must then provide a hearing at which interested persons may present their views on the proposed rule. In-

---

[43]*N.J.S.A.* 18A:4-3.

[44]*N.J.S.A.* 18A:4-4, 5, 6.

[45]*N.J.S.A.* 18A:4-7.

[46]*N.J.S.A.* 18A:4-8.

[47]*N.J.S.A.* 18A:4-9.

[48]*N.J.S.A.* 18A:4-10.

[49]*N.J.S.A.* 18A:4-15.

[50]*N.J.S.A.* 52:14B-1 *et seq.*

[51]*N.J.S.A.* 52:14B-4, 19.

terested persons must also be afforded an opportunity to submit data, views or arguments in writing to the state board. The only exceptions to the above-mentioned notice and hearing requirements occur when:

- The state board adopts rules prescribing its internal organization; or
- The state board, with the written concurrence of the governor, determines that an imminent peril to the public health, safety, or welfare requires immediate adoption of a rule.[52]

The state board is also given such incidental powers as may be needed to perform its duties.[53] The state board's presiding officer and each of its committees' presiding chairperson, has the power to administer oaths and to examine witnesses under oath in any part of the state regarding any matter pertaining to schools.[54] The state board has the power to compel by order the production at such times and places within the state as it designates, any and all books, papers and vouchers relating to the schools and the receipt or disbursement of school moneys.[55] It may also compel the attendance of any person in the employ of a board of education and suspend from office any person refusing to attend or to submit written material pursuant to an order of the state board.[56] In addition to the foregoing, the state board has complete subpoena power.[57]

Among its more express statutory mandates, the state board is required to prescribe a uniform system of bookkeeping for use in all school districts and to compel its maintenance and use.[58] Furthermore, the state board is required to report annually to the Legislature regarding all matters committed to its care.[59]

The Commissioner of Education

The Commissioner of Education is appointed by the governor, without regard to residence within or without the State of New Jersey, with the advice and consent of the senate. He serves at the pleasure of the governor during the governor's term of office and until his successor is appointed and qualified.[60] Any vacancy in the office of commissioner is filled for the

---

[52]N.J.S.A. 52:14B-4.

[53]N.J.S.A. 18A:4-16.

[54]N.J.S.A. 18A:4-17.

[55]N.J.S.A. 18A:4-18.

[56]N.J.S.A. 18A:4-18.

[57]N.J.S.A. 18A:4-19.

[58]N.J.S.A. 18A:4-14.

[59]N.J.S.A. 18A:4-20.

[60]N.J.S.A. 18A:4-21.

unexpired term, and his annual salary is fixed by law and paid as any other state salary.[61]

The commissioner is designated by law to be the chief executive and administrative officer of the department of education, having general charge and supervision of the work of the department.[62] He is the official agent of the state board for all purposes, and the budget request and approval officer of the department, with power to delegate the duties of these offices as may be required by law.[63] The commissioner is given the general supervision of all schools of the state which receive support or aid from state appropriations, excluding institutions of higher education.[64] He is required to enforce all rules prescribed by the state board.[65] By statute, the commissioner is granted the authority "to hear and determine...all controversies and disputes arising under the school laws..."[66]

The commissioner must, pursuant to rules and regulations of the state board, inquire into and ascertain the thoroughness and efficiency of operation of any of the schools and particular grades within such schools, of the public system of the state by such means as he deems proper.[67] He is further required to report to the state board the results of such inquiries and such other information with regard thereto as the state board may require or as he deems proper.[68] The statutes expressly say that the commissioner may, with the approval of the state board, prescribe minimum courses of study for the public schools and require boards of education to submit to him for approval or disapproval courses of study adopted by them, whenever he deems it advisable to do so.[69]

The commissioner may prepare, publish and distribute from time to time handbooks, materials and circulars for the guidance of teachers in the public schools. The commissioner is required to compile and publish for general distribution an annual report of comparative financial statistics of all school districts showing the capital and current costs, the cost of principal services, the amount of debt and other pertinent data for each school district.[70]

The commissioner, in consultation with the Commissioner of Health, must develop an inservice training program designed to enable public school teachers to recognize and respond to substance abuse by public

---

[61]*N.J.S.A.* 18A:4-21.

[62]*N.J.S.A.* 18A:4-22.

[63]*N.J.S.A.* 18A:4-22.

[64]*N.J.S.A.* 18A:4-23.

[65]*N.J.S.A.* 18A:4-23.

[66]*N.J.S.A.* 18A:4-24.

[67]*N.J.S.A.* 18A:6-9.

[68]*N.J.S.A.* 18A:4-24.

[69]*N.J.S.A.* 18A:4-25.

[70]*N.J.S.A.* 18A:4-28, 30.

school pupils. The commissioner also must establish guidelines for substance abuse education programs to be offered by boards to the parents or legal guardians of public school pupils.[71] Further, the commissioner must evaluate the effectiveness of the drug education program, and he may make grants to local school districts to assist in implementing substance abuse awareness programs aimed at elementary and secondary school students and at the general public.[72] In addition, he is required to develop and administer a program providing for the employment of substance awareness coordinators in certain school districts.[73]

The commissioner may appoint up to seven assistant commissioners, each of whom performs certain assigned duties such as:

- The supervision of curriculum and instruction;
- The supervision of vocational education;
- The hearing of controversies and disputes under the school laws;
- The supervision of business and financial matters; and
- The supervision of the Division of the State Library, Archives & History.[74]

Directors, inspectors, assistants, clerks and other employees may be appointed and assigned duties by the commissioner as he deems necessary to carry out the functions of the department.[75]

The commissioner is required to report to the state board once each month and annually at its December meeting on the operation and condition of the schools of the public school system and all educational institutions, other than institutions of higher education, which receive support or aid from state appropriations. His report must include appropriate statistical tables and such suggestions and recommendations for the improvement of the schools and the advancement of statewide public education as the commissioner deems expedient and of interest to the people of the state, especially those concerned with the operation of the public schools.[76]

The County Superintendent of Schools

In each county there is a county superintendent of schools, appointed by the commissioner with the approval of the state board, for a term of

---

[71]N.J.S.A. 18A:40A-16.

[72]N.J.S.A. 18A:40A-19, 20.

[73]N.J.S.A. 18A:40A-18.

[74]N.J.S.A. 18A:4-32, 34.

[75]N.J.S.A. 18A:4-35, 38.

[76]N.J.S.A. 18A:4-40.

three years.[77] The county superintendent must have been a resident of the state for at least three years immediately preceding his appointment, and must hold an appropriate certificate.[78] His salary is paid from state funds.[79] The commissioner may designate any one of his assistant commissioners or, with the approval of the state board, another suitable person to exercise the powers and perform the duties of the county superintendent during any period when the county superintendent is unable to perform his duties by reason of illness, physical disability, or for any other cause, and during any period when the office of the county superintendent is vacant by reason of death or resignation of the incumbent, or for any other cause.[80] The commissioner can withhold the payment of salary to any county superintendent who fails to perform faithfully all the duties imposed upon him by law.[81]

Each county superintendent is required to devote his entire time to the duties of his office, and he has the general supervision of all the public schools in the districts in his county, except those city school districts in which there has been appointed a full-time superintendent of schools.[82] The county superintendent maintains an office at a suitable location within the county which is open to the public as are other county offices, and which is supplied to him by the board of chosen freeholders of the county.[83] The school records of the county, maintained for the use of the county and state departments of education, the United States Office of Education and the United States Commissioner of Education, are kept in the county office.[84]

Each county superintendent is required to:

- Examine all the schools under his general supervision;
- Keep informed of the management, methods of instruction and discipline, course of study and textbooks in use, the condition of school libraries and of the real and personal property of the school districts with particular attention to the construction, heating, ventilation, and lighting of school buildings;
- Advise and counsel boards of education of local school districts under his general supervision on the performance of their duties;
- Report to the commissioner annually and as otherwise required; and

---

[77]N.J.S.A. 18A:7-1.

[78]N.J.S.A. 18A:7-1.

[79]N.J.S.A. 18A:7-3.

[80]N.J.S.A. 18A:7-2.

[81]N.J.S.A. 18A:7-4.

[82]N.J.S.A. 18A:7-5.

[83]N.J.S.A. 18A:7-6.

[84]N.J.S.A. 18A:7-6.

- Perform such other duties as are specifically prescribed by law.[85]

Helping teachers, whose duty it is to aid and direct teachers in the schools of the county, may be appointed by the commissioner whenever he deems advisable.[86] The helping teachers are part of the staff of the county superintendent, and work out of his office; their salaries are paid from state funds.[87]

A child study supervisor and the personnel for a child study team may be appointed by the commissioner whenever a survey of the handicapped children in a county indicates such a need. These employees serve under the direction and as part of the staff of the county superintendent, and their compensation is paid by the state.[88]

Education Coordinating Council

When the educational function of the state was divided into two separate departments, it became clear that a certain amount of mutual planning and cooperation was necessary. In response, the Legislature has established a New Jersey Education Coordinating Council. The council is an interdepartmental agency designed to facilitate the coordination of the educational policies and programs of the state in all fields of public education.[89] The council consists of six members: the president of the State Board of Education, the chairperson of the Board of Higher Education, the Commissioner of Education, the Chancellor of Higher Education, one citizen member of the State Board of Education and one citizen member of the Board of Higher Education, each of whom is selected by the state boards for terms of one year commencing July 1 and until the selection of their successors. Members of the council serve without compensation.[90] The council meets at the call of the governor with at least four regular meetings each year.[91] Its duties and responsibilities include reviewing and recommending programs and priorities to best meet the total educational needs of the state, reviewing the budgets of the departments of education and higher education and making fiscal recommendations to the State Board of Education and the Board of Higher Education.[92]

---

[85]*N.J.S.A.* 18A:7-8.

[86]*N.J.S.A.* 18A:4-36.

[87]*N.J.S.A.* 18A:4-36, 37.

[88]*N.J.S.A.* 18A:46-3, 4.

[89]*N.J.S.A.* 18A:5-1.

[90]*N.J.S.A.* 18A:5-2.

[91]*N.J.S.A.* 18A:5-3.

[92]*N.J.S.A.* 18A:5-4.

Interstate Compact for Education

The State of New Jersey has, by treaty duly enacted into law, entered into a compact with other states.[93] The compact has several purposes. Among its purposes is to provide a forum for the discussion, development, and recommendation of public policy alternatives in the field of education, and to provide a clearinghouse for information on matters relating to current educational problems at the state and national level.

As a vehicle to carry out these goals, the interstate compact has established the Education Commission of the States, whose task it is to develop the research data and proposals on educational problems, particularly in the area of adequate financing of education, and to arrange for such meetings or publications as may facilitate the dissemination of its work. New Jersey is represented on the Education Commission of the States by the governor, four citizens appointed by the governor, one state senator named by the president of the senate and one assemblyperson named by the speaker of the general assembly.[94]

New Jersey School Boards Association

In order to guarantee that local school boards have a voice at the state level, the Legislature has established an independent public corporation known as the New Jersey School Boards Association. All boards of education of the various school districts in the state are members of the association.[95] The association is empowered to investigate such subjects relating to education and its various branches as it may think proper, and to encourage and aid all movements for the improvement of the educational affairs of the state.[96] The powers of the state association to express its opinion and to intervene in public policy matters are broad.[97] The power of government of the state association resides in representatives selected from each local board of education, and the expenses of the association are paid for by dues which local boards assess of themselves.[98]

Local Educational Institutions

In addition to the institutions described in the foregoing sections, the Legislature has created a large number of local administrative units for

---

[93]*N.J.S.A.* 18A:75-1 *et seq.*

[94]*N.J.S.A.* 18A:75-11.

[95]*N.J.S.A.* 18A:6-45.

[96]*N.J.S.A.* 18A:6-47.

[97]See *N.J. State AFL-CIO v. State Federation of District Boards of Education*, 92 *N.J. Super.* 31 (Ch. Div. 1967).

[98]*N.J.S.A.* 18A:6-50.

various purposes, with a variety of formats for institutional governance, funding, and powers. These include local school districts, consolidated school districts, regional school districts, county vocational school districts and county special services school districts among others. An analysis of the general rules of law governing these districts, as well as a description of each of their legal structures, fills the subsequent chapters of this book.

Two institutions which are often overlooked in any account of local educational agencies are the county audio-visual aids center and the county educational services commissions.

The Legislature has authorized the boards of education of two or more school districts in any county to establish a county educational audio-visual aids center.[99] Such a center is governed by a commission consisting of three board of education members, three professional educators and a public librarian.[100] The commission is empowered to maintain and furnish educational audio-visual aids to the public schools of the participating school districts.[101] County audio-visual aids centers are funded by local participating school boards proportionately on the basis of pupil enrollment.[102]

The Legislature has also created the possibility for broader local cooperative enterprises by sanctioning the establishment of county educational services commissions. Any five or more local boards in any county or in any two or more counties may, with the approval of the commissioner, petition the State Board of Education to establish such a commission.[103] The commission, governed by a board of directors consisting of local board members and the county superintendent of schools, is a separate corporate entity with broad powers to hire personnel including certificated professionals, to apply for and receive private and public grants-in-aid,[104] to enter service contracts with member school districts for terms of up to 10 years,[105] and to expand its membership and its purposes.[106] However, it has been determined that an educational services commission does not have the authority to contract with a private firm to provide special educational services to local districts.[107]

The avowed legislative purpose of such commissions is to carry on programs of educational research and development and to provide public

---

99*N.J.S.A.* 18A:51-1.

100*N.J.S.A.* 18A:51-2.

101*N.J.S.A.* 18A:51-6.

102*N.J.S.A.* 18A:51-7.

103*N.J.S.A.* 18A:6-52.

104*N.J.S.A.* 18A:6-58, 59, 60, 65, 67.

105*N.J.S.A.* 18A:6-63.

106*N.J.S.A.* 18A:6-69, 70.

107*NJEA v. Essex County Educational Services Commission*, unpublished Appellate Division decision, Docket No. A-3986-80T2, decided October 15, 1981.

school districts such educational and administrative services as may be authorized by rules of the state board of education.

THE ADMINISTRATION OF THE SCHOOL LAWS

Any body of laws as complex as those which govern the public schools requires a system of review to insure their even application and effective implementation. The Legislature has responded with a system which places quasi-judicial power in local hands and favors in the first instance the local resolution of disputes. That system also provides for several levels of intermediate quasi-judicial administrative review before a dispute proceeds to the courts, thereby assuring a uniform application of the school laws statewide.

The Role of the Local Board

The local board of education is the prime enforcer of the school laws. Its obligation in this respect is unambiguous, arising under a legislative mandate that it enforce the rules of the state board and perform all acts consistent with law for the conduct, equipment and maintenance of the public schools.[108] Local boards have quasi-judicial powers. Any member of a local board may administer oaths to witnesses in any hearing in which the local board has jurisdiction.[109] The president of any local board of education may issue a subpoena at the request of any party to such a hearing, in order to compel the presence of witnesses or the production of documents.[110] The president or the board as a whole may apply to the courts for relief against recalcitrant witnesses.[111] Parties are guaranteed the right to be represented by counsel, to testify and produce witnesses on their behalf, and to cross-examine witnesses against them.[112]

Although the jurisdiction of local boards is not precisely listed and there may be some question as to the proper role of a local board in certain disputes,[113] the board itself will largely determine the extent of its jurisdiction, and in some cases, such as student expulsion, the exercise of quasi-judicial power is clearly called for.[114]

---

[108]*N.J.S.A.* 18A:11-1(b), (d).

[109]*N.J.S.A.* 18A:6-19.

[110]*N.J.S.A.* 18A:6-20.

[111]*N.J.S.A.* 18A:6-21 *et seq.*

[112]*N.J.S.A.* 18A:6-20.

[113]*Cf. Hoek v. Bd. of Ed. of Asbury Park*, 75 *N.J. Super.* 182 (App Div. 1962), application for rehearing denied 76 *N.J. Super.* 448 (App. Div. 1962); *In re Fulcomer*, 93 *N.J. Super.* 404 (App. Div. 1967).

[114]*N.J.S.A.* 18A:11-1(c), 6-26; *Tibbs v. Bd. of Ed. of Franklin Twp., Somerset County*, 114 *N.J. Super.* 287 (App. Div. 1971), aff'd 59 *N.J.* 506 (1971); *G.F. v. Washington Twp. Bd. of Ed.*, 1980 *S.L.D.* 20.

The local board's judgment on educational disputes is the first in time and largest by volume, as the vast majority of disputes are resolved locally. The Legislature has provided a series of subsequent steps which a dissatisfied party to a school law dispute may take as a matter of right.

Appeals to the Commissioner, the State Board and the Courts

The Commissioner of Education next has jurisdiction over controversies and disputes which are not resolved locally, and this jurisdiction covers all disputes arising under the school laws except those governing higher education.[115] It includes disputes concerning the rules of the commissioner and the state board of education.[116] With the exception of charges against tenured employees and school election disputes, proceedings before the commissioner are initiated by the filing of a petition setting forth the basis of the dispute and the relief requested.[117] In all instances, the actual hearing before the commissioner is conducted by an Administrative Law Judge (ALJ) assigned by the Office of Administrative Law. The ALJ makes findings of fact, conclusions of law and recommends a decision to the commissioner, who must adopt, reject or modify the initial decision within 45 days or the intitial decision becomes final.[118]

The commissioner's function in reviewing local decisions has been the subject of much litigation and conflict. The well-settled rule is that the commissioner can exercise his quasi-judical powers in three ways.[119] First, he may be called upon to determine whether a disputed local decision is improper as a matter of law. Second, he can decide whether the evidence available in a particular case is sufficient to sustain the factual conclusions which were reached locally, and if not, to find new conclusions of fact. Third, he will be required to determine, in those issues that entailed the use of local "discretion," whether that discretion was applied in an arbitrary, capricious or unreasonable manner. The comprehensive nature of the commissioner's quasi-judicial function has existed in our statutes since 1851, and has never been withdrawn or narrowed.[120] The commissioner himself has repeatedly been chastised for seeking to limit his own powers.[121]

---

[115]*N.J.S.A.* 18A:6-9.

[116]*Id.*.

[117]*N.J.A.C.* 6:24-1.1 *et seq.*, 5.1, 6.1.

[118]*N.J.S.A.* 52:14B-10.

[119]*Kopera v. West Orange Bd. of Ed.*, 60 *N.J. Super.*288 (App. Div. 1960); *Fanwood v. Rocco*, 59 *N.J. Super.* 306 (App. Div. 1960), aff'd 33 *N.J.* 404 (1960).

[120]*Bd. of Ed. of East Brunswick v. Twp. Council of East Brunswick*, 48 *N.J.* 94, 101 (1966).

[121]*In re Masiello*, 25 *N.J.* 590 (1958), where the Supreme Court said at 607: "Such self-imposed limitation does not appear to be proper upon a study of the broad statutory authority granted to him." See also *Jenkins, supra,* 58 *N.J.* at 503.

Nonetheless, controversy over the commissioner's use of these powers is likely to continue because the three functions outlined above differ vastly. The first two functions require the exercise of the commissioner's independent judgment in deciding questions of law and resolving questions of fact.[122] To some, this substitution of the state's judgment for local decision-making seems violative of the traditions of home rule, particularly when applied to budgetary decisions, even though the amount of money needed to maintain a "thorough and efficient" educational system is clearly a matter of state constitutional law rather than of purely local discretion. On the other hand, the third function, review for unreasonableness, entails a standard which is completely respectful of local decisions,[123] and is the only issue for the commissioner's review where the facts are not disputed and where there is no allegation that the local rule or decision violates some law.[124]

Any party aggrieved by any determination of the commissioner may appeal from his determination to the State Board of Education.[125] Such an appeal must be taken within 30 days after the decision appealed from is filed.[126] Rules of the state board set forth the procedures for perfecting an appeal.[127] Under law, a committee of the board may hear the appeal and report its conclusions to the full board, which decides the case by resolution at a public meeting.[128] Although theoretically the state board will not reverse the commissioner unless it is persuaded that he abused his discretion,[129] it is clear that the board has the authority to make a *de novo* review of the record and an independent decision when it chooses to do so.[130]

Finally, it must be noted that any party dissatisfied with the results of this extensive administrative review is guaranteed the opportunity to have at least one appellate court consider its claim. Appeals from decisions of the state board of education may be taken to the Appellate Division of Superior Court.[131] The Appellate Division sits in panels of two or

---

[122]*In re Masiello, supra,* 25 *N.J.* at 607.

[123]*Kopera, supra,* 60 *N.J. Super.* at 297; *Boult v. Bd. of Ed. of Passaic,* 39-49 *S.L.D.* 7, aff'd by State Board 39-49 *S.L.D.* 15, 135 *N.J.L.* 329 (Sup. Ct. 1947), 136 *N.J.L.* 521 (E. & A. 1948).

[124]See e.g., *Concerned Parents v. Bd. of Ed. of Howell Twp.,* 1972 *S.L.D.* 600.

[125]*N.J.S.A.* 18A:6-27.

[126]*N.J.S.A.* 18A:6-28; *N.J.A.C.* 6:2-1.1.

[127]*N.J.A.C.* 6:2-1.3.

[128]*N.J.A.C.* 18A:6-29.

[129]*Byers v. Bd. of Ed. of Bridgeton* 67 *S.L.D.* 341, 342.

[130]*Quinlan v. North Bergen Bd. of Ed.,* 73 *N.J. Super.* 40 (App Div 1962); *Pelletreau v. Bd. of Ed. of New Milford,* 67 *S.L.D.* 45; *Meyer v. Bd. of Ed. of Sayreville,* 70 *S.L.D.* 188, 192, decision on remand 1971 *S.L.D.* 140, rev'd by State Board 1972 *S.L.D.* 673.

[131]Rules Governing the Courts of the State of New Jersey, 2:2-3.

three judges each. It is at this level that the results are least predictable, as the nature of the issues to be considered largely determines the administrative decision-maker. "Our obeisance to that expertise and experience is not equally deep in all cases," one court has said. "It depends upon the issues of each case. If the case is one which he (i.e., the administrative agency) is plainly better equipped than we are to decide, because of his expertness, knowledge and experience, we naturally defer. In some cases that deference would be almost to the point of considering his judgment conclusive. On the other hand, where the issues are such that we can evaluate them as well as he, we do not defer to his expertness to the same degree."[132]

A party aggrieved by a decision of the Appellate Division has only a limited right of appeal to the New Jersey Supreme Court. In cases involving a substantial constitutional issue and in cases where there has been a dissent in the Appellate Division, the State Supreme Court must hear the appeal.[133] In other cases, a final judgment of the Appellate Division may be appealed only if the State Supreme Court grants "certification" of the action.[134] The Supreme Court will generally grant certification "only if the appeal presents a question of general public importance which has not been but should be settled by the Supreme Court or is similar to a question presented on another appeal to the Supreme Court, if the decision under review is in conflict with any other decision of the same or a higher court or calls for an exercise of the Supreme Court's supervision and in other matters if the interest of justice requires."[135]

Following any State Supreme Court action (including a denial of certification), there is an extremely limited right of appeal to the United States Supreme Court. Such appeals are limited to cases involving federal constitutional and federal statutory issues. Furthermore, the United States Supreme Court often has the discretion to refuse to hear such cases.[136]

---

[132]*Fanwood V. Rocco, Supra,* 59 *N.J. Super.* at 319; *Newark, v. Natural Resource Council, Dept of Environmental Protection,* 82 *N.J.* 530 (1980); *Biancardi v. Waldwick Bd. of Ed.,* 139 *N.J. Super,* 175 (App. Div. 1976).

[133]N.J. Const. art. 6, sec. 5, par. 1.

[134]*Id.*

[135]Rules Governing the Courts of the State of New Jersey, 2:12-4.

[136]28 *U.S.C.A.* section 1257.

2

THE LEGAL STRUCTURE OF LOCAL SCHOOL DISTRICTS

School districts in New Jersey are legally classified as Type I or Type II districts.[1] This system of classification provides a skeletal framework for school district organization, although it has been frequently criticized as being overly complex and inefficient.[2]

TYPE I SCHOOL DISTRICTS

Type I school districts include every district established in a city except where the district has changed its classification (see below).[3] As of October 1991, there were 23 Type I districts in the State.

In Type I districts, the board of education consists of five, seven or nine members[4] who are appointed to three year terms by the mayor or other chief executive officer of the municipality which constitutes the district.[5] If a vacancy occurs in the membership of the board, it is the duty of the board secretary to report it immediately to the mayor or other chief executive officer who then has 30 days in which to appoint a qualified person to fill the vacancy for the unexpired term.[6]

School appropriations in a Type I district are set by a board of school estimate.[7]

TYPE II SCHOOL DISTRICTS

Type II school districts include all districts established in municipalities

---

[1]N.J.S.A. 18A:9-1.

[2]See the Report of the State Committee to Study the Next Steps of Regionalization and Consolidation in the School Districts of New Jersey, April 1969.

[3]N.J.S.A. 18A:9-2. It should be noted that school districts in New Jersey have the same boundaries as cities, boroughs, villages, towns and townships, either singly or in combination.

[4]N.J.S.A. 18A:12-6.

[5]N.J.S.A. 18A:12-7.

[6]N.J.S.A. 18A:12-7.

[7]N.J.S.A. 18A:22-1.

other than cities and all regional school districts.[8] As of October 1991, there were 554 Type II districts, of which 68 were regional school districts. A Type II school district can have either an elected or appointed board of education.

Type II Elected Districts

In Type II districts having elected boards of education, the board consists of nine members, unless pursuant to law the number has been reduced to three, five or seven members.[9] Board members are elected at annual school elections for terms of three years.[10] Vacancies in board memberships are filled by the county superintendent, if the vacancy is caused by:

- The absence of candidates for election to the school board;
- Removal of a member because of a lack of qualifications;
- A failure to fill a vacancy within 65 days of its occurrence.

The county superintendent may also fill vacancies up to a number sufficient to make up a quorum if, by reason of vacancies, a quorum is lacking.

If, in the annual school election, two or more candidates qualified for board membership receive an equal number of votes, the vacancy is filled by a special election restricted to such candidates and held within 60 days of the annual school election. The special election is held only after a recount and certification of the annual election results by the commissioner. If, in this special election, two or more qualified candidates receive an equal number of votes, the vacancy is filled by the county superintendent.

If there is a failure to elect at the annual election due to improper election procedures, the vacancy is filled by a special election held within 60 days of the annual election and restricted to those persons who were candidates at the annual election.

If there is a failure to elect at the annual election due to improper campaign practices, the vacancy is filled by the commissioner. In all other cases vacancies are filled by the board itself.[11]

In Type II elected districts the board of education fixes and determines the amount of money in its budget,[12] and the budget is submitted for approval by the voters at the annual school election.[13]

---

[8]N.J.S.A. 18A:9-3.

[9]N.J.S.A. 18A:12-11.

[10]N.J.S.A. 18A:12-11.

[11]N.J.S.A. 18A:12-15.

[12]N.J.S.A. 18A:22-32.

[13]N.J.S.A. 18A:22-33.

Type II Appointed Districts

Any Type II district in a town having a population of more than 10,000 in which the members of the board of education were appointed by the mayor or other chief executive officer as of January 11, 1968, the date Title 18A became effective, continues to have an appointed board of education after that date, unless the voters in the district by referendum have determined that the members of the board of education shall be elected.[14] In Type II districts having appointed boards of education, board members are appointed by the mayor or other chief executive officer of the municipality for five year terms in the case of five member boards and three year terms for seven member and nine member boards.[15] Vacancies in the membership of the board must be reported immediately by the board secretary to the mayor or other chief executive officer of the municipality who then has 30 days to appoint a qualified person to fill the vacancy for the unexpired term.[16]

CHANGE OF CLASSIFICATION

School districts may change their classification from Type I to Type II or from Type II to Type I. The question of reclassification must be submitted to the voters of the district whenever the governing body of a municipality in a Type I district or the board of education in any district by resolution so directs, or whenever a petition, signed by the requisite number of voters, has been filed with the clerk of a municipality.[17]

Whenever such a resolution has been passed, or such a petition has been filed in a Type I district, the municipal clerk has the question submitted at the next municipal or general election held in the municipality following the expiration of 35 days from the date of adoption of the resolution or the filing of the petition.[18]

In a Type II district, the question is submitted to the voters at the next annual school election, which is held at least 15 days after the adoption of the resolution or the filing of the petition, unless the petition requests that the question be submitted at a special school election. If a request for a special school election is made, the board of education must call a special election to be held not more than 50 days after the filing of the petition.[19]

---

[14]*N.J.S.A.* 18A:12-16.

[15]*N.J.S.A.* 18A:12-9.

[16]*N.J.S.A.* 18A:12-7.

[17]*N.J.S.A.* 18A:9-4, 9-6.

[18]*N.J.S.A.* 18A:9-5.

[19]*N.J.S.A.* 18A:9-6.

If the voters of a Type I district decide that the district will become a Type II district, the district will immediately thereafter be governed by those laws relating to Type II districts. Board of education members at the time of the election can continue in office until the expiration of their respective terms, and the qualification in office of their respective successors.[20]

If the voters of a Type II district decide that the district will become a Type I district, the district will be governed by those laws relating to Type I districts after the following January 31, unless the district is one established in a city of the first class. In that case, the district will be governed as a Type I district after the following June 30.[21]

If the board of education of any district becoming a Type II district has less than nine members, it must be increased to nine at the next annual school election, or at a special school election in certain cases.[22] The terms of the additional members to be elected must be arranged by the members of the board holding over so that as soon as possible the term of each member of the board shall be three years, and the term of three members shall expire in each year.[23]

REGIONAL SCHOOL DISTRICTS

New Jersey allows two or more school districts to unite to provide educational services as a regional school district. Regional districts are governed by the same provisions as are Type II school districts unless otherwise provided by law.[24]

Regional school districts are of two types:

1. "All-purpose regional districts" organized to run all the schools of the municipalities included in the regional district; and

2. "Limited purpose regional districts" organized to provide and operate in the territory comprised within such districts of one or more of the following: elementary schools, junior high schools, high schools, vocational schools, special schools, health facilities or particular educational services or facilities.[25]

Regional school districts are under the supervision of the county superintendent of the county in which the constituent districts having the

---

[20]*N.J.S.A.* 18A:9-9.

[21]*N.J.S.A.* 18A:9-8.

[22]*N.J.S.A.* 18A:9-10.

[23]*N.J.S.A.* 18A:9-11.

[24]*N.J.S.A.* 18A:13-1.

[25]*N.J.S.A.* 18A:13-2.

greatest amount of ratables are situated.[26] The board of education of a regional district consists of nine members, unless there are more than nine constituent districts, in which case the number of members shall be one more than the number of districts.[27]

The apportionment of the members of a regional board having more than nine constituent districts, as well as the weight of their votes in all proceedings of the board, is determined by the appropriate county superintendent according to a complex apportionment formula, which attempts to assure as closely as possible that all the inhabitants of a regional district are equally represented. The current formula is a legislative response to a decision of the New Jersey Supreme Court holding the prior formula unconstitutional, based on a finding that it allowed a greater than 10 percent deviation from strict voter equality, thereby violating equal protection.[28]

If there are nine or fewer constituent districts, the members of the board of education are apportioned by the county superintendent among the districts according to the number of their inhabitants, except that each district must have at least one member.[29]

A portion of the current statute concerning apportionment in regional districts having nine or less constitutent districts, which excluded all military and civilian personnel stationed at or residing in a military installation from the calculation of the population of a constituent district, was ruled unconstitutional as denying equal protection of the laws.[30] Hence, military base inhabitants can no longer be excluded when determining the population of a constituent district.

Vacancies in board membership are filled from the constituent district in the same manner as vacancies in the membership districts are filled.[31] The first board of education of a newly created regional district is appointed by the county superintendent;[32] thereafter, board members are elected for three year terms at annual school elections.[33]

No regional school district may be created or enlarged unless the voters in each district in the existing or proposed regional district approve the regionalization at a special election.[34] However, the New Jersey Supreme Court has held that the Commissioner of Education has the power to cross

---

[26]*N.J.S.A.* 18A:13-4.

[27]*N.J.S.A.* 18A:13-8.

[28]*Franklin Twp. v. North Hunterdon Regional Bd. of Ed.*, 74 *N.J.* 345 (1977), *cert. den.* 435 *U.S.* 950 (1978).

[29]*N.J.S.A.* 18A:13-8.

[30]*Oceanport v. Hughes*, 186 *N.J. Super.* 109 (Ch. Div. 1982).

[31]*N.J.S.A.* 18A:13-11.

[32]*N.J.S.A.* 18A:13-37.

[33]*N.J.S.A.* 18A:13-10.

[34]*N.J.S.A.* 18A:13-34 *et seq.*

district lines for the purpose of effectuating a merger of school districts in order to avoid "segregation in fact," at least where there are no impracticalities, and where the concern is not with multiple communities but with a single community without visible or factually significant internal boundary separations.[35]

School appropriations in a regional district are fixed by the board of education and submitted to the voters at each annual school election.[36]

COUNTY VOCATIONAL SCHOOLS

New Jersey's education laws contain special provisions for the maintenance of vocational education at the county level. Vocational education means any education whose purpose is:

- To fit for profitable employment;
- To provide training which is supplemental to daily employment; or
- To fit for homemaking.[37]

A county vocational school may be established in one of three ways:

1. If the state board of education adopts a resolution that a need for a vocational school exists in a county and the board of chosen freeholders of that county by a majority vote favors the establishment of such school;[38]

2. If at least 15 percent of the registered voters of a county of fewer than 100,000 in population petition for a referendum on the question and the result of the referendum favors the establishment of a county vocational school;[39]

3. If the board of chosen freeholders in a second class county determines by a majority vote to establish a county vocational school.[40]

The board of education of the county vocational school system consists of five members, one of whom must be the county superintendent of schools. However, a county of the first class which has adopted provisions of government set forth in the Optional County Charter Law may establish a board of education consisting of seven persons appointed by

---

[35]*Jenkins v. Morris Twp. Bd. of Ed.*, 58 *N.J.* 483 (1971).

[36]*N.J.S.A.* 18A:13-17.

[37]*N.J.S.A.* 18A:54-1.

[38]*N.J.S.A.* 18A:54-12.

[39]*N.J.S.A.* 18A:54-13.

[40]*N.J.S.A.* 18A:54-14.

the county's chief elected executive officer. In all other counties, the four appointed members of the board are appointed by the chief elected executive officer of the county, or the director of the board of chosen freeholders, with the advice and consent of that board.[41]

School appropriations for county vocational schools are fixed and determined by a board of school estimate.[42]

COUNTY SPECIAL SERVICES DISTRICTS

The board of chosen freeholders of any county may establish a county special services school district for the education and treatment of handicapped children upon its findings that the need for such a special services school district exists.[43] If such a special district is established, first priority is given to courses of study not at the time available in any other school within the county, especially for those with unusually severe disabilities.[44] Once a special services school district has been established, all eligible pupils within the county must be accepted so far as the facilities permit. Children residing outside the county may be accepted if the facilities are available, but only after provision has been made for all eligible children within the county.[45]

The board of education for each county special services school district consists of a superintendent of schools, who serves as an *ex officio* member, and six other persons who are appointed by the director of the board of chosen freeholders with the advice and consent of that board.[46] Each board of education for a county special services school district shall organize annually by the election of a president and vice-president on any day, except a Sunday, during the first two weeks of July.[47] School appropriations in a special services district are fixed and determined by a specially appointed board of school estimate.[48]

---

[41]*N.J.S.A.* 18A:54-16.
[42]*N.J.S.A.* 18A:54-27, 28, 29.
[43]*N.J.S.A.* 18A:46-29.
[44]*N.J.S.A.* 18A:46-33.
[45]*N.J.S.A.* 18A:46-31.
[46]*N.J.S.A.* 18A:46-35.
[47]*N.J.S.A.* 18A:46-37.
[48]*N.J.S.A.* 18A:46-39, 40, 41.

THE LOCAL BOARD OF EDUCATION

3

AUTHORITY AND POWERS OF THE BOARD

The schools of each school district are governed through the supervision and control of a local board of education.[1] Because boards of education are created by statute to perform a state function at a local level, their powers are derived from the Legislature, and not from the people of the school district. Boards of education can perform only those acts for which express or implied authority exists in law or in the rules and regulations of the state board of education. (See Chapter I, The Legal Structure of N.J. Public Education, for amplification of these concepts.)

Every local board of education is required, as part of its mandatory powers and duties, to:

- Adopt an official seal;
- Enforce the rules of the state board of education;
- Make, amend and repeal rules for its own government, the transaction of business, the government and management of the public schools and public school property in the district, and for the employment, regulation of conduct and discharge of employees;
- Perform all acts and do all things, consistent with law and state board rules, necessary for the proper conduct, equipment and maintenance of the public schools.[2]

As legal entities, boards of education have been given by the Legislature the power to sue or be sued in the corporate name.[3] Where a suit is brought against an individual board member, the board may be responsible for the legal costs and other financial losses of the member.[4] (See Section B, Members of the Board).

As part of its permissive powers, a board of education may:

---

[1]*N.J.S.A.* 18A:10-1.

[2]*N.J.S.A.* 18A:11-1.

[3]*N.J.S.A.* 18A:11-2.

[4]*N.J.S.A.* 18A:12-20.

- Cause an exact census to be made annually of all of the school age children in the district and employ appropriate personnel for this purpose;[5]
- Accept and hold in trust real or personal property for the purpose of awarding scholarship grants for higher education in colleges, universities and graduate schools;[6]
- Join with one or more boards of education to establish a jointure commission to educate physically handicapped and mentally retarded children;[7]
- Join with one or more boards in any county to establish a "county educational audio-visual aids center";[8]
- Participate in the organization, operation and maintenance of a non-commercial, non-profit, educational television station, and contract for services, not to exceed for any one year more than $2.00 per pupil in resident enrollment;[9]
- Establish a nursery school or a nursery department in any school under its control, and admit to such nursery school or department any child who is under the age at which children are admitted to other schools or classes in the district;[10]
- establish and maintain a special school of instruction for the purpose of restraining, instructing, and caring for dependent and delinquent children under 16 years of age, committed to the school by any juvenile and domestic relations court or any court having jurisdiction over juvenile offenders;[11]
- Establish and maintain public evening schools for the instruction of persons over 16 years of age;[12]
- Establish and maintain a public evening school or evening schools for the instruction of foreign born residents of the district over 14 years of age, in the English language and in the form of government and the laws of New Jersey and of the United States;[13]

---

[5]*N.J.S.A.* 18A:11-2.
[6]*N.J.S.A.* 18A:71-27.
[7]*N.J.S.A.* 18A:46-25.
[8]*N.J.S.A.* 18A:51-1.
[9]*N.J.S.A.* 18A:51-13.
[10]*N.J.S.A.* 18A:44-1.
[11]*N.J.S.A.* 18A:47-1.
[12]*N.J.S.A.* 18A:48-1.
[13]*N.J.S.A.* 18A:49-1.

- Maintain a program of adult education and utilize buildings, equipment and other school facilities of the district for such purpose;[14]
- If located in a municipality containing a population of over 10,000 provide for the employment of lecturers on the natural sciences and kindred subjects in the public schools in any such municipality, in the evenings, for the benefit of working men and working women;[15]
- Provide by contract and appropriate funds for the support and maintenance of existing museum facilities and services for the educational or recreational use and benefit of pupils in the public schools;[16]
- Establish and maintain vocational schools;[17]
- Enter into contracts for vocational education courses with a state approved private vocational school when such courses cannot be provided by public vocational schools or other school districts or when the private vocational school can provide substantially equivalent training at a lesser cost. Boards must secure the written approval of the commissioner prior to execution of such contracts.[18]

Certain acts of a board of education require a majority vote of all members of the board. Before taking action on a particular matter, the specific section of the laws dealing therewith should be consulted to determine whether a majority vote of all the members is required. The following actions require a majority vote of the full membership of the board:

- Appointing a teaching staff member;[19]
- Transferring a teaching staff member;[20]
- Adopting or altering a course of study;[21]
- Selecting textbooks;[22]
- Withholding a prescribed employment or adjustment increment;[23]

---

[14]*N.J.S.A.* 18A:50-1.

[15]*N.J.S.A.* 18A:52-1.

[16]*N.J.S.A.* 18A:53-1.

[17]*N.J.S.A.* 18A:54-5.

[18]*N.J.S.A.* 18A:54-10.1 *et seq.*

[19]*N.J.S.A.* 18A:27-1.

[20]*N.J.S.A.* 18A:25-1.

[21]*N.J.S.A.* 18A:33-1.

[22]*N.J.S.A.* 18A:34-1.

[23]*N.J.S.A.* 18A:29-14.

- Determining the sufficiency of charges to dismiss or reduce the salary of a tenured employee;[24]
- Admitting pupils, who have never attended public or private school, after October 1 following the opening of school for the fall term;[25]
- Appointing and fixing the term of a superintendent of schools;[26]
- Appointing or removing an assistant superintendent of schools;[27]
- Appointing and fixing the term and salary of a board secretary;[29]
- Appointing and fixing the term and salary of an assistant board secretary;[29]
- Appointing, fixing the salary and defining the duties of a school business administrator;[30]
- Appointing or removing and fixing the salary of a business manager in a Type I school district;[31]
- Appointing an executive superintendent in districts in cities of the first class with a population over 325,000;[32]
- Restoring or removing an assistant superintendent, principal or teaching staff member, following suspension by the superintendent of schools;[33]
- Removing from office a president or vice president of a board for failure to perform a duty imposed upon him by law;[34]
- Directing the board secretary to make deductions for United States government bonds from salaries of participating employees;[35]
- Deciding to use voting machines in annual and special school elections in districts where they are used in general or municipal elections;[36]

---

[24]N.J.S.A. 18A:6-11.

[25]N.J.S.A. 18A:38-6.

[26]N.J.S.A. 18A:17-15.

[27]N.J.S.A. 18A:17-16.

[28]N.J.S.A. 18A:17-5.

[29]N.J.S.A. 18A:17-13.

[30]N.J.S.A. 18A:17-14.1.

[31]N.J.S.A. 18A:17-25.

[32]N.J.S.A. 18A:17A-1.

[33]N.J.S.A. 18A:25-6.

[34]N.J.S.A. 18A:15-2.

[35]N.J.S.A. 18A:16-8.

[36]N.J.S.A. 18A:14-39.

- Exchanging lands owned by the board;[37]
- Disposing of land owned by the board, or the rights or interests therein;[38]
- Deciding to establish, with other school districts of the county, a county educational audio-visual aids center;[39]
- Applying for membership in an already established county educational audio-visual aids center;[40]
- Applying to the county superintendent to investigate the advisability of withdrawing from a regional district;[41]
- Fixing and determining the amount of money in the budget to be submitted to the voters in a Type II district;[42]
- Approving capital projects for submission to voters in a Type II district;[44]
- Authorizing the issuance of school bonds in a Type II district.[44]

In rare instances an action of the board will require an affirmative vote of more than a majority of the full membership. Examples are:

- Awarding a contract without bidding after having twice advertised but receiving no bids or unreasonably high bids which the board rejected based on prior cost estimates—requires a two-thirds vote;[45]
- Adopting a refunding ordinance—requires a two-thirds vote;[46]
- Calling an emergency meeting of the board without providing adequate prior notice—requires a three-fourths vote.[47]

MEMBERS OF THE BOARD

Board of education members must be citizens and residents of their school districts, and must have been such for at least two years immediate-

[37]N.J.S.A. 18A:20-8.

[38]N.J.S.A. 18A:20-5.

[39]N.J.S.A. 18A:51-1.

[40]N.J.S.A. 18A:51-11.

[41]N.J.A.C. 6:3-3.1.

[42]N.J.S.A. 18A:22-28, 32.

[43]N.J.S.A. 18A:22-39.

[44]N.J.S.A. 18A:24-10.

[45]N.J.S.A. 18A:18A-5.

[46]N.J.S.A. 18A:24-61.4.

[47]N.J.S.A. 10:4-9.

ly preceding their appointment or election to the board. Board members must be able to read and write.[48]

Board members are forbidden by law to receive any compensation for their services on the board,[49] and they are further prohibited from having any direct or indirect interest in any contract with or claim against the board.[50] A board member cannot be appointed to a paid position in the district, during the term for which he is elected or appointed, unless he shall resign or cease to be a member six months prior to his appointment, except where appointment to a paid position is specifically authorized by statute.[51]

Whenever a board member ceases to be a resident of the district, or becomes mayor or member of the governing body of a municipality (or the member of the governing body of a county in the case of a county vocational or special services district), his membership on the board immediately ceases.[52]

Provision is also made for removal by the board, if it so chooses, of any board member who fails to attend three consecutive meetings of the board without good cause.[53]

Whenever a civil action is brought against a board member for an act or omission arising out of the performance of his official duties, the board of education must pay for the board member's reasonable legal expenses and must protect the board member from any resulting financial loss. The board must also pay reasonable legal fees and other financial losses of a member in a like criminal action if the disposition of the case is favorable to the board member. The board may arrange for and maintain appropriate insurance to cover all such damages, losses and expenses.[54]

A board of education member may be appointed secretary to the board, but he must serve without compensation while holding both positions.[55] In a regional or consolidated school district a board member may be appointed as treasurer or custodian of school moneys and receive compensation.[56]

For further information on the composition of boards of education refer to Chapter II, The Legal Structure of Local School Districts.

---

[48]*N.J.S.A.* 18A:12-1.

[49]*N.J.S.A.* 18A:12-4.

[50]*N.J.S.A.* 18A:12-2.

[51]*N.J.S.A.* 18A:12-1.1.

[52]*N.J.S.A.* 18A:12-3.

[53]*N.J.S.A.* 18A:12-3.

[54]*N.J.S.A.* 18A:12-20.

[55]*N.J.S.A.* 18A:17-5.

[56]*N.J.S.A.* 18A:13-14; 8-33.

MEETINGS OF THE BOARD

The board of education performs its functions at regular or special meetings. Under the Sunshine Law, all meetings of boards of education must be held in public, with certain exceptions. The public must also be given advance notice of meetings. (See Chapter IX, on the Sunshine Law).

In addition, board meetings must comply with a number of other statutory requirements. Each board of education must organize annually at a regular meeting held not later than 8:00 p.m.:

- In Type I districts on March 16, or on the following day if that day is Sunday;
- In Type II districts on any day of the first or second week following the annual school election;
- If the organization meeting cannot take place on the specified day, it must be held within three days thereafter.[57]

The organization meeting constitutes a regular meeting of the board of education for the transaction of business.[58] The board must elect a president and a vice president at the organization meeting. If such officers are not elected, the county superintendent appoints them.[59]

It is the duty of the secretary of the board to give notice of the organization meeting and of all other regular or special meetings of the board.[60]

Every board of education must meet to transact business at least once every two months during the period in which the schools are in session. All board meetings must commence no later than 8:00 p.m. If at that time a quorum is not present, the meeting may be recessed until a quorum is present, but not later than 9:00 p.m. If no quorum appears, the meeting may be adjourned until another day not more than seven days thereafter. Public announcement must be made of the time and date to which the meeting is adjourned. No further recess or adjournment is permissible.[61]

Special meetings of the board are called by the secretary of the board whenever the president of the board so directs, or whenever a majority of the whole membership of the board requests a calling of such a special meeting.[62]

It is the duty of the secretary of the board to record the minutes of all proceedings of the board.[63] Minutes of board meetings are public records

---

[57]*N.J.S.A.* 18A:10-3.

[58]*N.J.S.A.* 18A:10-5.

[59]*N.J.S.A.* 18A:15-1.

[60]*N.J.S.A.* 18A:10-4; 17-7.

[61]*N.J.S.A.* 18A:10-6.

[62]*N.J.A.C.* 6:3-1.9.

[63]*N.J.S.A.* 18A:17-7; *N.J.S.A.* 10:4-14.

which must be open to inspection at reasonable times and places by the public.[64] (See Chapter IX on the Sunshine Law and Right to Know Law).

Every board may make its own rules for the conduct of its meetings, as long as its rules are consistent with state law. Most actions of a board require a simple majority of those voting, but certain actions require a majority vote of the full membership of the board. (See Section A above.)

The commissioner has held that when a majority vote of the full membership is not required, an abstention is counted as an affirmative vote unless the member abstaining expressly dissents from taking affirmative action prior to the vote.[65] This ruling applies to those cases in which a local board has not previously adopted its own rule to govern the counting of an abstention. It would seem that where a local board adopts its own reasonable rules on abstentions, such local parliamentary rules would be upheld.

---

[64]*N.J.S.A.* 47:1A-2; *N.J.S.A.* 10:4-14.

[65]*King v. Bd. of Ed. of Asbury Park*, 39-49 *S.L.D.* 20; *Farmer v. Bd. of Ed. of Camden*, 1967 *S.L.D.* 287.

THOROUGH AND EFFICIENT —SCHOOL FINANCE AND EDUCATION QUALITY

4

ROBINSON V. CAHILL

In 1970, suit was brought in the Superior Court by a number of residents, taxpayers and officials of several municipalities challenging the constitutionality of New Jersey's system of financing public schools. The plaintiffs charged that the system was unconstitutional in that it relied too heavily on local property taxes and thus resulted in a great disparity in the quality of education offered in various districts. The plaintiffs argued, in part, that the financing method violated the specific directive of the New Jersey Constitution that:

> *The Legislature shall provide for the maintenance and support of a thorough and efficient system of free public schools for the instruction of all the children in the state between the ages of five and eighteen years.*[1]

On appeal, the New Jersey Supreme Court interpreted this "thorough and efficient" clause as a mandate that the state provide an equal educational opportunity for all children and the Court held that the system of school finance was not sufficiently geared to that mandate. The Court agreed that the heavy reliance on local property taxes produced a direct relationship between a community's wealth and the amount of funds available for public education in a district. The Court also accepted the view that the quality of educational opportunity depends in substantial measure upon the number of dollars expended, notwithstanding that a multitude of other factors, including teacher availability, individual and group disadvantages and curriculum decisions, play a vital role in the educational result.[2]

The Court noted that the state had never spelled out the content of educational opportunity which constitutes a "thorough and efficient" education and stated:

---

[1]N.J. Const. 1947, art. 8, sec. 4, par. 1.

[2]*Robinson v. Cahill*, 62 *N.J.* 473, 481, 515-16 (1973), *cert.* den. 414 *U.S.* 976 (1973); 69 *N.J.* 131, 141, n. 3 (1975).

Without some such prescription, it is even more difficult to understand how the tax burden can be left to local initiative with any hope that statewide equality of educational opportunity will emerge.[3]

The decision made clear that the state was not prohibited from delegating its fiscal responsibility for education to the local level.[4] However, the ultimate responsibility for meeting the constitutional requirement rests with the state itself and, if the state chooses to delegate some portion of its obligation, it must do so in a manner that will insure equality of educational opportunity.[5]

To at least a limited extent, the statutory financing system struck down in *Robinson v. Cahill* did attempt to set a minimum level of funding per pupil and to distribute state aid so as to compensate for differences of wealth among districts.[6] However, the Court noted that 67 percent of operating expenses were being met by local taxes, a situation inevitably resulting in gross disparities in per pupil expenditures among districts, and that the system as a whole did not adequately guarantee that the combination of local effort and state aid would yield a "thorough and efficient" education for all pupils in New Jersey's public schools.[7]

The Legislature's response to the *Robinson v. Cahill* decision was the Public School Education Act of 1975.[8] In enacting this statute, the Legislature declared its intention to fulfill the constitutional mandate by:

- Defining the overall goal of a thorough and efficient system of free public schools;
- Establishing guidelines and monitoring procedures to insure progress toward thorough and efficient educational goals; and
- Establishing a funding structure to insure adequate financial resources to implement a thorough and efficient public school system.[9]

In January, 1976 the New Jersey Supreme Court held that the act was constitutional on its face and had met the "T & E" mandate, assuming that full funding of the financial aid provisions would be forthcoming from the Legislature.[10] By enacting the Public School Education Act, the Legislature had acted to officially accept its constitutional responsibility for public education. However, the Legislature repeatedly was unable to

---

[3]*Robinson*, 62 *N.J.* at 516.

[4]*Id.* at 502-13.

[5]*Id.* at 509, 513.

[6]*N.J.S.A.* 18A:58-1 *et seq.* Repealed by L. 1975, c. 212 (eff. 7/1/75).

[7]*Robinson, supra,* 62 *N.J.* at 480, 515-19.

[8]*N.J.S.A.* 18A:7A-1 *et seq.*

[9]*N.J.S.A.* 18A:7A-2.

[10]*Robinson,* 69 *N.J.* 449 (1976).

agree upon a state taxation method to fund its financial obligations under the act.

Consequently, in May, 1976 the New Jersey Supreme Court enjoined the expenditure of funds for public schools, effective July 1, 1976, unless timely legislative action was taken to fund the act.[11] In an effort to avoid a very real crisis in New Jersey's public schools, the Legislature acted in July to adopt a tax package which included the New Jersey Gross Income Tax Act to meet the state's financial responsibility for "T & E" funding.[12] The Supreme Court dissolved the injunction against expenditure of funds, and further crisis was avoided.[13]

THE "T & E LAW"

The Public School Education Act of 1975 impacted upon local school districts in two major areas:

1. Local and state financial support of schools; and

2. Local and state planning and implementation of a thorough and efficient education.

The Legislature declared in the "T & E Law" that the goal of a thorough and efficient system of free public schools shall be to provide all children in New Jersey, regardless of socioeconomic status or geographic location, the educational opportunity which will prepare them to function politically, economically and socially in a democratic society.[14]

Under the "T & E Law" funding for public schools was a responsibility shared jointly by the state and local school districts. Because local districts were compelled to rely on local property taxes to meet their share of the obligation, the law provided for two types of state aid which attempted to equalize, to some extent, the resources available for education regardless of the amount of taxable property within a community: current expense equalization aid and capital outlay and debt service equalization aid.[15]

Both types of aid were computed under complex formulas set out by statute which, in general, provided for greater state aid to those districts which had less property wealth available for local taxation. The formula also provided for greater state aid to those districts which had a higher expenditure level per pupil, up to a state support limit. Funds spent by

---

[11]*Robinson, 70 N.J.* 155 (1976).

[12]*N.J.S.A.* 54A:1-1 *et seq.*

[13]*Robinson, 70 N.J.* 465 (1976).

[14]*N.J.S.A.* 18A:7A-4.

[15]*N.J.S.A.* 18A:7A-18; *N.J.S.A.* 18A:7A-19.

a district beyond the state support limit did not trigger any corresponding increase in state aid. The formula also contained a provision which guaranteed a minimum level of current expense equalization aid for districts with greater property wealth available for taxation. However, there was no minimum aid provision for capital outlay and debt service equalization aid.

The statute also provided categorical program aid which supplied additional state funding to help districts meet the extra costs of special education classes and other classes and services including bilingual education, compensatory education, approved local vocational education and private school tuition, and supplementary and speech instruction. The amount of categorical program aid received by each district depended on the number of pupils being provided special services and upon a weighting factor for each type of handicap or for the type of other special class or service.[16]

The state also reimbursed districts for 90 percent of the cost of approved transportation based upon each district's costs for the prior year. Approved transportation was defined as transportation for elementary school children who reside more than two miles from school, secondary pupils who live more than two and one-half miles from school,[17] and special education pupils who live closer than the minimum distance if transportation is necessary or advisable.[18] Also, pupils who attended private, nonprofit schools within 20 miles of their residence were eligible for the same transportation as provided by the district for public school children; however, if providing such transportation was too costly, the district had the option of reimbursing the parents for the cost of transportation up to a statutory limit.[19] Unapproved transportation was paid for entirely out of local funds.

Under the "T & E Law", the state also provided aid to local districts by absorbing the cost of each district's employer contribution to the Teachers Pension and Annuity Fund. (TPAF—See Chapter VIII). Districts were required to pay some administrative costs out of local funds.[20]

These state aid provisions increased the state's share of the financial burden for public education so that the state paid approximately 40 percent of the total cost of public education in New Jersey contrasted with approximately 28 percent prior to the passage of the "T & E Law". Because the amount of state aid due to districts under the equalization aid provisions was tied to the amount which local districts chose to spend on education, the Legislature placed upon the annual growth of school

---

[16]*N.J.S.A* 18A:7A-20.

[17]*N.J.S.A* 18A:58-7.

[18]*N.J.S.A* 18A:46-23.

[19]*N.J.S.A* 18A:39-1, 39-a.

[20]*N.J.S.A* 18A:66-33, 17

budgets a limit known as budget caps.[21] The caps were intended to limit state aid liability, to prevent large and inefficient expenditures by districts due to increased state aid and to insure local property tax relief.[22]

The statute authorized the commissioner to annually certify to each local board of education the amount by which the district could increase its budget for the next year. The amount was based upon a formula set out by statute which was calculated separately for each school district and resulted basically in a maximum percentage increase for each district based on the number of pupils enrolled during the pre-budget year. The maximum increase applied only to that portion of a district's budget that was funded through local taxes. Income from other sources such as transportation and categorical program aid, tuition and federal grants could be added to each district's budget cap figure.[23]

The statute also empowered the commissioner to approve the request of a local board for a greater increase than would be permitted under the statutory formula. This exception known as a "cap waiver" was granted on two bases. First, if an increased enrollment could reasonably be anticipated in the district. Second, if the commissioner determined that a reallocation of resources or other action taken within the budget cap spending level was insufficient to meet the goals, objectives and standards for a thorough and efficient education established under the "T & E Law".[24] The decision of the commissioner on a cap waiver could be appealed by a local board to the state board.[25]

ABBOTT V. BURKE

During its first few years, Chapter 212 seemed to be accomplishing its goal; the disparities between property-rich and property-poor districts began to narrow. After only a few years, however, the disparities again began to widen for a variety of reasons:

- The Legislature fully funded Chapter 212 in only two of its 15 years;
- Many lower-wealth school districts, particularly those in the urban centers, suffered from "municipal overburden," the excessive tax levy some municipalities found necessary to impose in order to meet governmental needs other than education;
- Prior year funding made it more difficult for property-poor

---

[21]N.J.S.A 18A:7A-25.

[22]Report on Budget Caps of the Joint Committee on the Public Schools, November 2, 1976.

[23]N.J.S.A. 18A:7A-25.

[24]Id.

[25]N.J.A.C. 6:2-1.7.

districts to implement new programs since the entire cost of these programs would be financed by property taxes in the first year;

In 1981, the Education Law Center, Inc., a New Jersey nonprofit, public interest law firm, filed a complaint in Superior Court on behalf of 20 children attending public schools in Camden, East Orange, Irvington, and Jersey City. The plaintiffs challenged the constitutionality of the school financing scheme under the "T & E" law. Specifically, plaintiffs argued that the financing scheme, because of its reliance on local property taxes, resulted in significant educational and program disparities between poor urban and wealthy suburban school districts, leaving poor urban districts unable to meet the educational needs of their students. These inequities, argued plaintiffs, violate the thorough and efficient and Equal Protection clauses of the state Constitution, as well as the Law Against Discrimination.

In 1983, the Superior Court granted the state's motion to dismiss the complaint on grounds that plaintiffs had failed to exhaust their administrative remedies. The Appellate Division reversed this decision in 1984, and on appeal, the New Jersey Supreme Court remanded the case to the Office of Administrative Law to determine the appropriate administration issues and to resolve the factual matters material to the ultimate constitutional issues.[26]

In 1988, Administrative Law Judge Steven L. Lefelt handed down a 607 page decision in which he determined that there were unmet educational needs in poor urban districts and vast program and expenditure disparities between property-rich suburban and property-poor urban school districts; that the plaintiffs' districts, and others were not providing the constitutionally mandated T & E education; that the inequality of educational opportunity statewide itself constituted a denial of a T & E education; and that the failure was systemic.[27] As an administrative law judge, Lefelt could not declare the state's educational system unconstitutional, but could only make a recommendation to the state's education commissioner. Judge Lefelt concluded that as the Public School Education Act was being applied, a court may find that it violates the New Jersey Constitution.[28] Under administrative law, the commissioner may affirm, modify or reject an Administrative Law Judge's recommended decision.

The commissioner rejected Judge Lefelt's recommendations, arguing that educational disparities were district-specific, and that the T & E clause did not require absolute sameness in financing or programming. He also rejected the finding that there was a strong relationship between educa-

---

[26]100 *N.J.* 269 (1985).
[27]1988 *S.L.D.* (August 24).
[28]*Ibid.*

tional expenditures and the quality of education.[29]

The State Board of Education affirmed the Commissioner's decision and plaintiffs appealed to the state Supreme Court.

The Supreme Court found that the Public School Education Act's system of school financing was unconstitutional, as Judge Lefelt recommended. However the Court's finding was limited to 28 poor urban districts. The court ruled that it could not find the system unconstitutional as it applied to other districts.[30] It was left to the Legislature, the State Board and the commissioner to identify the poorer urban districts. The court also declared minimum aid unconstitutional because it applied only to the wealthier districts. "Its [minimum aid's] sole function is to enable richer districts to spend even more, thereby increasing the disparity of educational funding between richer and poorer [districts]."[31] The court ordered a remedy that would raise the funding level of the 28 districts to the level of the property-rich suburban districts, but leave other districts untouched. In addition, the Court mandated that provisions be formulated, "similar to categorical aid, for the special educational needs of these districts in order to redress their extreme disadvantages."[32]

While minimum aid was declared counter-equalizing, and thus unconstitutional, categorical and transportation aid were upheld. Both have "educational justification" because "it [categorical aid] helps meet the cost of educating students with special needs, who reside in all districts, richer and poorer" and "[transportation aid] similarly goes to all districts and is distributed in a way that bears no relationship to the wealth of the district."[33]

The Court found state aid to fund the Teachers' Pension and Annuity Fund (TPAF) "in effect counter-equalizing", because teacher pension contributions are paid in greater amounts to richer districts because they tend to have more experienced and higher paid teachers. However, the court concluded that it would abide by its previous judgment in *Robinson v. Cahill, supra,* and allow TPAF contributions to remain as a state contribution.[34] The court cautioned, however, that it would not foreclose the possibility that such aid is "constitutionally infirm."[35]

The court delegated the formulation of the new funding mechanism to the Legislature. However, the court stated the funding must be certain every year and cannot depend on how much a poorer urban school district

---

[29]1989 *S.L.D.* (February 22).

[30]119 *N.J.* 297; 386-387 (1990).

[31]*Id.* at 382.

[32]*Id.* at 385-386.

[33]*Id.* at 383.

[34]*Id.* at 329; 384.

[35]*Id.*

is willing to tax.[36] The court declined to rule on the plaintiffs' state equal protection claim, and found that plaintiffs had failed to prove that the educational financing system violates the state Law Against Discrimination.

QUALITY EDUCATION ACT OF 1990

The Quality Education Act of 1990 ("QEA") was the administration's answer to eliminate the gross disparities found by the *Abbott* court.[37] The original QEA, championed by Governor Jim Florio, moved very rapidly through the Legislature and was signed into law on July 3, 1990. It provided $1.1 billion in new money for state aid to education and dramatically changed the way in which state aid to public education was distributed. According to the Governor, the new law was designed to provide sufficient resources and accountability measures so that all children, regardless of the wealth of the community in which they lived, would have access to a thorough and efficient education, as required by our state Constitution.[38] The intent of the QEA is to provide greater equality of educational opportunity throughout the state and also to achieve property tax relief in low and moderate wealth districts. To achieve this end, the original QEA was designed to allocate about 70 percent of total state aid in 1991-92 on an equalized basis, i.e. based on a district's wealth, with proportionately more aid going to poorer districts.

However, following a taxpayers revolt, a worrisome election and severe criticisms from many sides, the Legislature and the Governor made significant amendments to the Act that were signed into law on March 14, 1991.[39] The amendments shifted $360 million from state aid to education into municipal property tax relief. Through tighter budget caps, 7.5 to 9 percent for non-special needs districts, another $229 million was shifted into property tax relief. Special needs districts were permitted more liberal "equity spending caps" designed to permit them to reach spending parity by 1995-96. Cap waiver procedures were redesigned to require voter approval of most cap waiver requests.[40] The amendments also provided for state assumption of the employer's share of TPAF and social security costs for two years[41] and gave districts a two-year save harmless period for compensatory education aid.[42]

---

[36]*Id.* at 386.

[37]*N.J.S.A.* 18A:7D-1 *et seq.*

[38]N.J. Const. 1947, art. 8, sec. 4, para. 1.

[39]*P.L.* 1991, Ch. 62.

[40]*P.L.* 1991, Ch. 62, Sec. 19.

[41]*P.L.* 1991, Ch. 62, Sec. 29,30.

[42]*P.L.* 1991, Ch. 62, Sec. 32.

Much of the impact of the aid loss was felt by the 30 "special needs" districts—the 28 poor urban districts that the court had identified in *Abbott v. Burke* plus two others designed through criteria established under the QEA. While the $816 million increase in state aid for 1991-92 was hailed by the administration as record-breaking, it was roughly equal to the normal increase in state aid to schools over a two-year period under Chapter 212. Since there had been no increase in state aid in the previous year, that two-year leap was needed just to stay on track.

The QEA in Brief

QEA differs significantly from the former school funding system, Chapter 212 of the Public Laws of 1975.[43] The QEA is basically a *foundation program*. The state calculates how much it costs to provide an adequate education for regular pupils in each district, based on the number of pupils and their grade levels. This amount is known as the district's *maximum foundation budget*.[44] The state then calculates a *local fair share* for the district, based on the district's per pupil wealth in terms of property value and personal income.[45] The state subtracts the *local fair share* from the *maximum foundation budget* and provides *foundation aid* to make up the difference, if there is any.[46]

Under Chapter 212, which was a guaranteed tax base system, the state paid a portion of the district's budget for regular education up to a certain limit. The state's share was based on the district's property value behind each pupil, with the State share being highest in districts with the lowest property values per pupil.[47]

State aid for special education and bilingual education is very similar under Chapter 212 and the QEA.[48] Under the QEA, transportation aid was significantly altered[49] and compensatory education aid was eliminated following a two-year save harmless period.[50] A new categorical aid, known as at-risk aid, was established for low income students.[51]

The most dramatic aspect of the original QEA was the provision that local school districts were required to pay the employers' share of pension and social security costs, a major expenditure that had been fully paid

---

[43]*N.J.S.A.* 18A:7A-1 *et seq.*

[44]*N.J.S.A.* 18A:7D-6.

[45]*N.J.S.A.* 18A:7D-7.

[46]*N.J.S.A.* 18A:7D-4.

[47]*N.J.S.A.* 18A:7A-18.

[48]*N.J.S.A.* 18A:7D-16, 21.

[49]*N.J.S.A.* 18A:7D-18.

[50]*P.L.* 1991, Ch. 62, Sec. 32.

[51]*N.J.S.A.* 18A:7D-20.

by the state under prior funding systems.[52] Under the amended QEA, districts must still include these costs in their budgets as line items but the State will provide aid to cover the exact cost of pensions and social security for two years.[53] Beginning in 1993-94, however, districts will be responsible for the full cost of pensions and social security, with the state providing a share of the costs through either foundation aid or transition aid. Transition aid will cease in 1995-96.[54]

In response to the Supreme Court decision, the Legislature created a special category of districts known as special needs districts. These are the 28 poor urban districts cited by the Court, plus two others identified through legislatively designed criteria.[55] The law is intended to enable these districts to reach parity with the more affluent districts (socio-economic groups I and J) within five years.

COMPONENTS OF THE QEA

Foundation Program

For 1991-92 the base foundation amount for pupils in grades 1-5 is $6,640. The amount for pupils in other grade levels and in other school settings varies based upon assigned foundation weights. The foundation amount is increased by five percent for each pupil in a special needs district. The base foundation amount ($6,640) will increase each year by the average annual percentage increase in state per capita personal income (PCI) over the four prior fiscal years. A facilities foundation amount of $107 per pupil is provided for 1991-92 and will be increased annually by the PCI.[56] The maximum foundation budget is calculated for each district by multiplying the foundation amount by the foundation weights and pupil enrollment as of October 15 of the pre-budget year.[57] A local fair share is calculated for each district based, in equal parts, on property value and personal income per pupil in each district.[58] A district's foundation aid is determined by subtracting its local fair share, along with any surplus in excess of 7.5 percent, from its maximum foundation budget. Beginning in 1993-94 any district that retains excess surplus, over 7.5 percent, will experience a dollar for dollar reduction in foundation aid.[59]

[52]N.J.S.A. 18A:66-33.

[53]P.L. 1991, Ch. 62, Sec. 29,30.

[54]N.J.S.A. 18A:7D-33.

[55]N.J.S.A. 18A:7D-3.

[56]N.J.S.A. 18A:7D-6.

[57]Id.

[58]N.J.S.A. 18A:7D-7

[59]N.J.S.A. 18A:7D-4

Districts that are not eligible for or receive a minimum amount of foundation aid receive transition aid in amounts sufficient to ensure that their total state aid in 1991-92 is at least 6.5 percent higher than their total state aid in 1990-91. Transition aid will be phased out over a four-year period.[60]

Cost Containment Measures

The Quality Education Act, as amended, imposes tighter budget caps on non-special needs districts, 7.5 to 9 percent for 1991-92. The lower limit of the budget cap reflects the latest 4-year average percentage growth in statewide per capita income (PCI). The budget cap will change each year as the PCI rises or falls. Special needs districts have more liberal "equity spending caps" which will extend through the 1995-96 school year. These caps are designed to enable the special needs districts to achieve spending parity with the state's wealthiest districts by 1995-96.

Caps under the QEA have been extended to cover both current and capital expense as well as all programs supported by categorical aid. The QEA permits the commissioner of education to grant cap waivers under four very limited criteria:

- For the two years prior to the pre-budget year, the district has had an average annual increase in its resident enrollment of greater than two percent;
- The district has had an increase in special education costs in excess of five percent in the preceding year;
- The district has entered into a lease purchase agreement between July 1, 1990 and April 1, 1991;
- The district send pupils and pays tuition to a special needs district.[61]

The maximum level of state aid is capped at $4.1 billion for 1991-92, exclusive of transition aid.[62] Increases in state aid for education are linked to the annual increases in the state revenues which fund the aid program; the state income tax. Beginning with 1992-93 school year the maximum state school aid will be determined annually by a formula which takes into account the growth in per capita income (PCI) and adds 80 percent of that increase. Beginning in 1993-94 the Governor may set the annual increase anywhere between 80 to 100 percent of the state school aid inflater.[63] Limits are imposed on the amount of growth in a district's net

---

[60]N.J.S.A. 18A:7D-33
[61]N.J.S.A. 18A:7D-28
[62]N.J.S.A. 18A:7D-15.
[63]N.J.S.A. 18A:7D-3.

budget that is eligible for foundation aid. In 1991-92 and 1992-93 the district may increase this "aidable" portion of its budget by its budget cap. After 1992-93, the allowable increase in "aidable" portion of the net budget will be 20 percent.[64]

Additional State Aid

Foundation aid districts receive aid for debt service on a current year basis in the same percentage that they receive foundation aid.[65] Districts receive state aid for each special education pupil, with the amount of aid based on the student's handicapping condition. Special education aid for 1991-92 ranges from $820 for a perceptually impaired pupil to $11,616 for a chronically ill student.[66] Districts receive at-risk pupil aid for each pupil eligible for free lunch or free milk. The aid can be used for any flexible manner for pre-school programs, alternative education, reduced class size, counselling or other programs that will help disadvantaged students succeed. Although these funds replace compensatory education monies, their use is not limited to preventive or remedial programs in the basic skills. For 1991-92, this aid ranges from $1032 to $1380 per full day pupil, depending on grade level.[67] For each eligible pupil enrolled in a bilingual education program, as mandated by state law, districts receive bilingual education aid. In 1991-92 this aid is $1,203 per pupil.[68]

Transportation aid is based on three formulas that involve the number of regular and special education students required to be transported by state law, the average distance from home to school, district size, population density, and the county in which the district is located. Theoretically, the formulas are intended to produce sufficient aid to cover 100 percent of the costs for approved transportation.[69] For 1991-92 and 1992-93 school districts will, for the first time, pay the employer's share of pension and social securities costs. They will, however, receive state aid in the exact amount of this payment. Beginning in 1993-94, school districts will assume the entire costs of the employer's share of pension and social security, supported only by amounts of foundation aid and/or transition aid the districts receive.[70] Transition aid will cease after 1994-95.[71]

County vocational schools and county special services school districts receive state aid directly, including debt service, in much the same manner

---

[64]*N.J.S.A.* 18A:7D-29.

[65]*N.J.S.A.* 18A:7D-22.

[66]*N.J.S.A.* 18A:7D-16.

[67]*N.J.S.A.* 18A:7D-20.

[68]*N.J.S.A.* 18A:7D-21.

[69]*N.J.S.A.* 18A:7D-18, 19.

[70]*N.J.S.A.* 18A:66-33, 66

[71]*N.J.S.A.* 18A:7D-33, 34.

other high school districts are funded.[72] County special services school districts are not eligible for transportation aid while county vocational school districts will not become eligible for transportation aid until 1992-93.[73] County vocational school districts and county special services school districts may receive funds from the county board of freeholders and may charge local districts tuition to make up any difference between the state and county appropriations and their allowable costs.[74]

---

[72]*N.J.S.A.* 18A:54-20.2; *P.L.* 1991, Ch. 62, Sec. 26, 27.

[73]*N.J.S.A.* 18A:7D-18.

[74]*N.J.S.A.* 18A:46-31; 54-20.1.

THE EDUCATIONAL ENVIRONMENT

5

The prime focus of the discretionary powers of local boards of education is the decisions which directly determine the educational environment of the children in New Jersey's public schools. It is to those decisions that the bulk of school board activity and energy should be directed.

The previous chapter described a number of legal provisions under the "T & E Law" directly affecting both educational planning and content. This chapter describes other major elements of the law which apply as the board houses its students, provides for their attendance, health and safety, and establishes the school program.

SCHOOL LANDS AND BUILDINGS

The local school board has broad authority and responsibility for the establishment and maintenance of the school facilities. The board of education holds title to the property, real and personal, of the school district and has supervision, control and management of all such property.[1] The board generally may acquire, receive, hold, hold in trust and sell and lease real estate and personal property and may take and condemn lands and other property for school purposes.[2] In addition, it may accept any gift or grant of land, of money or of other personal property.[3] Finally, it may undertake capital projects the cost of which may be provided by taxes or the issuance of bonds appropriately authorized, such as:

- Acquisition by purchase or condemnation of lands;
- Grading, draining and landscaping of lands owned or to be acquired by the board;
- Acquisition, construction, reconstruction, remodeling, alteration, enlargement or major repair of buildings;
- Purchase or major renewal of the original furniture, equipment

---

[1]*N.J.S.A.* 18A:20-1.

[2]*N.J.S.A.* 18A:20-2, 3.

[3]*N.J.S.A.* 18A:20-4.

and apparatus for any building.[4]

The board in a Type II district, without prior approval of the voters, may:

- Rent buildings for school purposes, in case of emergency, on a year-to-year basis or for a term not to exceed five years; and
- Take an option not to exceed one year in duration and not to exceed the fair market value of such option, on the purchase of land. This option may be exercised only after purchase of the land has been approved by the voters.[5]

A district may also:

- Purchase, take and condemn lands within the district;
- Purchase, take and condemn lands not to exceed 50 acres in an adjoining municipality;
- Grade, drain, landscape and improve its lands;
- Erect, lease for a term not exceeding 50 years, enlarge, improve, repair or furnish buildings; and
- Borrow money for any of the above purposes in accordance with the statutory procedures applicable to the type of district.[6]

Any board may lease a building or enter into a lease-purchase agreement for a building and site. Any lease for a term exceeding one year and any lease-purchase agreement in excess of five years must be approved by the commissioner of education and the Local Finance Board in the Department of Community Affairs.[7]

A board may also acquire or lease a building with another governmental entity or business for the joint use of the district and the co-owner or lessee. In such joint ownership or leasing arrangements the non-educational uses of the building must be compatible with the establishment and operation of a school as determined by the commissioner. The portion of the building used as a school must conform to regulations of the Department of Education, and the board must comply with provisions of the law and regulations relating to the selection and approval of sites.[8] A board may also enter into a joint ownership arrangement with any individual or business authorized to do business in New Jersey, in which the individual or business agrees to construct or provide for the construction of a building on a site contributed by the board. A joint ownership

---

[4]N.J.S.A. 18A:21-1.

[5]N.J.S.A. 18A:20-4.1

[6]N.J.S.A. 18A:20-4.2.

[7]Id.

[8]N.J.S.A. 18A:20-4.2(e).

arrangement must be approved by the commissioner and the Local Finance Board of the Department of Community Affairs and must enable the building to be provided at reduced cost to the board. The agreement must also provide that the board is not responsible for costs associated with any portion of the building used for non-educational purposes. Again, all portions of a building used for educational purposes must comply with Department of Education regulations.[9]

Any board may dispose of unsuitable or no longer needed lands:

- By public sale which has been advertised at least once a week for two weeks.[10] Sale must be to the highest bidder but the board is permitted to set a minimum price and to provide for acceptance or rejection of bids not later than the second regular meeting after the sale;[11]

- By private sale to the state or one of its political subdivisions without advertisement;

- By transfer for a nominal consideration to the municipality or any agency thereof, to a volunteer fire company or rescue squad, to a U.S. veterans organization or to a nonprofit child care service organization incorporated under New Jersey law, to a nonprofit hospital or to a nonprofit organization duly licensed to provide emergency shelter for the homeless. The board may stipulate that if the property ceases to be used for the purposes intended, it shall revert to the board.[12]

In addition, a board may, by resolution, transfer land to the board of education of a county vocational school district for the purpose of constructing a vocational school on the land.[13]

In some instances, a board may determine that a piece of land, a building or a portion of a building is not necessary for school purposes, but may wish to retain the property in the event that it may in the future be required for school purposes. In these circumstances, a board may authorize the lease of the land or building for a term beyond the official life of the board.[14] The lease will be binding on a successor board if it is leased to the highest bidder after public advertisement. Also, the lease will be binding on a successor board if it is leased to the federal government, the state or one of its political subdivisions, another school district

---

[9]*N.J.S.A.* 18A:20-4.2(g).

[10]*N.J.S.A.* 18A:20-6.

[11]*N.J.S.A.* 18A:20-7.

[12]*N.J.S.A.* 18A:20-9.

[13]*N.J.S.A.* 18A:20-8.1.

[14]See *Foote v. Township of Wall Bd. of Ed.*, 1977 *S.L.D.* 462 re: Board's lack of authority to enter into a lease for a term beyond the life of the board unless specifically authorized by statute; see also *Wilson Coalition v. Summit*, 245 *N.J. Super.* 616 (1990).

or any board, body or commission of a municipality within the district, any volunteer fire company or rescue squad, to a U.S. veterans' organization, to a nonprofit child care service organization, to a nonprofit hospital or nonprofit organization duly licensed under the laws of the State of New Jersey to provide emergency shelter for the homeless, to a nonprofit senior citizen organization, or to a nonprofit historic preservation organization duly incorporated under New Jersey law. In the case of a lease to any of the enumerated organizations, the lease may be for a nominal fee and advertisement for bids is not required.[15]

Any lease in excess of five years must be approved by the commissioner of education, and where the lease involves joint occupancy, the noneducational uses of the building or land must be compatible with the establishment and operation of a school.[16] In addition, the board may exchange land not needed for school purposes for other lands located in the district and at least equal in value.[17]

A school district may establish public playgrounds and recreation places.[18] It may accept, maintain, manage and control public playgrounds and recreation places conveyed by the municipal governing body when such a transfer is agreed upon.[19] Further, it may join with a municipal governing body or the board of chosen freeholders in acquiring, improving, equipping, operating and maintaining playgrounds, playfields, gymnasiums, public baths, swimming pools, and indoor recreation centers and may appropriate money for them.[20] The statute provides that a board shall have full control over all lands, public playgrounds, and recreation places which it acquires or leases and may adopt rules for their use and for the conduct of persons while on or using them.[21]

A local board must obtain state approval of all plans and specifications for the erection of any building or part thereof before entering contracts.[22] The board must also follow the statutory procedure for drafting plans, advertising and awarding bids and completing construction contracts. A discussion of these subjects is included in Chapter XII, School Business Practices.

To protect the community's investment, the board must keep all insurable property, real and personal, insured against loss or damage by fire and against other loss and damage as it deems appropriate.[23]

---

[15]N.J.S.A. 18A:20-8.2.
[16]Id.
[17]N.J.S.A. 18A:20-8.
[18]N.J.S.A. 18A:20-17.
[19]N.J.S.A. 18A:20-18.
[20]N.J.S.A. 18A:20-22.
[21]N.J.S.A. 18A:20-20.
[22]N.J.A.C. 6:22-1.1.
[23]N.J.S.A. 18A:20-25.

Under rules adopted by it, the board may permit the use of the schoolhouse or rooms therein, or the school grounds, when not in use for school purposes, for:

- The meeting of persons giving and receiving instruction in any branch of education, learning, or the arts;
- Public library purposes;
- Holding such social, civic and recreational meetings and entertainments and for such other purposes as may be approved by the board;
- Such meetings, entertainments, and occasions where admission fees are charged as may be approved by the board; and
- Polling places, holding elections, the registration of voters, and holding political meetings.[24]

A board may allow religious groups to use school facilities on a *temporary* basis for religious services or educational classes, as long as the groups reimburse the board for all out of pocket expenses incurred as a result of their use of the facilities.[25]

Under prior law, a board was not liable for injury to the person from the use of any public grounds, buildings, or structures. That law was repealed by the enactment in 1972 of the New Jersey Tort Claims Act under which all governmental entities and public bodies were made subject to limited liability for such injuries.[26]

Under this law, a school district is liable for injuries caused by any dangerous condition existing on school district property where the negligent or wrongful act or omission of a district employee created the dangerous condition. The district is also liable if it had actual or constructive notice of the dangerous condition a sufficient time prior to the injury to have taken measures to protect against the dangerous condition or if the condition was of such an obvious nature that it should have been discovered.[27] Where it is asserted that a dangerous condition on school district property arose from the negligence of an employee, the standard of care is palpable unreasonableness, rather than ordinary negligence which is required under *N.J.S.A.* 59:2-2a and *N.J.S.A.* 59:3-1a.[28] The Supreme Court has defined "palpably unreasonable" as "imply[ing] behavior that is patently unacceptable under any given circumstances."[29]

---

[24]*N.J.S.A.* 18A:20-34.

[25]*Resnick v. East Brunswick Tp. Bd. of Ed.,* 77 *N.J.* 88 (1978).

[26]*N.J.S.A.* 59:4-2 *et seq.*

[27]*N.J.S.A.* 59:4-2, 3.

[28]*Pico v. State,* 116 *N.J.* 55, 63 (1989).

[29]*Kolitch v. Lindedahl,* 100 *N.J.* 485, 493 (1985).

The burden is on the school district both to plead and to prove the immunities and defenses provided by the Tort Claims Act. See Pressler, Current N.J. Court Rules, Comment *R.* 59:4-4.

ATTENDANCE AND TRANSPORTATION

Attendance at public school is free to the following persons over five and under 20 years of age:

- Anyone domiciled in the school district;
- Anyone living in the home of another person domiciled in the school district who provides support gratis as if the child were his own. The board may require a sworn statement that the child living there is wholly supported, with all the child's personal obligations assumed, and will be supported for the whole year and not merely the school term. A board of education may contest the validity of the sworn statement in proceedings before the commissioner. However, no child may be denied an admission during the pendency of any such proceedings before the commissioner. The resident has the burden of proving, by a preponderance of the evidence, that the child is eligible for a free education under the criteria in this subsection.
- Anyone whose parent or guardian is residing temporarily in the school district;
- Anyone for whom the New Jersey Division of Youth and Family Services is acting as guardian;
- Anyone whose parent or guardian moves from one school district to another as a result of being homeless and whose district of residence is determined pursuant to *N.J.S.A.* 18A:7B-12;[30]
- Anyone who is placed in the home of a resident by the courts or by any society, agency, or institution incorporated in this state and having as its object the care and welfare of neglected children, except that no board shall be required to accept an unreasonable number of such children.[31]

Anyone who fraudulently allows another's child to use her residence and is not the primary financial supporter of that child as well as anyone who fraudulently claims to have given up custody of her child to someone in another district commits a disorderly persons offense.

---

[30]*N.J.A.C.* 6:3-7 contains provisions for the education of homeless children and youth.

[31]*N.J.S.A.* 18A:38-1, 2. A board may also have an obligation to provide for educationally handicapped children under three or over 20.

The board may, if it chooses, admit persons over the age of 20 who, except for age, would be entitled to attend school.[32] The board may also admit non-residents upon such terms and with or without payment of tuition, as the board prescribes.[33]

Children between six and 16 years of age must regularly attend a public school or a day school where instruction equivalent to the public schools is provided.[34] Children who are so handicapped that they cannot attend school may receive equivalent instruction elsewhere.[35] Any attendance officer who finds a truant child between six and 16 years of age must take the child to his parent (or guardian) or to the teacher in the school he is required to attend.[36] The attendance officer may also proceed against the parents or guardians, in cases of willful and continued truancy.[37]

No child between the ages of four and 20 years may be excluded from any public school on account of race, creed, color, national origin, or ancestry. Board members who vote such an exclusion may be found guilty of a misdemeanor.[38]

Children who have never attended any public or private school may be admitted to public school on or before October 1 following the opening of the fall term, and at no other time except by a majority vote of all the board members.[39] The board of education is not required to accept by transfer from another public or private school any pupil who was not eligible by reason of age for admission on October 1 of that school year, but the board may admit such pupil in its discretion.[40] Pupils may be admitted to demonstration schools maintained in connection with a state teachers college. The tuition to be paid by the board shall be determined by the district board and the college board of trustees. Such pupils are counted in the calculation of state aid to the district.[41]

If a board of education has the necessary accommodations it may receive, and may be required to receive by order of the state board, pupils from another district lacking facilities.[42] Tuition for such pupils is paid by the sending district.[43] A child who lives remote from school in the

---

[32]*N.J.S.A.* 18A:38-4.

[33]*N.J.S.A.* 18A:38-3.

[34]*N.J.S.A.* 18A:38-25, 26.

[35]*N.J.S.A.* 18A:46-13, 14.

[36]*N.J.S.A.* 18A:38-28.

[37]*N.J.S.A.* 18A:38-31.

[38]*N.J.S.A.* 18A:38-5.1.

[39]*N.J.S.A.* 18A:38-6.

[40]*N.J.S.A.* 18A:38-5.

[41]*N.J.S.A.* 18A:38-24.

[42]*N.J.S.A.* 18A:38-8.

[43]*N.J.S.A.* 18A:38-19.

district in which he lives may, with the written consent of the county superintendent, attend school in an adjoining district.[44] A district which does not have a high school must designate a high school or schools for its pupils to attend.[45] Whenever two or more high schools have been designated, pupil allocation must be made. If the designation existed in the 1943-44 school year, the same apportionment as in that year remains in effect. If the first designation occurred after that year, then the apportionment of the first year remains in effect.[46] No designation or allocation of pupils to receiving high schools can be changed or withdrawn, nor can a designated high school refuse to continue to receive high school pupils from the sending district except upon application made to and approved by the commissioner.[47] Prior to submission of the application, the district desiring to end the relationship must submit a feasibility study which analyzes the impact of the requested termination.

A board of education may, in its discretion, permit pupils from its district to attend school in another district and pay tuition therefore:

- When the board does not furnish instruction in a particular high school course of study;
- For attendance at an approved evening high school;
- For instruction beyond the 12th grade.[48]

A board of education which receives pupils from another district is entitled to charge and collect tuition from the sending district not to exceed the actual cost per pupil, as defined in regulations of the state board.[49]

A district receiving pupils from other districts on a tuition basis cannot exclude such pupils because of nonpayment of tuition, provided that the sending board delivers to the receiving board a school warrant for the amount due, bearing interest at the legal rate. A sending district cannot withdraw such pupils during the year except with the consent of the receiving board.[50] When a receiving district must enlarge its facilities to accommodate pupils from another district, it may enter into an agreement with the sending district for the continuation of the sending-receiving relationship for up to 10 years.[51]

A board must provide for the round trip transportation of elementary pupils who live more than two miles from their public school of at-

---

[44]*N.J.S.A.* 18A:38-9.

[45]*N.J.S.A.* 18A:38-11.

[46]*N.J.S.A.* 18A:38-12.

[47]*N.J.S.A.* 18A:38-13.

[48]*N.J.S.A.* 18A:38-15, 16, 17, 18.

[49]*N.J.S.A.* 18A:38-19; *N.J.A.C.* 6:20-3.1.

[50]*N.J.S.A.* 18A:38-23.

[51]*N.J.S.A.* 18A:38-20.

tendance or secondary school pupils who live more than 2.5 miles.[52] When a district provides round trip transportation to school for public school pupils, it must also furnish transportation to its pupils who attend non-public schools provided the non-public school is non-profit, is within 20 miles, and the cost does not exceed an amount arrived at pursuant to a statutory formula. If the cost is more than this statutory figure, the board is relieved of providing the transportation but must pay the parent the statutory amount in lieu of such service. The board is also relieved of furnishing transportation to non-public school pupils if the only transportation provided is for handicapped children or pupils attending vocational schools.[53]

In addition to providing transportation for pupils pursuant to *N.J.S.A.* 18A:39-1 and *N.J.S.A.* 18A:46-23 a board of education may provide transportation for other pupils to and from school. Districts shall not receive state aid pursuant to *N.J.S.A.* 18A:7D-18 for this transportation of pupils.[54] However, a board of education must furnish transportation to handicapped children for lesser distances than remote if the board of education finds, upon the advice of the medical examiner, that the handicap is such as to make transportation necessary or advisable.[55]

Any local board of education may provide transportation for pupils by buses owned by it or it may contract for such transportation for a term not exceeding four years. All transportation contracts require the approval of the county superintendent.[56] Two or more boards may enter into an agreement to provide jointly for the transportation of pupils.[57]

School buses under the jurisdiction of public schools must be retired after a specific period of time which is fixed by statute and dependent on the gross vehicle weight of the bus.[58]

A board may authorize qualified school personnel, state employees or parents to transport school children to and from school related activities in a private vehicle with a capacity of eight or less. A person so authorized need not be licensed as a bus driver, and the transportation so provided is exempt from the registration, equipment, inspection and maintenance requirements applicable to the transportation of pupils by school bus.[59]

A board of education may permit school buses owned or leased by it to be used for transporting senior citizens in its own or a contiguous district. A board may also authorize the use of school buses for trans-

---

[52]*N.J.S.A.* 18A:39-1.

[53]*N.J.S.A.* 18A:39-1, 39-1a.

[54]*N.J.S.A.* 18A:39-1.1.

[55]*N.J.S.A.* 18A:46-23.

[56]*N.J.S.A.* 18A:39-2.

[57]*N.J.S.A.* 18A:39-11, 12, 13, 14, 15, 16.

[58]*N.J.S.A.* 39:3B-5.1 through 5.3.

[59]*N.J.S.A.* 18A:39-20.1; *N.J.A.C.* 6:21-10.1 *et seq.*

porting handicapped citizens in any district. In addition, it may authorize the transportation of children and adults participating in a recreation or other program operated by the municipality or municipalities in which the district is located. Each use of school buses for these purposes must be approved by the board.[60]

A board may not allow the use of buses by any of these groups to interfere with the transportation of school pupils, and the school buses so used must be operated by licensed bus drivers. A board must require such groups to reimburse it for all or part of any costs which it incurs in permitting such use.[61]

No school bus driver or substitute driver may be assigned to transport pupils until his name and social security number as well as certification of a valid school bus driver's license and criminal background check have been filed with the county superintendent.[62] A board or contractor who fails to forward such information may be found guilty of a misdemeanor and subject to a fine of not more than $500.00. However, a bus driver may be employed provisionally for up to six months during the pendency of a criminal history record check as long as the candidate submits to the commissioner a sworn statement attesting that he has not been convicted of any crime or disorderly persons offense specified in the statute.[63]

Prior to employment as a school bus driver and when applying to renew a school bus driver's license, a bus driver is required to submit to the commissioner her name, address and fingerprints. The mechanism for initiating the criminal background check requires the subject's written consent before the report is furnished. When the report is received, the commissioner is required to provide written notification to the applicant of the results. A school bus driver is disqualified from employment or service if convicted of:

- A sexual offense, child molestation or endangering the welfare of children or incompetents;
- The manufacture, transportation, sale, possession or habitual use of a controlled dangerous substance;
- The use of force or the threat of the use of force upon a person or property.

The revocation or suspension of one's bus driver's license is also a basis for disqualification.[64]

A school bus driver-applicant has 30 days from the receipt of written

---

[60]N.J.S.A. 18A:39-22

[61]N.J.S.A. 18A:39-22; N.J.A.C. 6:3-4.1 (senior citizens only).

[62]N.J.S.A. 18A:39-17, 18, 19.

[63]N.J.S.A. 18A:39-20.

[64]N.J.S.A. 18A:39-19.1.

notice of disqualification from the commissioner to petition the commissioner for a hearing on the accuracy of the criminal history check or to establish rehabilitation. The rehabilitation factors are specified in the statute.

Once a bus driver-applicant is disqualified, the conviction which constitutes the basis for disqualification is sent to the Division of Motor Vehicles and notice of disqualification is given to the local board of education, school bus contractor and county superintendent.

After notice of disqualification is received by the Division of Motor Vehicles, the special driver's license must be revoked without the necessity of a further hearing.

Records are kept by commissioner for one year following the date of determination of qualification/disqualification.

Finally, it must be noted that all pupil transportation must be furnished in accordance with rules and regulations of the state board.[65]

PUPIL HEALTH AND SAFETY

Every board of education must employ at least one physician licensed to practice medicine or surgery in New Jersey as its medical inspector as well as at least one school nurse.[66] With the approval of the county superintendent, a board may also employ para-professional aides to assist school nurses in performing clerical and routine first aid functions.[67] Every pupil must be examined by the medical inspector, the nurse or other licensed health care personnel under the immediate direction of the medical inspector, to learn whether any physical defects exist.[68] The scope and frequency of the examinations are determined by rules of the state board.[69] However, pupils between the ages of 10 and 18 must be examined annually for scoliosis,[70] and children in certain grades must have hearing examinations.[71] A pupil who presents a statement signed by his parent or guardian that a medical examination interferes with the free exercise of his religious beliefs may be examined only to the extent as may be necessary to determine whether he is ill or infected with a communicable

---

[65]*N.J.S.A.* 18A:39-21; *N.J.A.C.* 6:21-1 *et seq.*

[66]*N.J.S.A.* 18A:40-1.

[67]*N.J.A.C.* 6:11-4.9; *Bernards Tp. Ed. Assn., et al. v. Bernards Tp. Bd. of Ed.,* 1981 *S.L.D.* (September 29), aff'd St. Bd. 1982 *S.L.D.* (April 7), aff'd Superior Court of New Jersey, Appellate Division, unpublished opinion (Docket No. A-4211-81T3, decided May 18, 1983).

[68]*N.J.S.A.* 18A:40-4.

[69]*N.J.A.C.* 6:29-1.1 *et seq.*

[70]*N.J.S.A.* 18A:40-4.3.

[71]*N.J.S.A.* 18A:40-4; *N.J.A.C.* 6:29-8.1, 8.2.

disease or to determine his fitness to participate in the health, safety and physical education course.[72]

Upon the recommendation of the school physician or the school nurse, or in their absence on his own initiative, the principal may exclude from school any pupil who shows evidence of departure from normal health, who has been exposed to communicable disease, or whose presence is certified by the medical inspector to be detrimental to the health or cleanliness of other pupils. The principal must notify the parent or guardian of the reason for the exclusion.[73] The parent must take appropriate steps to remedy the cause of exclusion where the cause is within his control, and, if he fails to do so within a reasonable time, he may be proceeded against as a disorderly person.[74]

The Legislature has addressed the issue of substance abuse by providing through the statutes for a comprehensive education program on the nature and effects of drugs, alcohol and controlled dangerous substances. Instructional programs on drugs, alcohol and controlled dangerous substances and their effects are required for pupils from kindergarten through grade 12.[75] Minimum curriculum guidelines are set forth in the statute. The curriculum guidelines must be updated as needed to reflect the most current information available on the nature and treatment of drug, alcohol and controlled dangerous substance abuse.

The board is required to provide time during the usual school schedule for the inservice workshops and programs to train selected public school teachers to teach an education program on drugs, alcohol and controlled dangerous substances which are established by the commissioner. This requirement is to insure that appropriate teaching staff members are prepared to teach the education program in each grade in each school district.[76]

Using guidelines established by the commissioner, each board is required to establish a comprehensive substance abuse intervention, prevention and treatment referral program.[77] Each school district must develop a clear written policy statement outlining its program to combat substance abuse and identify, evaluate and refer for treatment and discipline those pupils who are substance abusers. At the beginning of each school year, copies of the policy statement must be distributed to pupils and their parents.

In accordance with the state board's regulations, a board must adopt a policy and procedure for the evaluation, referral for treatment and

---

[72]N.J.S.A. 18A:40-4.

[73]N.J.S.A. 18A:40-7, 8.

[74]N.J.S.A. 18A:40-9.

[75]N.J.S.A. 18A:40A-1.

[76]N.J.S.A. 18A:40A-3.

[77]N.J.S.A. 18A:40A-10.

discipline of pupils involved in incidents of possession or abuse which occur on school property or at school functions.[78]

Any teaching staff member, nurse or other educational employee who observes a pupil who appears to be under the influence of a controlled dangerous substance must report the matter to the medical inspector or school nurse and the school principal or his designee. The principal must notify the child's parent and arrange for an immediate examination of the child by a physician selected by the child's parent, or, if that doctor is unavailable, by the school's medical inspector. If the medical inspector is unavailable, the pupil must be taken to the emergency room of the nearest hospital for examination. A written report of the examination must be furnished to the parent and superintendent within 24 hours; if the report indicates that the pupil was under the influence of a dangerous substance, she may not return to school until she submits a physician's report that she is mentally and physically able to do so.[79]

A board may, on account of the prevalence of any communicable disease or to prevent the spread of communicable diseases, prohibit the attendance of any teacher or pupil and may specify the time during which the teacher or pupil shall remain away from school.[80]

A board is required to insure compliance with regulations established as part of the State Sanitary Code pertaining to the immunization of school children against disease and prohibiting attendance by a child who has not been immunized.[81] A board may provide at public expense the necessary equipment, materials and services for immunizing pupils from diseases against which pupils are required to be immunized by the State Sanitary Code or for diseases against which immunization may be recommended by the State Department of Health.[82] A pupil may be exempted from mandatory immunization upon presentation of a written statement of the parent or guardian objecting thereto on the ground that the proposed immunization interferes with the free exercise of the pupil's religious rights.[83]

The presence or absence of tuberculosis infection in any or all of the pupils must be determined periodically. The frequency, procedures and selection of pupils for the examination must be in accordance with the rules of the state board.[84] The board may provide the equipment, materials

---

[78]*N.J.S.A.* 18A:40A-12.

[79]*N.J.S.A.* 18A:40-4.1.

[80]*N.J.S.A.* 26:4-6; Commissioner of Education can override power of boards of education to exclude pupils from public schools, due to health reasons. *Bd. of Ed. of City of Plainfield v. Cooperman,* 105 *N.J.* 587 (1987).

[81]*N.J.S.A.* 26:1A-9.

[82]*N.J.S.A.* 18A:40-20.

[83]*N.J.S.A.* 26:1A-9.1.

[84]*N.J.S.A.* 18A:40-16; *N.J.A.C.* 6:29-4.2.

and services for the examination or it may contract with a hospital or public health agency approved by the State Department of Health.[85] Any pupil found to have communicable tuberculosis must be excluded from school. A report of each case must be filed by the school physician with the local board of health.[86] Any records and reports of tuberculosis testing are the confidential property of the board, but are open to officers of state and municipal boards of health.[87]

A health record of each pupil must be kept in which the findings of each examination must be entered. A pupil's health record is the property of the board of education. It must be forwarded to the school to which the pupil is transferred, if the school is known.[88]

The board of education of any school district may provide such equipment, supplies and services as in its judgment will aid in the preservation and promotion of the health of the pupils.[89] Whenever a board of health of any municipality deems the closing of schools necessary because of an epidemic or because of ill health, it must notify the board of education. The board of education may then close the schools under its control. The schools may not be reopened until the board of education is satisfied that the danger is removed.[90]

Every school of two or more rooms or of one room when located above the first story of a building, must have two fire drills each month.[91] Furnace room, hallway, or stairtower fire or smoke doors must be closed at all times the school building is occupied.[92]

Each pupil and teacher must wear industrial quality eye protective devices while attending classes in which any dangerous process is taught, exposure to which might have a tendency to damage the eyes. Visitors to such classes must also wear such protective devices.[93] The kind, type and quality of the protective devices must comply with standards set by the commissioner.[94]

A board may provide for the organization of school safety patrols and for the appointment, with the permission of parents, of pupils as members of these patrols. No liability attaches to the board or any individual teacher or principal by virtue of the organization, maintenance, or operation of a

---

[85]N.J.S.A. 18A:40-16.

[86]N.J.S.A. 18A:40-11.

[87]N.J.S.A. 18A:40-19.

[88]N.J.S.A. 18A:40-4.

[89]N.J.S.A. 18A:40-6.

[90]N.J.S.A. 18A:40-12.

[91]N.J.S.A. 18A:41-1.

[92]N.J.S.A. 18A:41-2.

[93]N.J.S.A. 18A:40-12.1.

[94]N.J.S.A. 18A:40-12.2; N.J.A.C. 6:3-1.14.

school safety patrol.[95] Safety patrol pupils, however, may not direct traffic.[96]

A board may arrange for and pay the premiums for policies of accident insurance with any authorized insurance company, to provide for payment to pupils injured while participating in, practicing or training for, or traveling to and from games or contests conducted by the school or school district, and for injuries in connection with either the conduct of regular curricular and extracurricular programs of the district or with student travel to and from the places where such programs are conducted where such travel is made necessary by such programs.[97] The pupils may be required to pay a proportionate share of the premium for the benefit of such insurance, but no pupil can be forced to make payment if she elects not to participate in the insurance coverage.[98] These provisions are not construed as imposing liability upon the board for any injuries sustained in connection with a game or physical education program.[99]

Public school law enforcement officers may be employed and stationed in the schools upon a finding of need, with the approval of the county superintendent and upon application to and authorization by the commissioner.[100]

Boards of education may be held liable for injuries sustained by students due to the existence of dangerous conditions existing on property owned or controlled by the district.[101] The board may also be held liable for certain negligent acts or ommissions of school district employees which result in injury to students.[102]

THE SCHOOL PROGRAM

Although the board members themselves may have little direct contact with the pupils in their schools, the impact of board decisions profoundly affects these pupils' lives. The board determines annually the dates between which the schools of the district will be open.[103] Courses of study suited to the ages and attainments of all pupils must be provided. No course of study may be adopted or altered except by a recorded roll call majority vote of the full membership of the board.[104] Textbooks are selected by

---

[95]*N.J.S.A.* 18A:42-1.

[86]*N.J.A.C.* 6:29-5.3(g).

[97]*N.J.S.A.* 18A:43-1.

[98]*N.J.S.A.* 18A:43-2.

[99]*N.J.S.A.* 18A:43-3.

[100]*N.J.S.A.* 18A:17-43.

[101]*N.J.S.A.* 59:4-2.

[102]*N.J.S.A.* 59:2-2.

[103]*N.J.S.A.* 18A:36-2.

[104]*N.J.S.A.* 18A:33-1.

a recorded roll call majority vote of the full membership of the board,[105] and are loaned to pupils free of charge.

The Legislature and the state board have mandated the teaching of particular areas of study in all public schools as follows:

1. A two-year course in the history of the U.S., including materials on black history recommended by the commissioner, is required for all high school students;[106]

2. A course in health, safety and physical education, adapted to the ages and capabilities of the pupils. Every pupil must take the course unless excused by the school medical inspector as being physically incapable. The time devoted to the course in physical education must aggregate at least 2.5 hours per school week;[107]

3. Minimum course requirements for graduation from high school including, in addition to the requirements in (1.) and (2.), course requirements established pursuant to the T&E Law. These requirements include:

   a. One credit year of communications for each year of enrollment, up to four credit years;

   b. Two credit years of computation;

   c. One credit year of natural or physical science;

   d. One credit year of fine, practical, and/or performing arts;

   e. And one-half credit year of career exploration or development.[108]

4. The study of community civics, the geography, history and civics of New Jersey, and the privileges and responsibilities of citizenship, in appropriate grades;[109]

5. The nature of alcoholic drinks and narcotics and their effect upon the human system in such manner as may be adapted to the age and understanding of the pupils and sufficiently emphasized in appropriate places in the curriculum;[110]

6. Instruction in accident and fire prevention in appropriate grades and classes;[111]

---

[105]*N.J.S.A.* 18A:34-1.

[106]*N.J.S.A.* 18A:35-1.

[107]*N.J.S.A.* 18A:35-5, 7, 8.

[108]*N.J.A.C.* 6:8-4.2(c).

[109]*N.J.S.A.* 18A:35-3.

[110]*N.J.S.A.* 18A:35-4.

[111]*N.J.S.A.* 18A:6-2.

7. Instruction in the Constitution of the United States beginning not later than seventh grade;[112]

8. A family life education program designed to develop an understanding of all facets of human development, sexuality, and reproduction. The curriculum must be designed to strengthen family life, and must be implemented through a coordinated sequential elementary/secondary program.[113]

In addition, each local board must develop minimum standards for high school graduation which must include attainment of state-determined proficiency levels in reading and computation and may also include demonstration of proficiencies other than those required by the state.[114]

A board may elect to establish a sexual assault prevention program in accordance with guidelines established by the Department of Education.[115]

The board may provide by contract and appropriate funds for the support and maintenance of existing museum facilities and services for the use and benefit of pupils.[116]

Appropriate exercises are to be held on the last school day before Lincoln's Birthday, Washington's Birthday, Decoration Day, Columbus day, Veterans Day, and Thanksgiving Day, and such other patriotic holidays as are established by law.[117] Appropriate exercises for Flag Day are to be held in every public school on June 14 of every year.[118] Arbor Day is to be observed in all public schools with appropriate programs prepared by the superintendent of schools.[119] Commodore John Barry Day is to be observed in each public school on September 13, or the nearest school day if the 13th occurs on a weekend, with appropriate exercises as prescribed by the commissioner.[120]

Every board must display a United States flag on or near the school building during school hours, and have a flag in each assembly room and classroom. The board must require the pupils to salute the flag and pledge the oath of allegiance on every school day. Children with conscientious scruples against such pledge and salute and children of accredited representatives of foreign governments may not be required to make the pledge and salute.[121]

---

[112]*N.J.S.A.* 18A:6-3.

[113]*N.J.A.C.* 6:29-7.1.

[114]*N.J.S.A.* 18A:7C-1 *et seq.*

[115]*N.J.S.A.* 18A:35-4.5.

[116]*N.J.S.A.* 18A:53-1.

[117]*N.J.S.A.* 18A:36-13.

[118]*N.J.S.A.* 18A:36-6.

[119]*N.J.S.A.* 18A:36-9.

[120]*N.J.S.A.* 18A:36-10, 11, 12.

[121]*N.J.S.A.* 18A:36-3.

THE HANDICAPPED PUPIL

Laws relating to the education of handicapped children in New Jersey are found at both the state and federal levels, with a considerable degree of overlap between these two sets of statutes and regulations. While the federal and state statutes concerning handicapped children are summarized separately below, it should be noted that the extensive and detailed state board regulations concerning handicapped children both amplify and supplement state statutes and incorporate federal requirements. These regulations thus provide a complete guide to a district's obligation with respect to handicapped students and will be cited where applicable in the discussion of both state and federal statutes.[122]

New Jersey Statutes and Administrative Code

Each board of education, according to rules prescribed by the commissioner, must identify and provide services for any children between the ages of three and 21 residing in the district and enrolled in the public or nonpublic schools of the state who cannot be properly accommodated through the school programs usually provided, because of handicaps.[123] Programs and services may be provided by a district board of education, at their option, to pupils below the age of three and above the age of 21.[124]

At a minimum, however, each board must provide information to parents of handicapped children below the age of three regarding services and programs available through other state, county, or local agencies which may prevent their handicap from becoming more debilitating.[125]

Each child between the ages of three and 21 who is identified as eligible for special education and/or related services must be classified under one of the following categories: mentally retarded, orthopedically handicapped, communication handicapped, visually handicapped, neurologically or perceptually impaired, chronically ill, emotionally disturbed, socially maladjusted, auditorily handicapped, autistic, multiply handicapped or pre-school handicapped. This determination is accomplished through procedures prescribed by the commissioner and approved by the state board.[126]

The category of mentally retarded children is further divided by statute into three subcategories: educable mentally retarded children, trainable mentally retarded children, and children eligible for day train-

---

[122]These regulations are codified at *N.J.A.C.* 6:28-1.1 *et seq.*. Pursuant to Executive Order No. 66 (1978), Chapter 28 was readopted as R. 1989, d. 239 and will expire on April 10, 1994.

[123]*N.J.S.A.* 18A:46-6; *N.J.A.C.* 6:28-1.1(c), 3.2(a).

[124]*Id.*

[125]*N.J.A.C.* 6:28-1.1(c); *N.J.A.C.* 6:28-10.1 *et seq.*

[126]*N.J.S.A.* 18A:46-2; *N.J.A.C.* 6:28-3.5.

ing (the most severely retarded children).[127] State board regulations subdivide the category of communication handicapped into the subcategories of communication handicapped and eligible for speech-language services and the category of visually handicapped into the subcategories of blind and partially sighted.[128]

Each district board of education, independently or through joint agreements with other boards of education or state agencies, must employ child study teams, speech correctionists or speech-language specialists and other school personnel, in numbers sufficient to ensure provision of required programs and services for handicapped children.[129] The basic child study team must be composed of a school psychologist, a learning disability teacher consultant and a school social worker. For the purposes of evaluation and classification, the child study team shall include pertinent information from certified school personnel making the referral.[130] For pupils ages three to five, the child study team shall also include a speech correctionist or speech-language specialist. The child study team shall act in consultation with a school physician when considering medical diagnostic services. At least one member of the child study team shall be knowledgable about placement options for educationally handicapped pupils.[131]

Consent of the parent or guardian of a child must be obtained prior to implementation of any proposed action concerning the referral, classification, evaluation, or educational placement of a handicapped child.[132] If the board cannot obtain parental consent or if the parent disagrees with the proposed or denied action, either party may request a due process hearing before an administrative law judge.[133]

After the initial evaluation is completed, a meeting shall be convened to determine the pupil's eligibility for special education and her appropriate classification category. For pupils age five through 21, the classification category that best describes the pupil's educational status and needs shall be assigned. For pupils age three through five who have an identified handicapping condition and/or a measurable developmental impairment who require and who would benefit from special education and related services, the classification of pre-school handicapped shall be assigned.[134]

---

[127]N.J.S.A. 18A:46-9.

[128]N.J.A.C. 6:28-3.5.

[129]N.J.A.C. 6:28-1.1(f).

[130]N.J.S.A. 18A:46-5.1.

[131]N.J.A.C. 6:28-3.1.

[132]N.J.A.C. 1:6A-1 et. seq.; N.J.A.C. 6:28-2.3. These procedural safeguards are more extensive than those suggested by N.J.S.A. 18A:46-8, which requires notice and consultation prior to implementation of a classification and not prior to the earlier stages of referral and identification.

[133]N.J.A.C. 6:28-2.7.

[134]N.J.A.C. 6:28-3.5.

A parent who disagrees with the evaluation provided by a board of education may request an independent child study team evaluation. This evaluation must be provided at no cost to the parents unless the board initiates a due process hearing to show that its evaluation is appropriate and a final determination to that effect is made following the hearing.[135] Any independent evaluation submitted to the district child study team shall be considered in making decisions regarding special education and/or related services.[136]

Whenever parental consent to an initial evaluation is requested or a parent identifies to the board a child age three to five as potentially preschool handicapped or a notice of reevaluation is sent to the parents of a handicapped child, that parent shall receive a copy of his procedural safeguard rights.[137] Additionally, upon determination of a pupil's eligibility for special education and/or related services, a copy of *N.J.A.C.* 6:28-2.1 *et seq.* shall be provided to the parent or adult pupil.[138] Upon request by a parent or adult pupil, each district board of education shall provide copies of special education statutes and rules, pupil records rules and information regarding the availability of free and low cost legal and other services relevant to due process hearings.[139]

A due process hearing may be requested in regard to the referral, classification, evaluation or educational placement of a pupil age three through 21 and/or the provision of a free, appropriate public education to that pupil.[140] The school district bears the burden at the due process hearing of demonstrating that the current or proposed individualized education program (IEP) is appropriate under state and federal law. The standard to be applied is whether that program would allow the child to best achieve success in learning.[141]

Each district board of education shall ensure that, to the maximum extent appropriate, an educationally handicapped pupil shall be educated with children who are not educationally handicapped. Special classes, separate schooling or other removal of educationally handicapped pupils from the regular education environment shall occur only when the nature or severity of the handicap is such that education in regular classes even with the use of supplementary aids and services cannot be achieved satisfactorily.[142]

---

[135]*N.J.A.C.* 6:28-2.5(b).

[136]*N.J.A.C.* 6:28-2.5(d).

[137]*N.J.A.C.* 6:28-2.1(d).

[138]*N.J.A.C.* 6:28-2.1(e).

[139]*N.J.A.C.* 6:28-2.1(f).

[140]*N.J.A.C.* 6:28-2.7.

[141]*Lascari v. Bd. of Ed.*, 116 *N.J.* 30 (1989).

[142]*N.J.A.C.* 6:28-1.1(h), 2.10, 4.1(k).

When an educationally handicapped pupil transfers from one New Jersey school district to another, or when a pupil classified as educationally handicapped by a State or local school district outside of New Jersey, transfers into a New Jersey school district, and immediate review of the classification and IEP cannot be conducted, the pupil shall be immediately placed in a program consistent with the goals and objectives of the current IEP for a period not to exceed 30 calendar days.[143]

A child whose mental retardation is so severe that she has been diagnosed and classified as eligible for day training may be excluded from the district.[144] Day training programs shall be provided by the Department of Human Services through state operated or contracted facilities.[145] For pupils placed in day training centers, the district board of education must develop, with participation of the curriculum consultant for the proposed day training center, the pupil's individual education program (IEP). The board is also responsible for all services related to identification, referral, evaluation, eligibility, the IEP and reevaluation for pupils classified as eligible for day training.[146]

Each board, either independently or by contract, must provide suitable facilities and programs for all handicapped children other than those classified as eligible for day training. Tuition rates for providing these services through another school district or through a private school for the handicapped, are governed by statute and the administrative code.[147] These programs and facilities may be provided for each eligible child by one or more of the following:

- A special class or classes in the district, including a class or classes in hospitals, convalescent homes, or other institutions;
- A special class in the public schools of another district in this state or any other state;
- Joint facilities provided by agreement between school districts;
- A jointure commission program;
- A State of New Jersey operated program;
- Supplementary instruction at school.[148]

If the board of education, with the consent of the commissioner, determines that it is impractical to provide the required services by the above

---

[143]*N.J.A.C.* 6:28-4.1(h).

[144]*N.J.S.A.* 18A:46-16.

[145]*N.J.S.A.* 18A:46-18.1; *N.J.A.C.* 6:28-8.4(e).

[146]*N.J.A.C.* 6:28-3.2-3.7, 3.9(a), 8.4(f).

[147]*N.J.S.A.* 18A:7B-1 *et seq.*; *N.J.A.C.* 6:20-3.1 *et seq.*; 6:20-4.1 *et seq.*

[148]*N.J.S.A.* 18A:46-13, 14; *N.J.A.C.* 6:28-4.2.

means, it may either send children capable of benefiting from a day school instructional program to privately operated nonsectarian day classes approved for the handicapped in New Jersey or another state, or provide individual instruction at home or in a school.[149]

Whenever a child study team determines that a suitable special education program cannot be provided for a student by any of the above means and that the most appropriate placement for the child is in an academic program in an accredited non-sectarian, non-public school that has *not* been approved as a school for the handicapped, that child may be placed in that program with the consent of the commissioner or by order of a court of competent jurisdiction.[150]

Programs and facilities for preschool handicapped children may be provided by one or more of the following:

- Parent training and counseling;
- Special programs and services offered by other districts as programs in hospitals, homes or other institutions;
- Special programs and services offered by other districts as provided by agreement between one or more districts;
- A Jointure Commission;
- A county special services school district; and
- Such other methods as shall be approved by the commissioner with the approval of the state board.[151]

The state board has provided guidelines for pre-school programs indicating that a district board of education's pre-school handicapped programs shall be provided in one of the following settings:

- An approved public or private program;
- An accredited non-public school.
- An early intervention program in which the child has been enrolled for the balance of the school year in which the child turns age three.[152]

The commissioner may require boards which have the necessary facilities for handicapped students to receive pupils from other districts needing such services.[153] Any board of education, jointure commission, state operated facility or private school which receives handicapped pupils

---

[149]Id.

[150]*Id.*

[151]*N.J.S.A.* 18A:46-6.1.

[152]*N.J.A.C.* 6:28-4.2(b).

[153]*N.J.S.A.* 18A:46-20.

may charge tuition which is payable by the sending board of education. The tuition rate may not exceed the actual cost per pupil as determined under rules prescribed by the commissioner and approved by the state board.[154] A board of education which sends handicapped pupils to another district may not withdraw such pupils for the purpose of entering them in the schools of another district except for good and sufficient reason and after an application to and approval by the commissioner. If either the sending or receiving district disapproves of the commissioner's determination, it may appeal to the state board.[155]

The district board of education shall provide transportation for those handicapped pupils whose IEP's so require and where prescribed by the school physician. This related service may include special equipment, transportation aides and other special arrangements as necessary. For handicapped pupils below the age of five, safety belts or restraint systems are required.[156]

Two or more school districts may provide jointly for the facilities, examinations or transportation required for handicapped children under an agreement adopted by each board and approved by the commissioner.[157] The agreement may provide for the establishment of a jointure commission composed of representatives of each board with power to provide and maintain the necessary facilities, employ staff, administer the educational program and other required services, to accept pupils from school districts, set tuition rates and apportion the costs among the participating districts.[158]

At the county level, the board of chosen freeholders may establish a county special services school district for the education and treatment of handicapped children.[159] The board of education for such a district consists of the county superintendent of schools, ex officio, and six persons to be appointed by the director of the board of chosen freeholders with the advice and consent of the remaining members of such board.[160] The board of education of the county special services school district has all the powers provided by law for other school districts, subject to the additional restrictions provided by statute.[161]

Programs for educationally handicapped pupils in special education intermediate units such as jointure commissions, county special services

---

[154]N.J.S.A. 18A:46-21; N.J.A.C. 6:20-3.1 *et seq.*; N.J.A.C. 6:20-4.1 *et seq.*

[155]N.J.S.A. 18A:46-22.

[156]N.J.S.A. 18A:46-23; N.J.A.C. 6:28-3.8(a)(5).

[157]N.J.S.A. 18A:46-24.

[158]N.J.S.A. 18A:46-25, 26, 27, 28.

[159]N.J.S.A. 18A:46-29.

[160]N.J.S.A. 18A:46-35.

[161]N.J.S.A. 18A:46-38.

school districts and county educational services commissions shall be planned jointly with the personnel of participating district boards of education. The educational program and services provided shall be the responsibility of the local district board of education.[162]

Boards of education of school districts within the county may contract with the county special services school district of their county, if one exists, in order to send pupils to schools established by the latter. The sending districts must pay tuition, the amount not to exceed the lesser of the actual cost per pupil as determined for each special education category or the foundation amount per pupil plus the appropriate per pupil special education aid. County special services school districts must accept all eligible pupils within the county, so far as facilities permit. Pupils residing outside the county may also be accepted if facilities are available.[163]

Each district board of education in which a nonpublic school is located must provide remedial and auxiliary services for handicapped pupils enrolled in those nonpublic schools.[164] These services may be provided by the board itself, through joint agreements with other boards or through contracts with educational services commissions or other approved agencies.[165] These services include the identification, referral, evaluation, determination of eligibility and development of IEP's, provision of speech correction for articulation disorders, home instruction and supplementary instruction as well as bilingual education programs and compensatory education.[166] If transportation or the maintenance of vehicular classrooms is required, the board of education of the district in which the non-public school is located shall provide the transportation and maintenance. The board will receive state aid to help defray these costs.[167]

Educationally handicapped pupils are subject to the same district board of education disciplinary policies and procedures as non-handicapped pupils, unless the pupil's IEP includes exemptions to those policies or procedures. However, prior to effecting any discipline which would result in a significant change in placement, the child study team shall conduct a reevaluation. The following standards are used in determining if a proposed discipline constitutes a significant change in placement:

- If the proposed discipline involves expulsion or suspension for an indefinite period of time or for more than 10 consecutive school days, the expulsion or suspension constitutes a significant change of placement;

---

[162]N.J.A.C. 6:28-7.4.

[163]N.J.S.A. 18A:46-31.

[164]N.J.S.A. 18A:46-19.1 et seq.; N.J.S.A. 18A:46A-1 et seq.

[165]N.J.A.C. 6:28-6.1.

[166]N.J.S.A. 18A:46A-2; N.J.A.C. 6:28-6.2.

[167]N.J.A.C. 6:28-6.2.

- If the proposed discipline involves suspension of more than 10 non-consecutive school days, the suspension shall be reviewed to determine if it creates a pattern of exclusion which constitutes a significant change in placement.

On completion of the reevaluation, the child study team shall determine if the pupil's behavior was primarily caused by his or her educational handicap and, if so, whether the pupil's current educational placement is appropriate. If the pupil's behavior is determined to be primarily caused by the pupil's educational handicap, the district may not discipline the pupil. If it is determined that the pupil's behavior is not related to his or her educational handicap, the district board of education may discipline the pupil. However, at no time shall the district board of education cease educational services to that pupil. If there is ongoing peril of physical harm to self or others or of substantial disruption to the educational process, and the suspension would result in a significant change in placement, the pupil may be temporarily suspended while the district immediately seeks emergency relief.[168]

Federal Statutes

The primary federal statute that imposes obligations on school districts with respect to the education of children with disabilities is the Individuals with Disabilities Education Act (IDEA).[169] IDEA is the new name given the former Education for All Handicapped Children Act (EHA) as part of the October, 1990 reauthorization of EHA federal grant programs. IDEA consists of the Education of the Handicapped Act of 1970 as amended by the Education for All Handicapped Children Act of 1975, by the Handicapped Children's Protection Act (HCPA)[170] and the 1990 IDEA amendments. Under IDEA, all references to "handicapped children" are now "children with disabilities." These include children with mental retardation, hearing impairments, including deafness, speech or language impairment, visual impairments including blindness, serious emotional disturbance, orthopedic impairments, autism, traumatic brain injury, other health impairments, or specific learning disabilities who by reason thereof need special education and related services.[171]

The second significant federal statute that imposes obligations on school districts with respect to the education of handicapped children is section 504 of the Rehabilitation Act of 1973.[172] (Section 504).

---

[168]N.J.A.C. 6:28-2.8.

[169]20 U.S.C.A. § 1400 et seq.

[170]20 U.S.C.A. § 1415(e)(4)(B)-(f)

[172]20 U.S.C.A. § 1401.

[172]29 U.S.C.A. § 794.

These statutes impose requirements as a condition for, respectively, the receipt of federal assistance for children with disabilities (IDEA)[173] or the receipt of any form of federal assistance (Section 504).[174] It should be noted however, that the requirements of these statutes have been incorporated into the state board regulations on special education pupils which pertain to all New Jersey school districts.[175] Accordingly, a district is in fact subject to the federal requirements even if it does not receive any federal aid.

In addition to these two statutes, the Americans with Disabilities Act, 42 *U.S.C.* 12101 *et seq.,* imposes many of the same obligations on local boards of education irrespective of their receipt of federal aid. (See Chapter 8.)

The Education of the Handicapped Act of 1970 created within the United States Office of Education a bureau for the education and training of the handicapped in order to administer and implement programs for such education and training. With the creation of the Department of Education in 1979, all functions of the Office of Education and the Commissioner of Education were transferred to the Department of Education and the Secretary of Education.[176] Under IDEA, within the Office of Special Education and Rehabitive Services in the Department of Education, there exists an Office of Special Education Programs that administers and implements all programs and activities concerning the education and training of individuals with disabilities.[177]

Under IDEA, the Secretary of Education is authorized to make grants for part, or all, of the cost of altering existing buildings and equipment for removal of architectural barriers to children with disabilities. Applications for such funds may be made by any state or local educational agency or intermediate educational unit (e.g. a county special services district).[178]

Subchapter II of IDEA, "Assistance to States for Education of Handicapped Children,"[179] establishes maximum amounts which may be granted to states after Congress has enacted annual appropriations. These maximums are based on a sliding-scale percentage of the average per pupil expenditure in public elementary and secondary schools in the United States multiplied by the number of children receiving special education and related services in the school districts of the state.[180] Seventy-five percent of the aid granted to each state is allocated to local education agen-

---

[173]20 *U.S.C.A.* § 1400 *et seq.*

[174]20 *U.S.C.A.* § 794.

[175]*N.J.A.C.* 6:28-1.1 *et seq.*

[176]20 *U.S.C.A.* § 3441.

[177]20 *U.S.C.A.* § 1402.

[178]20 *U.S.C.A.* § 1406.

[179]20 *U.S.C.A.* § 1411 *et seq.*

[180]20 *U.S.C.A.* § 1411(a).

cies and intermediate educational units. The state agency may use five percent of its share or $350,000, whichever is greater, for administrative costs, with the remainder used to provide support services and direct services to children with disabilities and for the administrative costs of monitoring and complaint investigation.[181]

Each local district is entitled to a share of these federal funds based upon its percentage of the total statewide number of children with disabilities ages three to 21 receiving special education and related services.[182] In order to receive federal assistance under IDEA, each state must meet certain requirements. A state must have in effect a policy that assures all children with disabilities the right to free appropriate education.[183] A free appropriate education consists of special education and related services,[184] terms which are themselves defined as, respectively, specially designed instruction, at no cost to parents or guardians, to meet the unique needs of a child with a disability,[185] and transportation and such developmental, corrective and other supportive services (including speech pathology and audiology, psychological services, physical and occupational therapy, recreation and medical and counseling services) which may be required to assist a child with a disability to benefit from special education.[186]

A free appropriate education also includes the requirement that an individualized education program for each child with a disability be established at the beginning of each school year, and be reviewed and revised periodically but not less than annually.[187]

The state must also establish procedures to assure that, to the maximum extent appropriate, children with disabilities are educated with children who are not disabled and that separate schooling occurs only when the nature and severity of the disability is such that education in regular classes, even with the use of supplementary aids and services, cannot be achieved satisfactorily.[188] However, if a placement in a private school or facility is necessary to provide a child with a disability an appropriate education, the state must ensure that the program is provided at no cost to the parents or guardian.[189]

The state must assure that testing and evaluation materials are

---

[181]20 *U.S.C.A.* § 1411(c).

[182]20 *U.S.C.A.* § 1411(d).

[183]20 *U.S.C.A.* § 1412.

[184]20 *U.S.C.A.* § 1401(18).

[185]20 *U.S.C.A.* § 1401(16).

[186]20 *U.S.C.A.* § 1401(17).

[187]20 *U.S.C.A.* § 1401(18); 1414(a) (5).

[188]20 *U.S.C.A.* § 1412(5)(B).

[189]20 *U.S.C.A.* § 1413(a)(4)(B); 34 *C.F.R.* 104.33, 300.302.

selected and administered so as not to be racially or culturally discriminatory and are provided and administered in the child's native language or mode of communication unless it is clearly not feasible to do so.[190] The State must adopt procedures for consultation with individuals involved in or concerned with the education of children with disabilities, including individuals with disabilities and parents or guardians of such children.[191] As previously noted, state board regulations on children with disabilities incorporate these requirements.[192]

In order to receive federal assistance under IDEA, a local education agency or intermediate unit must submit an application to the state educational agency. The district's application must provide that all children who are residing within the local educational agency or intermediate unit who are disabled and who are in need of special education and related services will be identified, located and evaluated. The application must assure that payments will be used for the excess costs of providing special education and related services to children with disabilities. Payments shall be used to supplement and, to the extent possible, increase the level of state and local funds expended for the education of children with disabilities. In no case shall federal funds supplant state and local funds.[193]

The local programs must also establish the goals of providing full educational opportunities to all children with disabilities, including:

- The establishment of priorities for providing a free appropriate public education to all children with disabilities, first with respect to children with disabilities who are not receiving an education, and second with respect to children with disabilities, within each disability, with the most severe disabilities who are receiving an inadequate education;
- The participation and consultation of the parents or guardians of such children; and
- To the maximum extent practicable, the provisions of special services to enable such children to participate in regular educational programs.[194]

Every state educational agency, local educational agency or intermediate educational unit receiving assistance under IDEA must establish and maintain procedures to assure that children with disabilities and their parents are guaranteed procedural safeguards. These procedures include, but shall not be limited to:

---

[190]20 *U.S.C.A.* § 1412(5)(C).

[191]20 *U.S.C.A.* § 1412(7).

[192]*N.J.A.C.* 6:28-1.1 *et seq.*

[193]20 *U.S.C.A.* § 1414.

[194]20 *U.S.C.A.* § 1414(a)(1)(c).

- An opportunity for the parents or guardians of a child with a disability to examine all relevant records pertaining to the identification, evaluation and educational placement of such child and the provision of a free and appropriate education to such child and to obtain an independent educational evaluation of the child;

- Procedures to protect the rights of the child whenever the parents or guardian of the child are not known, unavailable, or the child is a ward of the state;

- Written prior notice to the parents or guardian whenever the agency or unit proposes to initiate or change, or refuses to initiate or change, the identification, evaluation or educational placement of the child or the provision of a free appropriate public education to the child;

- Notice which fully informs the parents in the parents' native language, unless it is clearly not feasible to do so, of all procedures available to them; and

- An opportunity to present complaints with respect to any matter relating to the identification, evaluation, or educational placement of the child, or the provision of a free appropriate public education to such child.[195] When parents register a complaint, they are entitled to an impartial due process hearing.[196]

In New Jersey, the due process hearing is conducted by an Administrative Law Judge (ALJ), in the Office of Administrative Law. The decision of the ALJ is final, binding on both parties and is to be implemented without undue delay unless stayed.[197] The ALJ's decision may be appealed to the Law Division of Superior Court of New Jersey or to the federal district court.[198]

During the pendency of any appeal proceedings, unless the State or local educational agency and the parents or guardian otherwise agree, the child shall remain in the then current educational placement. If the child is applying for initial admission to a public school, the child, with the consent of the parents or guardians, shall be placed in the public school program until all such proceedings have been completed.[199]

---

[195] 20 U.S.C.A. § 1415; N.J.A.C. 6:28-2.1 et seq.

[196] Id.

[197] N.J.A.C. 6:28-2.7(g).

[198] 20 U.S.C.A. § 1415(e); N.J.A.C. 1:6A-1 et seq.; Minguet v. Bd. of Ed. of North Brunswick, unpublished Appellate Division decision, Docket No. A-1483-82T3, decided October 20, 1983.

[199] 20 U.S.C.A. § 1415(e)(3).

In 1986, Congress enacted the Handicapped Children's Protection Act (HCPA), currently codified at Section 1415(e)(4)(f) of IDEA. This provision permits the court, in any action or proceeding under IDEA, to award reasonable attorneys' fees as part of the costs to the parents or guardian of a child with a disability who is a prevailing party.[200] The HCPA was Congress' reaction to the U.S. Supreme Court decision in *Smith v. Robinson*, which held that an award of attorney fees was not available under the Education for all Handicapped Children Act (EHA) as the EHA did not specifically provide for the recovery of attorney fees. The Court stated that the EHA was the exclusive avenue under which parental claims of this sort could be brought, making recovery of fees under another statute impossible.[201]

Numerous federal appeals courts have interpreted the HCPA to permit fee recovery not only in court proceedings but in administrative proceedings as well.[202] A separate legal action for fee recovery in the courts is necessary as IDEA does not authorize administrative hearing officers to award attorney fees.[203] Some federal courts have also ruled that attorneys' fees are recoverable for work done prior to an administrative proceeding, including pre-hearing settlement conferences.[204] Fees charged by lay advocates (non-attorneys) who represent parents at administrative hearings are not recoverable under the HCPA. However, these lay advocates may charge a fee as an expert witness or educational consultant that might be recoverable.[205]

Along with changing all references to "handicapped children" to "children with disabilities," IDEA amended the EHA in several significant areas. These amendments include:

- Abolishing state immunity under the eleventh amendment. This provision will permit suits against states and state agencies in federal court;[206]
- All IEP's for eligible students must provide for transition services. These services are defined as a coordinated set of ac-

---

[200]20 *U.S.C.A.* § 1415(e)(4)-(f).

[201]*Smith v. Robinson*, 468 *U.S.* 992 (1984).

[202]*Moore v. District of Columbia*, 907 F.2d. 165 (D.C. Cir. 1990), *McSombodies v. San Mateo Cty. School District*, 886 F.2d. 1559 (9th Cir. 1989), supplemented 897 F.2d. 975 (9th Cir. 1990); *Duane M. v. Orleans Parish School Board*, 861 F.2d. 115 (5th Cir. 1988); *Mitten v. Muscogee Cty. School District*, 877 F.2d. 932 (11th Cir. 1989).

[203]20 *U.S.C.A.* § 1415(e)(4)(B).

[204]*Shelly C. v. Venus Ind. School District*, 878 F.2d. 862 (5th Cir. 1989); *E.P. v. Union Cty. Reg. High School No. 1*, 741 F. Supp. 1144 (D. N.J. 1989).

[205]*Arons v. New Jersey State Board of Education*, 842 F.2d. 58 (3rd Cir. 1988); *N.J.A.C.* 1:6A-4.2.

[206]20 *U.S.C.A.* § 1403.

tivities for a student designed within an outcome-oriented process which promotes movement from school to post-school activities;[207]

- "Autism" and "traumatic brain injury" are new categories of disability;[208]
- Rehabilitation counseling and social work services are now related services;[209]
- Programs for deaf-blind children[210] and outreach preschool early intervention programs[211] are expanded and new grant programs are authorized for provision of transition services[212] and serving children with serious emotional disturbances.[213]

The second federal statute pertaining to handicapped pupils is the Rehabilitation Act of 1973. Section 504 of that act states: "No otherwise qualified handicapped individual...shall, solely by reason of his handicap, be excluded from the participation in, be denied the benefits of, or be subjected to discrimination under any program or activity receiving Federal financial assistance."[214]

Regulations implementing Section 504 became effective on June 3, 1977.[215] In 1979, the Department of Health, Education and Welfare was split into the Department of Health and Human Services and the Department of Education. The Department of Education became responsible for administration of the regulations leading to their recodification.[216] These regulations are administered by the Office for Civil Rights created within the Department of Education.[217]

The regulations specify that no qualified handicapped person shall, on the basis of handicap, be excluded from participation in, be denied the benefits of, or otherwise be subjected to, discrimination under any program or activity which receives or benefits from Federal assistance.[218] A "qualified handicapped person" means, with respect to preschool, elementary, or secondary educational services, a handicapped person:

---

[207]20 *U.S.C.A.* § 1401(a)(19).

[208]20 *U.S.C.A.* § 1401(a)(1).

[209]20 *U.S.C.A.* § 1401(a)(17).

[210]20 *U.S.C.A.* § 1422.

[211]20 *U.S.C.A.* § 1423.

[212]20 *U.S.C.A.* § 1425.

[213]20 *U.S.C.A.* § 1426.

[214]29 *U.S.C.A.* § 794.

[215]45 *C.F.R.* § 84.11, § 84.14.

[216]34 *C.F.R.* § 104.1 *et seq.*

[217]20 *U.S.C.A.* § 3441(a)(3), 3413(1).

[218]34 *C.F.R.* § 104.4.

- Of an age during which nonhandicapped persons are provided such services; or
- Of an age during which it is mandatory under state law to provide such services to handicapped persons to whom a state is required to provide a free appropriate public education under IDEA.

A "qualified handicapped person" means, with respect to post-secondary and vocational education services, a handicapped person who meets the academic and technical standards requested to admission or participation in the recipient's education program or activity.[219]

The regulations require that each educational agency which operates a public elementary or secondary program provide a free and appropriate public education to each qualified handicapped person who is in the agency's jurisdiction, regardless of the nature or severity of the person's handicap.[220] They require that the agency place handicapped students in the regular educational program unless it is demonstrated that the education of that person cannot be achieved satisfactorily in the regular setting, even with the use of supplementary aids and services.[221] The educational agency must also establish a system of procedural safeguards with respect to actions regarding the identification, evaluation or placement of persons who are believed to need special education or related services. These safeguards must include notice, an opportunity for the parents or guardian to examine relevant records, an impartial hearing with opportunity for participation by the person's parents or guardian and representation by counsel, and a review procedure.[222]

The regulations also require that an educational agency provide handicapped pupils an equal opportunity for participation in nonacademic and extracurricular services and activities. These services and activities may include counseling services, physical recreational athletics, transportation, health services, recreational activities, special interest groups or clubs and employment of students. If personal, academic, or vocational counseling is being provided, the district must ensure that qualified handicapped students are not counseled toward more restrictive career objectives than are nonhandicapped students with similar interests and abilities.[223]

The Section 504 regulations also deal with subjects not covered by IDEA and its implementing regulations. Subpart C of the 504 regulations addresses the problem of program accessibility based on building design

---

[219] 34 *C.F.R.* § 104.3(k).
[220] 34 *C.F.R.* § 104.33(a).
[221] 34 *C.F.R.* § 104.34.
[222] 34 *C.F.R.* § 104.36.
[223] 34 *C.F.R.* § 104.37

and establishes several requirements.[224] It provides that all newly constructed facilities and most alterations to existing facilities must be made readily accessible to and usable by handicapped persons.[225] The regulations do not go so far, however, as to require that every room, stairway, office, etc. of an existing or newly constructed facility be accessible to handicapped students. The critical requirement is that each program or activity, when viewed in its entirety, must be readily accessible to handicapped students.[226] These building design requirements have also been incorporated into the state board regulations.[227]

---

[224]34 C.F.R. § 104.21.

[225]34 C.F.R. § 104.23.

[226]34 C.F.R. § 104.22.

[227]N.J.A.C. 6:22-1.1 et seq.

STUDENTS' RIGHTS AND RESPONSIBILITIES

6

The right to a free public school education for all New Jersey children between the ages of five and 18 is guaranteed by the New Jersey Constitution.[1] The statutes provide that public schools are to be free to any person over 5 and under 20 years of age who is domiciled within the school district.[2] State law also requires compulsory education for children between the ages of six and 16.[3]

This right to education is subject to certain restrictions: students must submit to the authority of their teachers; they must pursue their prescribed courses of study; and they must comply with those rules that have been established by law for the governance of their schools.[4] Those students who do not obey the reasonable rules of the school system or who otherwise act in a manner so as to disrupt the school system are subject to punishment, including suspension or expulsion from school.[5]

The sections which follow focus on suspension and expulsion and other areas affecting the rights and responsibilities of students.

SUSPENSION AND EXPULSION

Conduct which constitutes good cause for a student's suspension or expulsion includes, but is not limited to:

- Continued and willful disobedience;
- Open defiance of any teacher's authority or person having authority over the student;
- Conduct of such character as to constitute a continuing danger to the physical well-being of other people;
- Physical assault on another pupil;

---

[1]*N.J. Const.* 1947, art. 8, sec. 4, par. 1.
[2]*N.J.S.A.* 18A:38-1.
[3]*N.J.S.A.* 18A:38-25.
[4]*N.J.S.A.* 18A:37-1.
[5]*N.J.S.A.* 18A:37-2.

- Taking, or attempting to take personal property or money from another pupil, or from her presence, by means of force or fear;

- Willfully causing, or attempting to cause, substantial damage to school property;

- Participating in an unauthorized occupancy by any group of pupils or others of any part of any school or other building owned by any school district, and failure to leave such school or other facility promptly after being directed to do so by the principal or other person in charge of such building or facility;

- Incitement which is intended to and does result in unauthorized occupation by any groups of pupils or others of any part of a school or other facility owned by any school district;

- Incitement which is intended to and does result in truancy by other pupils; and

- Knowing possession or knowing consumption without legal authority of alcoholic beverages or controlled dangerous substances on school premises, or being under the influence of intoxicating liquor or controlled dangerous substances while on school premises.[6]

In addition, a board *must* immediately suspend a student who commits an assault (as defined in the state's criminal code) on a board member, teacher, or other employee of the board of education. Expulsion proceedings before the local board of education must take place no later than 21 days following the suspension of the student.[7]

The terms "suspension" and "expulsion" are often used interchangeably, but there is a difference in their meanings. "Suspension" refers to the temporary denial of the student's right to attend school. A suspension is normally imposed by the school principal and is usually of short duration. "Expulsion," in contrast, refers to the permanent denial of the student's right to attend school and may be imposed only by the local board of education.

The principal may suspend any student from school for good cause, but the suspension must be reported immediately to the district superintendent, who in turn must report the suspension to the district board of education at its next regular meeting.[8] The suspended student may be reinstated by the principal or superintendent prior to the second regular meeting of the board after suspension unless the board has reinstated the student

---

[6]*Ibid.*

[7]*N.J.S.A.* 18A:37-2.1; *N.J.S.A* 2C:12-1. (It may not be possible to adhere to this statute in the case of handicapped students. See discussion later in this chapter.)

[8]*N.J.S.A.* 18A:37-4.

at its first regular meeting after suspension.[9] No suspension may be continued beyond the second regular meeting of the board of education after such suspension unless the board continues it.[10] The power to reinstate, continue any suspension or expel a student from the school system is vested solely in the board of education.[11]

A student may appeal a suspension or expulsion decision of the board of education to the commissioner of education.[12] An appeal from a decision of the commissioner is made to the state board of education.[13] Decisions of the state board are reviewable by the courts.[14]

A board's statutory authority to suspend or expel a student, is also affected by two sources of federal law. The first and more well established of these is the set of constitutional principles concerning the due process rights of students. These principles were articulated in several court decisions in the 1960's and 1970's. The second is the Education for All Handicapped Children Act, now known as the Individuals with Disabilities Act (IDEA),[15] whose procedural protections may, in some circumstances, limit a board's authority to expel a student who is classified as educationally handicapped.

Regarding the due process rights of students, the landmark decision in *Dixon v. Alabama State Board of Education*[16] recognized that the requirements of procedural due process under the Fourteenth Amendment of the United States Constitution are applicable to the suspension or expulsion of students from public education institutions.

The *Dixon* case involved students expelled from a state college without providing the students with any of the procedural safeguards required by due process. The guidelines stated by the court in *Dixon* are important and are worth repeating here. The court said:

> *For the guidance of the parties in the event of further proceedings, we state our views on the nature of the notice and hearings required by due process prior to expulsion from a state college or university. They shall, we think, comply with the following standards. The notice should contain a statement of the specific charges and grounds which, if proper, would justify expulsion under the regulations of the board of education. The nature of the hearing should vary depending upon the circumstances of the particular case. The case before us required*

---

[9]*Ibid.*

[10]*N.J.S.A.* 18A:37-5.

[11]*Ibid.*

[12]*N.J.S.A.* 18A:6-9.

[13]*N.J.S.A.* 18A:6-27.

[14]Rules Governing the Courts of the State of New Jersey, 2:2-3.

[15]20 *U.S.C.A.* Section 1400 *et seq.*

[16]294 *F.2d* 150 (5th Cir. 1961), *cert.* denied 368 *U.S.* 930 (1961).

something more than an informal interview with an administrative authority of the college. By its nature, a charge of misconduct, as opposed to a failure to meet the scholastic standards of the college, depends upon a collection of the facts concerning the charge of misconduct, easily colored by the point of view of the witnesses. In such circumstances, a hearing which gives the board or the administrative authorities of the college an opportunity to hear both sides in considerable detail is best suited to protect the rights of all involved. This is not to imply that a full dress judicial hearing with a right to cross-examine witnesses is required. Such a hearing, with the attending publicity and the disturbance of college activities might be detrimental to the college's educational atmosphere and impractical to carry out. Nevertheless, the rudiments of an adversary proceeding may be preserved without encroaching upon the interests of the college. In the instant case, the student should be given the names of the witnesses against him and an oral or written report on the facts to which each witness testified. He should also be given the opportunity to present to the board, or at least to an administrative official of the college, his own defense against the charges and to produce either oral testimony or written affidavits of witnesses in his behalf. If the hearing is not before the board directly, the results and findings of the hearing should be presented in a report open to the student's inspection. If these rudimentary elements of fair play are followed in a case of misconduct of this particular type, we feel that the requirements of due process of law will have been fulfilled.[17]

These guidelines were quoted as setting forth the minimum requirements for a suspension hearing in a subsequent New Jersey case.[18] That case involved a high school student who was given neither a preliminary hearing nor a full hearing before he was suspended from school. The court held that the New Jersey statutes relating to suspension and expulsion must be construed so as "to afford students facing disciplinary action involving the possible imposition of serious sanctions, such as suspension or expulsion, the procedural due process guaranteed by the Fourteenth Amendment."[19] The court went on to say that when school authorities have reasonable cause to believe that a student presents a danger to himself, to others or to school property, they may temporarily suspend the student for a short period of time pending a full hearing which will afford the student procedural due process. Under ordinary circumstances, however, the student must be afforded a preliminary hearing

[17]294 *F.2d* at 158-59.
[18]*R.R. v. Bd. of Ed., Shore Regional High School*, 109 *N.J. Super.* 337 (Ch. Div. 1970).
[19]*Id.* at 347.

before he may be suspended.[20] The preliminary hearing may be completely informal, but the full hearing "clearly depends upon the circumstances of the case."[21] At a minimum, the student must be afforded the procedural rights as mandated by *Dixon*.[22] In no case, the court held, should the full due process hearing take place more than 21 days from the date of the suspension.[23]

A 1971 case which was decided by the state's highest court held that in a suspension or expulsion hearing before the local board of education, the accused student always has the right to demand that his accusers appear in person to answer questions.[24] This right of confrontation exists even if the penalty to be imposed is less than expulsion or a severe term of suspension.[25]

The issue of students' rights in suspension procedures reached the United States Supreme Court in 1975. In *Goss v. Lopez*[26] the Supreme Court announced the minimum procedural requirements of the due process clause of the Fourteenth Amendment. The Court held that for short-term suspensions, a student must be given oral or written notice of the charges against her and, if she denies them, an explanation of the evidence the authorities have and an opportunity to present her side of the story.[27] It must be stressed that these minimum requirements apply only in cases where the suspension is for 10 days or less. The Court stated: "Longer suspensions or expulsions for the remainder of the school term, or permanently, may require more formal procedures. Nor do we put aside the possibility that in unusual situations, although involving only a short suspension, something more than the rudimentary procedures will be required."[28]

The informal notice and hearing required under *Goss* should generally precede the removal of the student from school. The Court, however, recognized that in cases where the student poses a danger to persons or property, or where he presents "an ongoing threat of disrupting the academic process," such student may be immediately removed from school.[29] In these cases, the school authorities should satisfy the notice and hearing requirements "as soon as practicable."[30]

---

[20]*Id.*

[21]*Id.* at 348.

[22]*Id.* at 350.

[23]*Id.*

[24]*Tibbs v. Bd. of Ed. of the Twp. of Franklin, Somerset County*, 114 *N.J. Super.* 287 (App. Div. 1971), affirmed 59 *N.J.* 506 (1971).

[25]114 *N.J. Super.* at 302.

[26]419 *U.S.* 565 (1975).

[27]*Id.* at 581.

[28]*Id.* at 584.

[29]*Id.* at 582.

[30]*Id.* at 583.

The Supreme Court further stated that under the due process clause, students do not have a right to the assistance of counsel in connection with short term suspension hearings. Nor do students have the right to confront adverse witnesses or to call their own witnesses. The school disciplinarian, however, has the discretion to permit the participation of counsel and the confrontation of witnesses in order to make a better-informed decision.[31]

From the cases discussed above and from pertinent statutes, some conclusions may be drawn concerning the procedural due process guarantees which are applicable to suspensions and expulsions of students *who are not classified as educationally handicapped*:

- New Jersey statutes relating to suspension and expulsion must be construed to require public school officials to afford students facing serious disciplinary action the procedural due process guaranteed by the Fourteenth Amendment;

- A principal has the power to suspend a student for a period of ten days or less following an informal hearing where the student is apprised of the charges against him and is given an opportunity to present a defense. (Such hearing may follow suspension in emergency situations.);

- Where the suspension is for more than ten days, or where a short suspension involves an "unusual situation," the student must be afforded both a preliminary and a full hearing. The preliminary hearing should conform to the requirments set forth above. The full hearing should conform to the requirements set forth below;

- Under no circumstances may a suspension by a principal be continued beyond the second regular meeting of the board of education, unless the board so continues the suspension, and only the local board of education has the power to expel a student;

- A full due process hearing, whether before the principal in a suspension matter or before the board in a continuation of a suspension matter or an expulsion matter, includes the accused student's right to:

   a. Notification of the charges against him (written is better);

   b. The names of the adverse witnesses;

   c. Copies of the statements and affidavits of the adverse witnesses;

   d. The opportunity to be heard in her own defense;

---

[31]*Id.* at 584.

e. The opportunity to present witnesses and evidence in her own defense;

f. The opportunity to cross-examine adverse witnesses; and

g. The opportunity to be represented by counsel.

In addition to the safeguards mandated by constitutional considerations, one additional prerequisite must be met before a student who is not already classified as educationally handicapped may be expelled: the student must be evaluated by the district's child study team in order to determine if he is eligible for the services described in the state board's special education regulations.[32]

When a board seeks to expel a student who is classified as educationally handicapped, the foregoing procedural protections will probably not be sufficient. The IDEA was enacted in 1977 in response to Congress' findings that the special educational needs of the more than 8,000,000 children with disabilities were not being fully met. Specifically, Congress found that in school districts across the country, one million children with disabilities were excluded from classes.[33] As a condition of federal financial assistance, IDEA requires states to ensure a "free appropriate public education" for all children with disabilities within their jurisdictions.[34]

IDEA establishes a comprehensive system of procedural protections designed to ensure parental involvement in decisions concerning the education of their children with disabilities. It also provides administrative and judicial review of any decisions with which the parent disagrees. Among these protections is a "stay put" provision which directs that the child "shall remain in the then current educational placement of such child..." pending the completion of the proceedings unless the State or local educational agency and parents otherwise agree.[35]

A series of federal cases has interpreted this "stay put" provision to imply that an expulsion of a handicapped student for disciplinary reasons is a change in placement, and thus triggers the procedural protections of IDEA and Section 504 of the Rehabilitation Act of 1973.[36] Moreover, and as will be illustrated below, the extension of the IDEA's procedural protections also places significant restrictions on a board's actual authority to expel a handicapped student at all. *Kaelin v. Grubbs*, a 1982 case concerning the discipline of handicapped students, synthesizes the principles

---

[32]*N.J.A.C.* 6:28-2.8(g).

[33]20 *U.S.C.* Section 1400(a)(1) and (2).

[34]20 *U.S.C.* Section 1400(c).

[35]20 *U.S.C.* Section 1415(e)(3).

[36]*Kaelin v. Grubbs*, 682 *F.2d* 595 (6th Cir. 1982); *S-1 v. Turlington* 635 *F.2d* 342 (5th Cir.), cert. denied, 454 *U.S.* 1030 (1981); *Doe v. Koger*, 480 *F.Supp.* 225 (N.D., Ind. 1979), *Sherry v. New York State Education Dept.*, 479 *F. Supp.* 1328 (W.D.N.Y., 1979).

articulated in previous cases and an examination of the facts and analysis in that case is useful here.

In *Kaelin*, a 15 year old mentally retarded student was suspended immediately after he caused a disturbance in class and assaulted his teacher. The board subsequently held a hearing and determined that the student should be expelled pursuant to a state statute authorizing removal from school for willful disobedience and assault on school personnel. The sixth circuit held that the action was improper because the board did not follow the procedures necessary to effect a change in placement under the EHA.[37] *Kaelin* followed previous cases in holding that the expulsion was a change of placement, and commented that the EHA's, now IDEA's, emphasis on individualized educational planning would be eviscerated if schools could expel handicapped pupils using traditional expulsion procedures.[38] It further held that, prior to expulsion of a handicapped child, a district's child study team must reconsider the appropriateness of the student's placement and determine the relationship, if any, between the child's handicap and the disruptive behavior.

If the disruptive behavior is found to be a manifestation of the student's handicap, *Kaelin* follows *S-1 v. Turlington* and *Doe v. Koger* in holding that the student may not be expelled, (although he may be moved to a more restrictive environment after following the appropriate procedures for a change in placement). Moreover, even where expulsion is appropriate—*i.e.*, there is no relationship between the disturbance and the handicap, *Turlington* and *Kaelin*, state, without amplification, that the EHA, now IDEA, does *not* permit a complete cessation of educational services.[39] Presumably, then, when a handicapped child is removed from a school he must either be placed in a more restrictive educational institution or provided with home instruction.

School officials have maintained that they have a right to exclude any student who is *clearly dangerous* even if that student is handicapped. A few federal courts have agreed.[40] However, the U.S. Supreme Court held in *Honig v. Doe*,[41] that Congress did not intend to exclude dangerous handicapped children from the "stay put" provision of the statute. In this case, Doe and Smith, two emotionally disturbed students, were suspended indefinitely for violent and disruptive behavior related to their disabilities, pending expulsion hearings. Doe filed suit alleging that the suspension and proposed expulsion violated the EHA, now IDEA; Smith joined the

---

[37]*Kaelin v. Grubbs, supra*, at 597.

[38]*Id.* at 602.

[39]*Id.*

[40]*See, Victoria L. v. District School Board*, 741 *F.2d.* 369 (11th Cir. 1984); *Jackson v. Franklin County School Board*, 765 *F.2d.* 535 (5th Cir. 1985).

[41]484 *U.S.* 305 (1988).

suit. The district court held, *inter alia*, that the school district could not expel handicapped students whose behavior was a manifestation of their handicap. The Appeals Court affirmed in part, but held that handicapped children were not totally immune from the disciplinary process. According to the court, school districts wishing to expel a handicapped student had to adhere to the change in placement guidelines established by the Education for All Handicapped Children Act, now IDEA.[42] The Superintendent, Bill Honig appealed, alleging a "dangerousness" exception existed allowing school officials to exclude handicapped students whose presence posed a threat to the safety of other students. The Supreme Court rejected this argument stating:

> *We think it clear, however, that Congress very much meant to strip schools of the* unilateral *authority they had traditionally employed to exclude disabled students, particularly emotionally disturbed students, from school. In so doing, Congress did not leave school administrators powerless to deal with dangerous students; it did, however, deny school officials their former right to "self-help," and directed that in the future the removal of disabled students could be accomplished only with the permission of the parents or, as a last resort, the courts.*[43]

While *Kaelin, Honig* and the body of cases they follow impose significant restrictions on a board's authority to *expel* a handicapped student, they also stress that a handicapped student may be suspended on a *short-term* basis in accordance with the same procedures which are applicable to other students under *Goss v. Lopez*.[44]

From the cases' discussion above, a few alternatives emerge concerning procedural due process rights for educationally handicapped children:

- A child with disabilities displaying violent or disruptive behavior shall be maintained in her current educational placement until parental consent is secured or an administrative hearing and appeal process is completed or a court order for alternative placement is obtained;
- Temporary suspension (10 days or less) may be utilized for immediate danger situations;
- Parental consent for interim placement may be sought; or
- Current relief under 20 *U.S.C.* Section 1415(e)(2) and *N.J.A.C.* 1:6A-12.1 may be sought.

In addition to the federal constitutional, state and federal statutory

---

[42]*Doe v. Maher*, 793 *F.2d.* 1470 (9th Cir. 1986).

[43]*Honig*, 108 *S. Ct.* at 604.

[44]*Kaelin v. Grubbs, supra*, at 602; *Goss, supra*.

provisions which a board must consider before suspending or expelling a student, the commissioner has urged boards to consider the appropriateness and effectiveness of these measures as approaches to student discipline. The commissioner recognized the importance of these considerations in a decision in which he said:

> *Termination of a pupil's right to attend the public schools of a district is a drastic and desperate remedy which should be employed only when no other course is possible. It is obvious that a board of education cannot wash its hands of a problem by recourse to expulsion. While such an act may resolve an immediate problem for the school it may likewise create a host of others involving not only the pupil but the community and society at large. The commissioner suggests, therefore, that boards of education who are forced to take expulsion action cannot shrug off responsibility but should make every effort to see that the child comes under the aegis of another agency able to deal with the problem. The commissioner urges boards of education, therefore, to recognize expulsion as a negative and defeatist kind of last-ditch expedient resorted to only after and based upon competent professional evaluation and recommendation.*[45]

Most expulsion cases in fact involve neither a permanent removal of a student from a school system, nor a termination of a board's obligation to the student during the period when he is barred from attendance. Boards often "expel" students for a lengthy but definite period of time such as a semester,[46] and even where a board itself seeks to permanently deny a student the right to attend school, the commissioner may confine the expulsion to a specific period of time.[47] Further, the commissioner frequently finds that the board must provide a student with home instruction during the time she is prohibited from attending classes.[48]

USE OF GRADES FOR DISCIPLINARY PURPOSES

Every legitimate suspension affects grades to some extent because class time is lost and absence from class ordinarily tends to reduce grades. The commissioner has on several occasions considered a board's authority to compound this incidental, inevitable effect by reducing a student's

---

[45]*Scher v. Bd. of Ed., West Orange*, 1968 *S.L.D.* 92.

[46]*See, e.g., J.W. v. Hammonton Bd. of Ed*, 1975 *S.L.D.* 776; *E.M. v. Hammonton Bd. of Ed.*, 1975 *S.L.D.* 791; *H.A. v. Warren Hills Bd. of Ed.* 1976 *S.L.D.* 336.

[47]*G.C. v. Egg Harbor Bd. of Ed.*, 1980 *S.L.D.* (May 8).

[48]*J.W. v. Hammonton Bd. of Ed., supra; H.A. v. Warren Hills Bd. of Ed., supra.*

grade because of unexcused absences or for absences attributable to suspensions.

The commissioner has held that a board may impose penalties for unjustifiable tardiness, improper absences from classes, truancy, and other unexcused absences.[49] He has sustained a board policy which imposed a percentage reduction in a student's classroom participation grade for each unexcused absence,[50] as well as policies which denied students course credit after a student was late or absent a specified number of times.[51]

However, in the context of suspension, the commissioner has held that a board may not impose a double penalty on a student who has been suspended either by giving her a zero for the days she was absent due to the suspension,[52] or by giving her a failing grade on an examination which she missed due to the suspension.[53] The commissioner has held that in instances where a student has missed an examination because of a suspension, the student's grade should be computed as if she had taken the examination at the usual time.[54] More recently, the Commissioner found improper a district's policy which arbitrarily imposed an automatic grade of F/40 based upon "attendance failures" because grades may not be used as a disciplinarian sanction.[55]

CORPORAL PUNISHMENT

A board of education may make no rules or regulations permitting corporal punishment of students, and no person employed by the board may inflict corporal punishment upon a student.

A board employee may, within the scope of his duties, use such force as is reasonable and necessary:

- To quell a disturbance which threatens physical injury to others;
- To obtain possession of weapons or other dangerous objects which a student has in his control;
- For the purpose of self defense; and
- For the protection of persons or property.

Such acts do not constitute corporal punishment.[56]

---

[49]*Wetherell v. Bd. of Ed. of Burlington Twp.*, 1978 *S.L.D.* 794, 800.

[50]*Id.*

[51]*Wheatley v. Bd. of Ed. of Burlington City* 1974 *S.L.D.* 851.

[52]*Wermuth v. Board of Education of Livingston*, 1965 *S.L.D.* 121.

[53]*Haddad v. Bd. of Ed. of the Twp. of Cranford*, 1968 *S.L.D.* 98.

[54]*Minorics v. Bd. of Ed. of the Town of Phillipsburg*, 1972 *S.L.D.* 86; *Haddad, supra.*

[55]*V.J.H. v. Board of Education of the City of Orange Township*, 1987 *S.L.D.* (July 23).

[56]*N.J.S.A.* 18A:6-1.

FREEDOM OF SPEECH

Symbolic Expression of Opinion

Students have a constitutional right to freedom of speech and expression which protects them even while in attendance at school. In order for a board of education to justify prohibiting a particular symbolic expression of opinion, it must be able to show that the prohibition is necessary and not a mere desire to avoid the discomfort and unpleasantness that accompany unpopular or controversial viewpoints. Where there is no showing that the symbolic expression would materially and substantially interfere with the requirements of appropriate discipline in the schools, the prohibition cannot be sustained.[57] In accordance with these principles, the U.S. Supreme Court has upheld a student's right to wear armbands or buttons as a sign of protest,[58] and a federal district court has held that a male homosexual student has a first amendment right to express his views by attending a school dance with another male student.[59]

Distribution of Literature

The commissioner of education has held that a board of education has the authority to develop reasonable regulations, consistent with constitutional safeguards, governing the time, place and manner of distribution of published materials by pupils on school property, together with guidelines or criteria which will serve to protect the legitimate concerns of school administrators for the orderly operation of the educational program. In a case involving the distribution of leaflets by high school students, the commissioner stated in 1969:

> *There is a common sense middle ground between the extremes of total proscription and absolute liberty which represents a sound approach to a solution of this problem. Such a plan would not provide an outright ban of all leaflet distribution but would seek to accommodate the maximum degree of freedom of expression by means consistent with the good order of the school. Guidelines for such purpose, cooperatively developed by pupils and faculty, would define the times and places when materials could be distributed without interfering with the work of the school. They would also include criteria by which the appropriateness of the material to be handed out can be judged. But such guidelines and the criteria to implement them need not constitute a censorship procedure. Certainly some decision-making is called for to determine the suitability of materials to be passed out*

---

[57]*Tinker v. Des Moines Independent School District*, 393 *U.S.* 503 (1969).

[58]*Id.*

[59]*Fricke v. Lynch*, 491 *F. Supp.* 381 (D. R.I. 1980).

to pupils in the schools. Suitability in this context should not be read to mean only non-controversial, popular, majority point of view expressions of opinion, but might well include materials representing many kinds of opinions on a variety of subjects. It is beyond argument, however, that so called "hate literature" which scurrilously attacks ethnic, religious and racial groups, other irresponsible publications aimed at creating hostility and violence, hardcore pornography, and similar materials are not suitable for distribution in the schools. Such materials can be banned without restricting other kinds of leaflets by the application of carefully designed criteria for making such judgments. In the commissioner's opinion, such a program does not constitute the kind of prior censorship which suppresses freedom of expression but represents, instead, the kind of accommodation which can be made in order to achieve the maximum degree of liberty consistent with the preservation of good order.[60]

While retaining jurisdiction, the commissioner remanded the case to the local board for the development of guidelines. A student-staff committee prepared a set of guidelines which were subsequently approved, with the exception of one provision, by the commissioner.[61] However, the students who had been suspended for leafleting then appealed to the Appellate Division which affirmed the decision of the commissioner.[62] The students finally appealed to the New Jersey Supreme Court which in 1975 held, over a vigorous dissent by Justice Clifford, that the case was moot since the students had graduated.[63] Thus, the constitutionality of the regulations adopted by the local board, and of the guidelines announced by the commissioner in 1969 (quoted above) was never addressed by the Court.

Justice Clifford's dissent in the *Oxfeld* case should be carefully considered, however, since he did reach a decision rather than vacate the case on grounds of mootness, because it presented issues of great importance. He noted that one of the regulations adopted by the board and approved by the commissioner required prior approval by the school principal of all materials which students desired to distribute. Such prior approval constituted an impermissible "prior restraint" on the students' First Amendment right of free speech.[64] Justice Clifford argued that such "prior restraints" on speech have been held valid by the United States Supreme Court *only* when the speech creates a clear and present danger of disruption. Thus, any system requiring prior approval of *all* materials intended

---

[60]*Goodman v. Bd. of Ed. of South Orange-Maplewood*, 1969 *S.L.D.* 88, 96-7.

[61]*Goodman v. Bd. of Ed. of South Orange-Maplewood*, 1971 *S.L.D.* 106.

[62]*Oxfeld v. Bd. of Ed. of South Orange-Maplewood*, 1973 *S.L.D.* 770.

[63]*Oxfeld v. New Jersey State Bd. of Ed.*, 68 *N.J.* 301 (1975).

[64]*Id.* at 322 (1975) (dissenting opinion).

to be distributed by students is unconstitutional.[65]

Clifford's reasoning and analysis of the First Amendment rights of students is supported by numerous cases in jurisdictions other than New Jersey.[66] In fact, should a similar case be presented again to the New Jersey Supreme Court where the issue is not moot, the weight of authority suggests that Clifford's views would prevail, and that restraints on distribution of student literature will be subjected to strict judicial scrutiny.

While the courts in other jurisdictions have indicated that some narrowly drawn restraints will be upheld, the board bears a heavy burden in justifying their legality. Boards of education were found to have met this burden in two federal cases. In one case, a federal appeals court held that a school could prohibit a student newspaper from distributing a sex questionnaire to high school students. The prohibition was upheld on the grounds that the school authorities had reasonable grounds to believe that the distribution might be disturbing and might result in emotional harm to some students.[67] A concurring opinion expressly stated that the distribution of the questionnaire, which implicated the rights and sensibilities of others, was distinct from a simple dissemination of reading material dealing with sex.[68] In another case, a court upheld a board's ban on the distribution of one issue of a student newspaper which advertised drug paraphenalia. The court held that this ban on literature which encouraged the use of materials dangerous to the health and safety of students did not violate the First Amendment.[69]

Until the 1980's, the rule regarding distribution of materials seemed to restrict school officials' intervention to situations where the distribution caused a "substantial and material disruption."[70] The legal status of student distribution on school premises of publications not related to the curriculum was unclear. In 1988, the U.S. Supreme Court sharply distinguished between school-created and school-sponsored expression. In *Hazelwood School District v. Kuhlmeier*,[71] the court held that the First

---

[65]*Id.* at 317.

[66]*See Burch v. Baker*, 861 *F.2d.* 1149 (9th Cir. 1988); *Nitzberg v. Parks*, 525 *F.2d* 378 (4th Cir. 1975); *Jacobs v. Bd. of School Commissioners, Indianapolis*, 490 *F.2d* 601 (7th Cir. 1973), vacated as moot, 420 *U.S.* 128 (1975); *Fujishima v. Bd. of Ed.*, 460 *F.2d* 1355 (7th Cir. 1972); *Riseman v. School Commission of the City of Quincy*, 439 *F.2d* 148 (1st Cir. 1971); *Butts v. Dallas Independent School District*, 436 *F.2d* 728 (5th Cir. 1971); *Hernandez v. Hansen*, 430 *F.Supp.* 1154 (D. Neb. 1977); *Leibner v. Sharbough*, 429 *F.Supp.* 744 (E.D. Va. 1977); *Pliscou v. Holtville Unified School District*, 411 *F.Supp.* 842 (S.D. Cal. 1976); *Poxon v. Bd. of Ed.*, 341 *F.Supp.* 256 (E.D. Cal. 1971); *Zucker v. Panitz*, 299 *F.Supp.* 102 (S.D. N.Y. 1969).

[67]*Ankner v. Trachtman*, 563 *F.2nd* 512, *cert.* den. 435 *U.S.* 925 (1977).

[68]*Id.* at 520.

[69]*Williams v. Spencer*, 662 *F.2d* 1200 (4th Cir. 1980).

[70]*Tinker, supra.*

[71]484 *U.S.* 260 (1988).

Amendment does not prevent educators from exercising editorial control over the style and content of student speech in school-sponsored newspapers, provided such restrictions are "reasonably related to legitimate pedagogical concerns."[72]

In *Hazelwood*, the principal prohibited the publication of pages containing two articles which he considered inappropriate. The articles were submitted by the journalism class. One story featured three students' experiences with pregnancy and the other story discussed the impact of her parents' divorce on one student.

The court expressed the following views regarding the broad scope of a school's authority to control school-sponsored expressive activities:

- School-sponsored activities (e.g., school newspapers, school plays) may be considered "part of the school curriculum" regardless of whether they occur in an actual classroom setting;[73]

- Educators may exercise editorial control over the style and content of school-sponsored expressive activities, so long as they do so for a LEGITIMATE PEDAGOGICAL REASON. For example, they may prevent students from publishing articles that are ungrammatical, poorly written, prejudiced, vulgar or "unsuitable for immature audiences;"[74]

- A school should be able to "disassociate itself" from student speech which might reasonably be perceived to advocate drug use, "irresponsible sex," etc., or to associate the school itself with a particular position on controversial political issues;[75]

- Student speech and writing in school-sponsored activities is distinguishable from student's personal speech that happens to occur on school premises, like the wearing of armbands protesting the U.S. involvement in the Vietnam war. The school may exercise far more control over the former, but must be more tolerant of the latter.[76]

Thus, the key to publication control is the degree of school involvement. It is worth noting the distinctions:

- *Curricular publications*—school officials have broad authority to exercise reasonable "editorial control" over the style and content of student periodicals, provided they are part of the established curriculum;

---

[72]*Id.*

[73]*Id.*

[74]*Id.*

[75]*Id.*

[76]*Id.*

- *Extra-Curricular publications*—must look at the amount of school support. The more support (i.e. school funding or faculty supervision) the more likely it will be subject to the school's control. This would apply to school-sponsored plays too;

- *Underground publications*—schools do *not* have authority to control the style or content. "Material disruption" rule applies if there is evidence to forecast its occurrence. Promotion of illegal activities is sufficient reason to prohibit distribution of any publication.

A policy which would restrict publication and circulation on school property to literature prepared under school sponsorship and supervision is an unlawful and improper restraint upon students' rights of free expression.[77]

HAIR LENGTH AND DRESS CODES

Conventions change the time, and the conventional hair styles of today are shallow reasons for denying otherwise eligible students from participation in any school programs.[78]

Boards of education and school administrators have the right to adopt and enforce rules governing student dress, but these rules must have a rational and substantial relationship to some legitimate purpose, such as the protection of health and safety or the maintenance of order in the educational process.[79]

As the commissioner has observed in a case involving such a dress code:

It can hardly be disputed that school authorities are vested with the power to regulate pupil appearance in instances where it is, or threatens to become so extreme as to be the obvious cause of indiscipline and disruption of the school program. Boards of education and their staffs have a responsibility by statutory mandate to provide and maintain conditions under which learning can take place most effectively. The power to adopt rules and regulations having as their purpose the creation of an optimum climate for learning and the elimination of distracting or disruptive elements is an entirely proper and necessary adjunct of that responsibility.[80]

---

[77]*Burke v. Bd. of Ed. of the Twp. of Livingston*, 1970 *S.L.D.* 319.

[78]*Harris v. Bd. of Ed. of the Twp. of Teaneck*, 1970 *S.L.D.* 311, 316.

[79]*Cuci v. Bd. of Ed. of the Town of Hammonton*, 1980 *S.L.D.* 73; *Pelletreau v. Bd. of Ed. of the Borough of New Milford*, 1967 *S.L.D.* 45, reversing 1967 *S.L.D.* 35; *Bertin v. Boyle*, 1968 *S.L.D.* 24; *Sylvester v. Bd. of Ed. of the Watchung Hills Regional High School*, 1969 *S.L.D.* 67; *Singer v. Bd. of Ed. of the Borough of Collingswood*, 1971 *S.L.D.* 594.

[80]*Pelletreau*, 1967 *S.L.D.* at 40-41.

Pelletreau also emphasized, however, that a board may not act unreasonably or capriciously in adopting a dress code, and may not promulgate a code which is designed to produce conformity among pupils, or which attempts to impose its own standards of good taste.[81]

The state board decision in *Pelletreau* commented in detail on that portion of the dress code which prohibited long hair, and made the following comment:

> *We recognize that students live most of their lives outside the walls of their schools. During their out-of-school hours, they are subject to the discipline of their parents and must abide by the laws of the community. A school regulation forbidding long hair in effect regulates outside of school conduct. It is not possible to have short hair in school and revert to longer hair at home. A regulation relating to dress does not have this effect. A student may well comply with regulations as to what may or may not be worn during school hours and dress as he or his parents see fit during his non-school hours.*[82]

The state board then came to the conclusion that the portion of the school regulations forbidding long hair was invalid. It was not convinced that the rule had a substantial relationship to a legitimate purpose. It could not conceive that the threat to school discipline was sufficiently great to justify interference with the "relatively harmless experimentation of students in the field of hair styling."[83]

Applying the standards of *Pelletreau*, a 1980 Commissioner decision invalidated a dress code on the grounds that it contained so many restrictions and inconsistencies that it was arbitrary. (*e.g.*, a particular style of garment was permissible when made of one material, but prohibited when made of another.)[84]

The commissioner has held that the opportunity to try out for a school team or to participate in other extracurricular activities must be open to all and selection for participation must be based on talent and potential contribution to the team or activity. The reasonable limits of any rules of eligibility should not include regulations on hair style and length, which are matters of personal taste, unless it can be shown that such styles create disorder, present a clear and present danger to that student or her fellow participants or are detrimental to good health and hygiene.[85]

---

[81]*Id.* at 41.

[82]*Id.* at 48.

[83]*Id.*

[84]*Cuci v. Bd. of Ed. of the Town of Hammonton*, 1980 *S.L.D.* 73.

[85]*Harris, supra; Bramwell v. Bd. of Ed. of the Twp. of Franklin, Somerset County*, 1970 *S.L.D.* 331, affirmed by State Board 1971 *S.L.D.* 662.

STUDENT RECORDS

In 1975, the state board adopted regulations regarding pupil records in order to comply with the federal Family Educational Rights and Privacy Act of 1974.[86] Pupil records are broadly defined to include any information gathered within or without the school system and maintained within the school system, regardless of the physical form in which it is maintained. Any information maintained for the purpose of second party review is considered a pupil record. Thus, information recorded by school personnel solely as a memory aid, not for the use of a second party, is not considered a pupil record.[87]

A school district may not compile any pupil records, other than the mandated and permitted records defined in state board regulations. Mandated records are those records which districts have been directed to compile by New Jersey statute, regulation, or authorized administrative directive. Permitted pupil records are those which a local board of education has authorized the district to collect by resolution adopted at a regular public meeting to promote the educational welfare of the pupil.[88]

Pupil records may contain only such information as is relevant to the education of the pupil, and is objectively based on the personal observations or knowledge of the originator of the recorder. All permitted records must be reviewed annually by certified school personnel to determine the educational relevance of the material contained therein. Material no longer relevant or descriptive of the pupil is to be deleted.[89]

The rules of the state board on access to pupil records provide that the following persons and organizations shall have the right to view, make notes and/or have a reproduction made of a pupil record:

- A parent, legal guardian, foster parent or parent surrogate of a pupil under the age of 18;
- Pupils under 18 having the written permission of such parent or guardian;
- Pupils at least 16 years of age who are terminating their education by graduating at the end of the term or planning to discontinue their education;
- Adult pupils (18 years of age and older);
- Parents or guardians of adult pupils where:
  a. they have the written permission of the pupil; or

---

[86]Title IV of Public Law 90-247, as amended.

[87]*N.J.A.C.* 6:3-2.1.

[88]*N.J.A.C.* 6:3-2.2.

[89]*N.J.A.C.* 6:3-2.2(c) and (i).

b. the pupil is financially dependent on them;

- Certified school personnel who have assigned educational responsibility for the pupil;
- Accrediting organizations, the Department of Education and officials of other school districts in which the student is registered or intends to enroll;
- A state agency investigating the need for protective services or supervision and organizations or persons on presentation of a court order;
- Organizations and persons outside the school with the written consent of the parent or adult pupil;
- Bona fide researchers under strict conditions of anonymity and confidentiality.[90]

It is important to note that there is no similar right to view those records alluded to above which are excluded from the definition of "pupil records" in the New Jersey regulations.

A record may be withheld from an authorized parent or pupil only when the chief school administrator is convinced that disclosure would create a substantial risk of harm to the pupil or to a person with whom the record is concerned.[91] Pupil records are subject to challenge by parents or adult pupils on grounds of inaccuracy, irrelevancy, impermissive disclosure or denial of access, and appeal may be made to the board of education or to the commissioner.[92]

The chief school administrator or a designee shall be present during inspection to provide interpretation where necessary and to prevent record alteration, damage or loss.[93]

The state board regulations on pupil records also contain detailed requirements pertaining to the time period within which requests to see records must be reviewed, procedures by which parents and pupils may challenge the contents of pupil records, and requirements concerning the retention and destruction of student records.[94]

STUDENT SEARCHES

The Fourth Amendment to the U.S. Constitution safeguards the privacy of individuals by protecting them against unreasonable searches

---

[90]*N.J.A.C.* 6:3-2.5.
[91]*N.J.A.C.* 6:3-2.6(a)5.
[92]*N.J.A.C.* 6:3-2.7.
[93]*N.J.A.C.* 6:3-2.6(a)3.
[94]*N.J.A.C.* 6:3-2.7, 2.8.

and seizures by government officials. It is a well-established principle of criminal law that the Fourth Amendment, with limited exceptions, permits the police to conduct a search of an individual or her home only after a warrant has been obtained upon a showing of probable cause.

In the context of criminal law, it is also well-established that evidence obtained as a result of an illegal search of an individual may not be used in criminal proceedings against him. This practice is termed the "exclusionary rule."

While there are court-imposed safeguards on students' constitutional rights, school officials still have greater leeway in conducting searches than police officers. Police officers must have a warrant to conduct a search and must meet a probable cause standard that incriminating evidence will be found. School officials have successfully argued that such a rigid requirement would seriously impair the schools' ability to maintain discipline and a safe school environment.

The U.S. Supreme Court has developed standards applicable to searches of students in a case which originated in New Jersey. In *New Jersey v. T.L.O.*,[95] the Supreme Court rejected the argument that the Fourth Amendment applies only to searches or seizures conducted by law enforcement officers and held instead that searches based upon reasonable suspicion that are reasonable in scope may be conducted by school officials to detect infractions of school rules.

This "reasonable suspicion" standard was expressly stated to be a lesser standard than probable cause.[96]

The court established a two-part test to determine the reasonableness of the search:

- The search must be reasonable at its inception (e.g. that there are reasonable grounds for suspecting that the search will turn up evidence that the student has violated or is violating either the law or the rules of the school); and

- The search must be reasonably related in scope to the circumstances which justified the interference in the first place.[97]

The court stated that for the latter criterion, "when measures adopted are reasonably related to the objectives of the search and not excessively intrusive in light of the age and sex of the student and nature of the infraction," the search will be permissible.[98]

In order to place the Supreme Court's general guidelines in perspec-

---

[95]105 *S. Ct.* 733 (1985).
[96]*State in the Interest of T.L.O.*, 94 *N.J.* 331, 346 (1983), rev'd 105 *S. Ct.* 733 (1985).
[97]*Id.* at 744
[98]*Id.*

tive, it is useful to analyze the fact situations considered by the court in
T.L.O.

In *T.L.O.*, a teacher accused a student of violating school rules by
smoking cigarettes in the girls' restroom. (Smoking was prohibited in
restrooms but allowed in designated areas.) When the student denied that
she had been smoking, the teacher took her to the principal's office where
she met with the assistant vice principal. The assistant vice principal opened the student's purse and discovered a pack of cigarettes and admonished
the student for lying to him. Upon removing the cigarettes, he observed
a pack of rolling papers. Suspecting the presence of drugs, he searched
further and discovered a plastic bag of marijuana as well as evidence ten-
ding to show that the student was dealing in drugs. All of these items
were turned over to police and formed the basis for the student's adjudica-
tion as a juvenile delinquent.

The Court reasoned that school children have legitimate expectations
of privacy. But striking the balance between those expectations and the
school's need to maintain an environment in which learning can take place
requires relaxation of the normal restrictions to which searches by public
authorities are ordinarily subject.[99]

Under the "reasonable suspicion" standard, the court found that the
initial search for cigarettes was reasonable. "The report to the Assistant
Vice Principal that respondent had been smoking warranted a reasonable
suspicion that she had cigarettes in her purse..."[100] Secondly, the
presence of rolling papers "then gave rise to a reasonable suspicion that
respondent was carrying marijuana as well as cigarettes in her purse, and
this suspicion justified the further exploration that turned up more
evidence of drug-related activities."[101]

The lesson for school boards from the *T.L.O.* case is that while school
officials have more leeway than police in conducting searches, it is wise
to have policies and procedures in place to assure that every effort is made
to ascertain reasonable grounds *before* a search is conducted. A possible
approach would be to prohibit staff from conducting a search until an appropriate administrator is advised and gives authorization, except where
an immediate search is required to protect students, e.g., where a teacher
sees a student conceal a weapon.

New Jersey statutes authorize school officials to inspect student
lockers or other storage facilities provided notice is sent to students at
the beginning of each school year of such inspections.[102]

---

[99]*Id.* at 743.

[100]*Id.* at 746.

[101]*Id.* at 747.

[102]*N.J.S.A.* 18A:36-19.2.

SECRET FRATERNITIES

Every fraternity, sorority or secret society or organization which is composed in whole or in part of public school students and which seeks to organize itself by taking in student members upon the basis of decision of the organization's membership rather than from the free choice of any students who are otherwise qualified to fill the special aims of the organization, has been declared by law to be inimical to the good of the school system and to the democratic principles and ideals of public education and the public good.[103]

No such fraternity, sorority or secret organization may be formed or maintained in any public high school, and the board of education of every district must adopt rules providing for the necessary disciplinary measures to enforce this prohibition.[104]

The prohibition does not apply to any state college.[105]

FLAG SALUTE AND PLEDGE OF ALLEGIANCE

Every board of education must require the students in each school in the district on every school day to salute the United States flag and repeat the pledge of allegiance to the flag.

A New Jersey statute provides that students who have conscientious scruples against the pledge or the salute, or who are children of accredited representatives of foreign governments to whom the United States government extends diplomatic immunity, cannot be required to salute or pledge allegiance but shall be required to show full respect to the flag while the pledge is being given by standing at attention, the boys removing the headdress.[106] However, a New Jersey federal district court has held that the requirement that such students stand at attention during the pledge is unconstitutional but that such students can be required to sit quietly throughout the pledge.[107]

---

[103]N.J.S.A. 18A:42-5.

[104]N.J.S.A. 18A:42-6; *Milligan v. Bd. of Ed. of Manchester Regional High School District*, 1961-62 *S.L.D.* 197; *Angelillo v. Bd. of Ed. of Manchester Regional High School District*, 1964 *S.L.D.* 74.

[105]*Id.*

[106]N.J.S.A. 18A:36-3; *Holden v. Elizabeth Bd. of Ed.*, 46 *N.J.* 281 (1966).

[107]*Lipp v. Morris*, 579 *F.2d* 834 (1978); *Goetz v. Ansell*, 477 *F.2d* 636 (2d Cir. 1973); *Banks v. Bd. of Public Instruction of Dade County*, 314 *F.Supp.* 285 (S.D. Fla. 1970), aff'd 450 *F.2d* 1103 (5th Cir. 1971).

STUDENT VANDALISM

It has long been the public policy in New Jersey to hold parents or guardians liable when their minor children vandalize school district property. New Jersey statutes originally provided that the parents or guardians of any pupil who injured school property was liable for damages for the amount of the injury, which was to be collected by the board of education or the owner of the premises in any court of competent jurisdiction, together with the costs of suit.[108] The New Jersey Supreme Court subsequently upheld a predecessor parental liability statute against a challenge that it violated the due process provisions of the U.S. Constitution because it imposed liability without fault.[109] The Court held that the statute was valid, finding that the existence of the parent-child relationship provided a rational basis for imposing liability and that the statute was a reasonable means to accomplish the statutory purpose of deterring vandalism and compensating school districts for property damage.[110] The Court construed the statute as imposing liability only where a child's actions are willful or malicious.[111] Subsequent to the *Piscataway* decision, the Legislature amended the statute reviewed by the Court in order to specify that it applies to damage to both public and non-public schools and imposes liability on all parents whose minor children damage school property, whether or not those children are enrolled in school.

---

[108]*N.J.S.A.* 18A:37-3. *See also N.J.S.A.* 2A:53A-15, which imposes liability on a parent who fails to exercise reasonable supervision over his child, and whose child willfully or maliciously damages the real or personal property of another.

[109]*Piscataway Twp. Bd. of Ed. v. Caffiero*, 86 *N.J.* 308 (1981) appeal dismissed 454 *U.S.* 1025 (1981).

[110]*Id.*

[111]*Id.*

THE MANAGEMENT OF
THE SCHOOLS

7

A comparison of the statutory powers of a local board of education[1] with those of certain school officials reveals an unmistakable legislative design to place the policy-making responsibility on the local board, and executive responsibility on the school officials. The statutes provide the minimal requirements for the school district's top managers, and local boards are left with the responsibility of filling out the details of the interrelationship among its key employees. Local boards are also left with the responsibility of specifying the obligations of their middle-echelon managers, such as building principals, since the statutes, other than for an occasional functional mandate, are silent. It is clear that the legislative scheme leaves much to the discretion of the local board, which would be remiss in not providing guidance to its management team.

THE SUPERINTENDENT OF SCHOOLS

Perhaps the most important duty any board performs is the selection and appointment of a capable superintendent for the school system. The laws relating to the superintendent of schools state that the board of education, in all Type I districts and Type II districts in which the position has been established, may appoint a superintendent of schools for a term not exceeding five years by a recorded roll call vote of the full membership.[2] A board may require a superintendent to devote herself exclusively to the duties of her office.[3] The superintendent has a seat on the board and the right to speak on all educational matters at meetings of the board, but not the right to vote.[4] Statutes give the superintendent general supervision over the schools, and she must report as directed by the board. She has such other powers and performs such other duties as the board may prescribe.[5]

---

[1]N.J.S.A. 18A:11-1, 2. See Chapters III and VII herein.

[2]N.J.S.A. 18A:17-15.

[3]N.J.S.A. 18A:17-18.

[4]N.J.S.A. 18A:17-20.

[5]Ibid.

A superintendent candidate must have the proper certification. The State has enacted rigorous requirements for superintendent candidates to attain a standard school administrator's certificate. Effective September 1, 1991, each candidate must:

- Possess a provisional certificate (requires a master's degree in administration, pass the state written exam, undergo an assessment of performance conducted by state-approved assessors, and obtain an offer of employment which requires a school administrator's endorsement);
- Complete a one-year state-approved district residency program; and
- Be evaluated by a mentor on at least three occasions.[6]

The mentor shall submit his recommendation regarding certification of the candidate to the Division of Teacher Preparation and Certification.[7] Candidates who receive a recommendation of "approved" will be issued a standard certificate. These recommendations are not subject to review or approval by local boards of education.[8] Persons who enrolled in formal state-approved New Jersey college preparation programs prior to September 1, 1991 will be permitted until September 1, 1997 to attain standard certification by completing the college program in which they are enrolled.[9]

A superintendent, in the performance of her duties, is required to keep herself informed of the condition and progress of the schools under her jurisdiction and shall report to the board as directed.[10] State regulations require superintendents to have a school administrator's endorsement. This endorsement authorizes superintendents to:

- Direct the formulation of district goals, plans, policies, and budgets;
- Recommend their approval by district board of education;
- Direct their implementation;
- Recommend all staff appointments and other personnel actions for board approval including terminations, suspensions and compensation (this includes the school business administrator's appointment);
- Direct district operations and programs;
- Supervise and evaluate building administrators and central of-

---

[6]*N.J.A.C.* 6:11-9.4(a) and (b).

[7]*N.J.A.C.* 6:11-9.4(f).

[8]*Id.*

[9]*N.J.A.C.* 6:11-9.4(i).

[10]*N.J.S.A.* 18A:17-20.

fice staff, including school business administrators; and

- Oversee the administration and supervision of school-level operations, staff and programs.[11]

The superintendent may appoint and, subject to tenure status, may remove the clerks in her office, but their number and salaries are determined by the board.[12] On or before August 1 the superintendent must submit a report annually to the commissioner and the county superintendent in prescribed form.[13]

Upon the superintendent's nomination, the board, by a recorded roll call majority vote of the full membership, may appoint assistant superintendents and fix their salaries. They may be removed by a similar vote, subject to tenure status.[14] Each assistant superintendent performs such duties as are prescribed by the superintendent with the approval of the board.[15]

The superintendent may, with the approval of the president, suspend any assistant superintendent, principal or teaching staff member, and must report such suspension to the board, after which the board may take, by recorded roll call majority vote of all members, whatever action it may deem proper, subject to tenure laws.[16]

A Type II district in which the position of superintendent has not been established may make application to the county superintendent. If the application is approved in writing by the county superintendent and is approved by the commissioner and the state board, the board of education may thereafter appoint a superintendent.[17] Boards of two or more districts may make joint application for a superintendency and, if approved, may unite in employing a superintendent. In such cases, the superintendent is appointed by the commissioner with approval of the state board.[18]

No person may be appointed, or act as, or perform the duties of superintendent or assistant superintendent unless he holds an appropriate certificate.[19]

At the time of this writing, the Governor signed legislation ending superintendent tenure. This new law replaces tenure entitlements with three to five year contracts.[20] Although effective immediately, the new

---

[11]N.J.A.C. 6:11-9.3(a).

[12]N.J.S.A. 18A:17-24.

[13]N.J.S.A. 18A:17-21.

[14]N.J.S.A. 18A:17-16, 19.

[15]N.J.S.A. 18A:17-22.

[16]N.J.S.A. 18A:25-6.

[17]N.J.S.A. 18A:17-15.

[18]Ibid.

[19]N.J.S.A. 18A:17-17.

[20]Ch. 267, Laws of 1991.

law does not apply to superintendents who have already attained tenure in their current positions. The law also requires a unit control system of administration where the chief school administrator is directly accountable to the board on all matters, including financial matters. The latter provision does not apply to districts that employ superintendents who have already gained tenure.

THE BOARD SECRETARY

Every board of education must have a secretary to perform the duties and functions assigned to him by law and which only he can perform. The secretary is appointed by a majority roll call vote of the full membership of the board for a term to expire not later than June 30 of the calendar year next succeeding that in which the board was organized. His compensation is fixed by the board. A board member may be appointed secretary but without compensation while holding both offices.[21] A vacancy in the office of the secretary must be filled by the board within 60 days or, if not, the county superintendent appoints a secretary.[22] The secretary must be bonded in an amount not less than $2,000 and with surety approved by the board. The board may pay the premium.[23]

It is the secretary's duty to notify board members of all meetings, to post and give notices of all school elections, and to record all proceedings of the board and of school elections in suitable minute books.[24] As general accountant of the board, the secretary is required to:

- Collect tuition fees and other moneys due the board and transmit them to the custodian of school moneys;[25]

- Examine and audit all accounts and demands against the board, present them to the board at its meetings, indicate the board's approval and send them to the custodian for payment;[26]

- Keep accounts of the school district's financial transactions including a correct detailed account of all expenditures;[27]

- Report to the board at each regular meeting the amount of the total appropriations and cash receipts for each account, the

---

[21]*N.J.S.A.* 18A:17-5.

[22]*Ibid.*

[23]*N.J.S.A.* 18A:17-6.

[24]*N.J.S.A.* 18A:17-7.

[25]*N.J.S.A.* 18A:17-8a.

[26]*N.J.S.A.* 18A:17-8b; 19-4.

[27]*N.J.S.A.* 18A:17-8c; 19-4.

amount of warrants drawn against each account, and the amount of orders or contractual obligations incurred and chargeable against each account;[28]

- Keep all contracts, records and documents belonging to the board;[29]

- Give the board a detailed report of its financial transactions at the close of each fiscal year and file a copy with the county superintendent and make an annual report by August 1 to the commissioner;[30]

- Report to the commissioner annually by August 1 the amount of unpaid school debt, the interest rate payable, the dates of issue and the due dates of bonds or other indebtedness;[31]and

- Prepare a summary of the annual audit and recommendations prior to the meeting of the board to act thereon and make copies of the summary available to interested persons.[32]

The secretary is authorized to administer oaths relevant to school matters, without charge.[33]

The secretary in a Type I district may appoint and remove, subject to tenure, clerks in his office to the number and at salaries as set by the board.[34]

When authorized by the board, the secretary may make purchases or negotiate and award contracts for services or supplies where the annual cost of such services or supplies does not exceed $10,700.[35]

The secretary has important responsibilities in preparing for school elections. He:

- Receives all petitions nominating candidates for board membership;[36]

- Notifies the candidate when a defective nominating petition is filed and permits its amendment, except as to the number of signatures, before ballots are printed;[37]

---

[28]N.J.S.A. 18A:17-9a.
[29]N.J.S.A. 18A:17-9b.
[30]N.J.S.A. 18A:17-10.
[31]N.J.S.A. 18A:17-12.
[32]N.J.S.A. 18A:23-4.
[33]N.J.S.A. 18A:17-11.
[34]N.J.S.A. 18A:17-14.
[35]N.J.S.A. 18A:18A-3.
[36]N.J.S.A. 18A:14-9.
[37]N.J.S.A. 18A:14-12.

- Withdraws the name of any nominee who so requests;[38]
- Conducts a drawing for position of candidates on the ballot;[39]
- Receives nominations of challengers and issues certificates of appointment to challengers;[40]
- Gives notice of all elections by posting at least seven public notices 10 days prior to the election and by newspaper notice;[41]
- Furnishes each polling place with proper equipment in ample time for the election;[42]
- Publishes notices of the election for absentee voters, including military service absentee voters, and receives the canvass of the absentee votes and adds them to the tally at the polls;[43]
- Prepares sample ballots, mails them to each registered voter, and posts them in each polling place when directed by resolution of the board to do so;[44]
- Prepares official ballots and furnishes them to the election officials, if paper ballots are used;[45]
- Notifies the appropriate county official, when the board decides to use voting machines, of the number of machines to be used, the location of the polling places and the hours they will be open at least 40 days before the election; furnishes, at least seven days before the election, official ballots to be used in the machines; and makes such other arrangements as are necessary to hold the election by use of voting machines;[46]
- Declares the polls open at the appropriate time, in the absence of a member of the board of education or the election judge;[47]
- Gives written notice to the county registration commissioner at least 10 days before the election, of the election districts in the school district; receives from her the signature copy registers, delivers them to the election board at each polling place, and returns them to the registration commissioner the

---

[38]*N.J.S.A.* 18A:14-12.1.

[39]*N.J.S.A.* 18A:14-13.

[40]*N.J.S.A.* 18A:14-15, 16.

[41]*N.J.S.A.* 18A:14-19.

[42]*N.J.S.A.* 18A:14-20.

[43]*N.J.S.A.* 18A:14-25, 27, 28.

[44]*N.J.S.A.* 18A:14-29, 30, 31.

[45]*N.J.S.A.* 18A:14-32.

[46]*N.J.S.A.* 18A:14-40, 41.

[47]*N.J.S.A.* 18A:14-46.

day after the election;[48]

- Receives the report of the election and the sealed package of ballots, poll list and tally sheets from each polling place; adds the votes cast by absentee ballot as certified by the county board of election; combines the reports from all polling places and announces the result; certifies the accuracy of the count as required;[49]
- Forwards the sealed election packages and statement of results to the county superintendent within 5 days of the election;[50] and
- Performs any duties, not in conflict with those imposed upon any other officer by law, necessary for the proper conduct of a school election.[51]

In districts having a board of school estimate, he serves as secretary of such board without additional compensation.[52] The board may appoint, by a recorded roll call majority vote of all members, an assistant secretary to assist the secretary and to serve in his stead during the absence or inability of the secretary to act.[53]

Board secretaries and assistant secretaries are subject to tenure entitlements and may not be dismissed or reduced in compensation except for reasons of neglect, misbehavior or other offense provided in their contract of employment.[54]

SCHOOL BUSINESS OFFICIALS

Type I Districts—The Business Manager

A business manager may be appointed in any Type I school district and, subject to tenure status, may be removed by a majority vote of all members.[55] The business manager has a seat on the board and the right to speak on all matters pertaining to her functions but has no right to vote.[56] The business manager must be bonded in an amount not less than $2,000, with surety approved by the board. The premium may be paid

---

[48]N.J.S.A. 18A:14-47.

[49]N.J.S.A. 18A:14-61.

[50]N.J.S.A. 18A:14-62.

[51]N.J.S.A. 18A:14-63.

[52]N.J.S.A. 18A:22-2, 4.

[53]N.J.S.A. 18A:17-13.

[54]N.J.S.A. 18A:17-1, 2.

[55]N.J.S.A. 18A:17-25.

[56]N.J.S.A. 18A:17-27.

by the board as a current expense.[57]

It is the duty of the business manager to:

- Have charge and care of the school buildings and property of the district and their repair and maintenance;[58]

- Order repairs not exceeding $1,000 when so authorized by the board between board meetings without previous order or advertisement;[59]

- Draw or supervise the drawing of all plans and specifications for the erection, improvement or repair of the school buildings, subject to board approval;[60]

- Oversee all advertisements for bids in the letting of contracts for the board;[61]

- Supervise the construction and repair of all school buildings, inspect all work done and materials furnished and, subject to board approval, condemn or reject work or materials which do not conform to specifications;[62]

- Report monthly to the board progress on construction or repair work;[63] and

- Perform other duties as may be required by the board.[64]

Type II Districts—The School Business Administrator

The board of a district without a business manager may delegate to any appropriate officer employed by the board, the duties and powers of the business manager listed above.[65]

If the county superintendent agrees to the necessity for the position and the commissioner and state board approve, a board or the boards of two or more districts, may appoint a school business administrator, define his duties and fix his salary. One of his assigned duties may be to serve as secretary to the board.[66]

The school business administrator must hold an appropriate certificate.

---

[57]N.J.S.A. 18A:17-26.

[58]N.J.S.A. 18A:17-28a.

[59]N.J.S.A. 18A:17-28a.

[60]N.J.S.A. 18A:17-28b.

[61]N.J.S.A. 18A:17-28c.

[62]N.J.S.A. 18A:17-28d.

[63]N.J.S.A. 18A:17-28e.

[64]N.J.S.A. 18A:17-28f.

[65]N.J.S.A. 18A:16-1.2.

[66]N.J.S.A. 18A:17-14.1.

He is considered a member of the professional staff.[67] It must be noted that a board secretary or business manager who has acquired tenure in the district and is appointed school business administrator continues to hold that tenure while in the new position.[68]

School business administrators are authorized to perform duties at the district level in the areas of financial budget planning and administration, insurance/risk administration, purchasing and financial accounting and reporting, and may include other responsibilities such as: plant planning, construction and maintenance; personnel administration; administration of transportation and food services; and central data processing.[69]

THE CUSTODIAN OF SCHOOL MONEYS

The custodian of the moneys of the municipality is by reason of such office the treasurer of school moneys of the school district unless the board of education designates the municipal tax collector to perform this duty. If both the treasurer of moneys of the municipality and the municipal tax collector submit written notifications to the board that they do not wish to serve as treasurer of school moneys, the board shall appoint any other suitable person, except a member or employee of the board, with a term of office fixed by the board.[70] In school districts containing more than one municipality, the custodian of moneys of the municipality having the largest amount of taxable property is treasurer of school moneys unless and until the board appoints any other suitable person except a member or employee of the board.[71] In a regional or consolidated district, the board may appoint a suitable person, who may be a member of the board, as treasurer of school moneys.[72]

If the bond given by the treasurer for the faithful performance of her municipal duties is sufficient and is certified to cover her school duties, no additional bond is required. If otherwise, the treasurer must give additional bond, as the board shall direct, to secure performance of her school duties. In determining the amount of coverage the board must be guided by a schedule of minimum limits set by the state board.[73] The board determines the compensation to be paid the treasurer.[74]

---

[67]N.J.S.A. 18A:17-14.2; N.J.A.C. 6:11-9.7.

[68]N.J.S.A. 18A:17-14.3.

[69]N.J.A.C. 6:11-9.3(d).

[70]N.J.S.A. 18A:17-31.

[71]Ibid.

[72]N.J.S.A. 18A:13-14; 8-33.

[73]N.J.A.C. 6:3-1.5; N.J.S.A. 18A:17-32.

[74]N.J.S.A. 18A:17-33.

It is the duty of the treasurer to:

- Receive and hold in trust all school moneys, except funds from school athletic events and pupil organization activities, and deposit them in the banks designated by the board;[75]
- Pay out school moneys only on warrants made payable to the person entitled to receive payment and specifying the object for which it is issued and signed by the president and secretary of the board and the treasurer;[76]
- Receive school employee payrolls and a warrant for the full amount of each payroll certified by the president and secretary of the board, deposit the warrants in a separate payroll account, and issue individual checks drawn on such account to each employee;[77]
- Give public notice when funds are on hand for payment of interest bearing warrants issued for which no funds were available;[78]
- Keep a record of moneys received and paid out by him in books provided for that purpose and in accordance with a bookkeeping system prescribed by the state board;[79]
- Pay over the balance of school funds in her hands to her successor;[80]
- Render a monthly report to the board giving a detailed account of all receipts, the amounts of all warrants issued, the accounts from which they were drawn, and the balance in each account;[81] and
- Render an annual report by August 1 showing the amounts received and disbursed by her during the school year and file a copy with the county superintendent.[82]

When the school treasurer is also the municipal treasurer, school payroll checks may be signed by her deputy, if the deputy is properly bonded.[83]

---

[75]*N.J.S.A.* 18A:17-34.

[76]*N.J.S.A.* 18A:19-1.

[77]*N.J.S.A.* 18A:19-9, 10.

[78]*N.J.S.A.* 18A:19-12.

[79]*N.J.S.A.* 18A:17-35; *N.J.A.C.* 6:20-2.1 *et seq.*

[80]*N.J.S.A.* 18A:17-35.

[81]*N.J.S.A.* 18A:17-36.

[82]*Ibid.*

[83]*N.J.S.A.* 18A:19-11.

THE SCHOOL DISTRICT AUDITOR

Every board of education is required to employ a public school accountant to make an annual audit of the school district's accounts and financial transactions, which must be completed within four months of the close of the fiscal year.[84] The auditor must be a New Jersey registered municipal accountant or a New Jersey certified public accountant who holds a valid license as a New Jersey public school accountant issued by the New Jersey State Board of Public Accountants.[85]

Each annual audit must cover the books, accounts and moneys of the board, all officers and employees, all athletic events, and all pupil organizations conducted under board auspices as well as contracts entered into for the purchase of materials, supplies and equipment for the district.[86] The auditor must file a report of his audit and recommendations with the board and two copies with the commissioner.[87]

The report of the auditor must be received and acted upon by the board and his recommendations read and discussed at a public meeting within 30 days of receipt of the audit. The discussion must be noted in the board's minutes. A summary of the audit, prepared by the board's secretary, must be available for distribution to interested parties.[88] The commissioner is required to publish annually a summary of the auditor's recommendations for each school district and the steps which have been taken in each district for their implementation.[89] The commissioner may order an audit made by an accountant designated by him at the board's expense, if the board fails to have an audit made and completed in the prescribed time.[90]

THE SCHOOL BOARD ATTORNEY

Often overlooked in any catalogue of school management personnel, the school board attorney has, in practice, become a vital member of the management team. The power of a local board to hire counsel has been affirmed by the courts.[91] Attorneys may be employed by the board just

---

[84]N.J.S.A. 18A:23-1.

[85]N.J.S.A. 18A:23-8.

[86]N.J.S.A. 18A:23-2.

[87]N.J.S.A. 18A:23-3.

[88]N.J.S.A. 18A:23-4, 5.

[89]N.J.S.A. 18A:23-3.

[90]N.J.S.A. 18A:23-6.

[91]Merry v. Board of Education of Paterson, 100 N.J.L. 273 (Sup. Ct. 1924).

as any other professional, but do not normally acquire tenure.[92] The attorney's duties may be specified by the board, and should include:

- Legal representation of the board, individual board members and appropriate staff in judicial and administrative proceedings;
- Attendance at all board meetings at which the need for assistance of counsel is anticipated;
- Legal drafting or review of legal documents, legal notices, proposed policies, etc.; and
- Availability for consultation on all legal questions confronting the board and/or selected staff.

---

[92]*Koribanics v. Clifton Board of Education*, 48 *N.J.* 1 (1966); *Perella v. Jersey City Board of Education*, 51 *N.J.* 323 (1968); *Taylor v. Hoboken Board of Education*, 187 *N.J. Super* 546 (App. Div. 1983).

STAFF PERSONNEL

Every school board member should know the provisions of state law concerning the employment, transfer, retirement, discharge and compensation of personnel.

TENURE

Teaching Staff Members

All teachers, principals other than administrative principals, assistant principals, vice principals, assistant superintendents, school nurses and all other members of the teaching staff who are required to hold appropriate certificates are protected by tenure after employment in the district:

- For three consecutive calendar years or any shorter period set by the employing board; or
- At the beginning of the fourth consecutive academic year, or
- For the equivalent of more than three academic years within a period of four consecutive academic years.[1]

When a teaching staff member is transferred or promoted with her consent to a new position, she acquires tenure in the new position:

- After two consecutive calendar years, or
- At the beginning of the third academic year, or
- After more than the equivalent of two academic years in a period of three consecutive academic years.[2]

No teaching staff member may acquire tenure in any position unless she is the holder of an appropriate certificate,[3] and unless she is, or until she becomes, a citizen of the United States.[4] Any teaching staff member

[1]N.J.S.A. 18A:28-5.
[2]N.J.S.A. 18A:28-6.
[3]N.J.S.A. 18A:28-4.
[4]N.J.S.A. 18A:28-3.

who does not hold an appropriate certificate may be dismissed without charges or a hearing.[5] Substitute teachers hired because of the temporary absence of an employee may not acquire tenure.[6] Part-time remedial or supplemental teachers may acquire tenure if they otherwise meet the statutory criteria for tenure acquisition.[7]

Tenure for superintendents and administrative principals was eliminated in August of 1991 by *P.L.* 1991, Ch. 267. Boards of education may by contract appoint, for a term of not less than three nor more than five years and expiring July 1, a superintendent of schools by the recorded roll call majority vote of the full membership of the board. Superintendents and administrative principals who acquired tenure before the effective date of the new law are not affected by the change in law.[8]

Tenure of teaching staff members is not affected by any change in the method of government of the school district.[9] All principals, teachers and other employees in a school district which is dissolved as the result of the formation of a regional or consolidated district must be continued in their employment in the new district with their rights to tenure, pension and accumulated sick leave unaffected.[10]

Tenured teaching staff members shall be evaluated annually. The teaching staff member's supervisor shall prepare an annual written performance report, which must include, among other things, an individual professional improvement plan developed by the supervisor and the teaching staff member, and there shall be an annual summary conference between the supervisor and the teaching staff member.[11]

Other Board Employees

Any secretary, assistant secretary, school business administrator or business manager who devotes full time to the duties of his office and any person holding any secretarial or clerical position acquires tenure:

- After three consecutive calendar years of employment, or
- At the beginning of the fourth consecutive academic year.[12]

Attendance officers in city districts acquire tenure after employment for one year.[13]

---

[5]*N.J.S.A.* 18A:28-14.

[6]*N.J.S.A.* 18A:16-1.1.

[7]Spiewak v. Rutherford Bd. of Ed., 90 *N.J.* 63 (1982).

[8]*N.J.S.A.* 18A:17-15, 20; 28-5.

[9]*N.J.S.A.* 18A:28-15.

[10]*N.J.S.A.* 18A:8-34; 13-49; 30-3.1.

[11]*N.J.A.C.* 6:3-1.21, 1.22.

[12]*N.J.S.A.* 18A:17-2.

[13]*N.J.S.A.* 18A:38-33.

Any janitor, unless he is appointed for a fixed term, enjoys tenure status. A janitor who is appointed for a definite term does not acquire tenure,[14] except that a janitor so appointed may acquire tenure if so provided by the collective bargaining agreement.[15] A board of education may reduce the number of janitors employed. A tenured janitor so dismissed must be the one with the least number of years of employment in the district and he must be placed upon a preferred eligibility list for reemployment as vacancies occur.[16]

Reduction of Persons Under Tenure

The law relating to tenure does not impede the ability of a board of education to reduce the number of teaching staff members employed in the district whenever in the board's judgment it is advisable to do so for reasons of economy or because of a reduction in the number of pupils or a change in the administrative or supervisory organization of the district or for other good cause.[17] Reduction of tenured teaching staff members must be made on the basis of seniority according to standards established by the commissioner and the state board. The seniority regulations emphasize actual work experience with respect to the accumulation of seniority in specific categories of employment. Tenured teachers dismissed due to a reduction in force must be placed on a preferred eligibility list for reemployment when vacancies occur.[18] Seniority rights only accrue to tenured teaching staff members. A tenured teaching staff member is entitled to preference in a reduction in force as against non-tenured individuals in any teaching assignment covered by the endorsements on the tenured employee's certificate.[19] Reduction in the number of teaching staff members or janitors may not be made for reasons of residence, age, sex, marriage, race, religion or political affiliation. The only applicable standards for effectuating a reduction in force are those set forth by the commissioner and approved by the state board.[20]

Dismissal of Tenured Employees

No employee of a board of education who has acquired tenure status may be dismissed except for inefficiency, incapacity, unbecoming conduct

---

[14]*N.J.S.A.* 18A:17-3.

[15]*Wright v. East Orange Bd. of Ed.*, 194 *N.J. Super.* 181 (App. Div. 1983), aff'd 99 *N.J.* 112 (1985).

[16]*N.J.S.A.* 18A:17-4.

[17]*N.J.S.A.* 18A:28-9.

[18]*N.J.S.A.* 18A:28-10 *et seq.*; *N.J.A.C.* 6:3-1.10.

[19]*Capodilupo v. West Orange Bd. of Ed.*, 218 *N.J. Super.* 510 (App. Div. 1987), *certif. den.* 109 *N.J.* 514 (1987).

[20]*N.J.S.A.* 18A:28-10; 17-4.

or other just cause and then only after written charges have been proferred against him and a hearing held before the commissioner.[21]

Written charges must be filed with the board secretary, and a written statement of evidence made under oath in support of the charges must be presented to the board. The board must forthwith provide the employee with a copy of the charge and of the statement of evidence and must give the employee an opportunity to submit a written statement of position and a written statement of evidence under oath.

If the charge is inefficiency, the board must also provide the employee with a written notice specifying the nature of the alleged inefficiency and must allow the employee at least 90 days in which to correct the inefficiency. At the time of such notice, the board shall direct that there be a modification of the individual professional improvement plan.

After consideration of the documents presented to it, the board must determine, by a majority vote of its full membership:

- Whether there is probable cause to credit the evidence in support of the charge; and
- Whether the charge, if credited, is sufficient to warrant a dismissal or reduction in salary.

Where the board makes this determination, it must forward the charge together with a certificate of such determination to the commissioner for a hearing. The board is required to forthwith notify the employee of its determination, either in person or by certified mail.[22] If the board makes no determination within 45 days after the receipt of the written charge, or within 45 days after the expiration of the time for correction of the inefficiency, if the charge is of inefficiency, the charge is deemed dismissed.[23] The consideration and actions of the board as to any charge shall not take place at a public meeting.[24]

Upon certification of a charge, the board may suspend the employee with or without pay but, if a final determination by the commissioner is not made within 120 days after certification by the board, then the board must resume payment of the employee's full salary beginning on the 121st day and continuing until such determination is made. However, any sums received by the suspended employee as pay or salary from any substituted employment assumed during the suspension period are deducted from this full salary. If the charges are eventually dismissed by the commissioner,

---

[21]*N.J.S.A.* 18A:6-10.

[22]*N.J.S.A.* 18A:6-11; *N.J.A.C.* 6:24-5.1.

[23]*N.J.S.A.* 18A:6-13.

[24]*N.J.S.A.* 18A:6-11.

the employee must be reinstated with full pay from the date of suspension.[25]

The commissioner may dismiss the charges if he deems them insufficient to warrant dismissal or reduction of salary. Otherwise he must conduct a hearing on the charges within 60 days.[26]

The board which certified the charges is a necessary party in the hearing before the commissioner.[27]

The commissioner is required to render a written decision within 60 days after the close of the hearing and to serve a copy of his decision upon each party. The commissioner's decision is binding unless and until reversed upon appeal.[28]

In a tenure hearing, each party may be represented by counsel and has the right to testify, to produce witnesses in his own behalf, to cross-examine witnesses against him, and to compel the attendance of witnesses.[29]

Whenever a school employee is dismissed or suspended, and such dismissal or suspension is upon appeal decided to have been without good cause, the employee is entitled to compensation for the period covered by his dismissal or suspension, if written application is made within 30 days after final determination.[30]

Transfer of Tenured Employees

In order to promote the overall goal of providing students a thorough and efficient education, a board of education may transfer or reassign tenured staff members, without their consent, to any position within the scope of their certification.[31] Transfers made for disciplinary as opposed to educational reasons are prohibited.[32] A board may not transfer staff without consent if it involves dismissal or reduction in compensation since reductions in compensation and dismissal may only be made for reasons and according to procedures set forth in statute.[33] When a transfer is made because of a reduction in force, the reassignment must be made in accordance with the individual's seniority rights.[34]

---

[25]*N.J.S.A.* 18A:6-14.

[26]*N.J.S.A.* 18A:6-16.

[27]*N.J.S.A.* 18A:6-17.

[28]*N.J.S.A.* 18A:6-25.

[29]*N.J.S.A.* 18A:6-20.

[30]*N.J.S.A.* 18A:6-30.

[31]*N.J.S.A.* 18A:25-1; *Ridgefield Park Ed. Ass'n. v. Ridgefield Park Bd. of Ed.*, 78 *N.J.* 144 (1978).

[32]*N.J.S.A.* 34:13A-25.

[33]*N.J.S.A.* 18A:28-5.

[34]*N.J.S.A.* 18A:28-11.

NONTENURED TEACHING STAFF MEMBERS

All nontenured teaching staff members must be observed and evaluated in the performance of their duties at least 3 times during each school year but not less than once during each semester. Boards must provide for these evaluations to be completed before April 30 of each year; however, evaluations may cover that period between April 30 of one year and April 30 of the succeeding year, with the exception of the first year of employment where all three evaluations must be completed prior to April 30. The number of required observations and evaluations may be reduced proportionately when an individual teaching staff member's term of service is less than one academic year. Following each evaluation the teaching staff member has a conference with his or her superior. Recommendations regarding continued employment, identification of deficiencies and assistance in the correction thereof and improving professional competence are major considerations in the implementation of this procedure.[35] The state board has adopted rules for the supervision of instruction, observation and evaluation of nontenured teaching staff members. These rules provide that the term "evaluation" shall be construed to mean a written evaluation prepared by the administrative or supervisory staff member who visits the work station for the purpose of observing a teaching staff member's performance of the instructional process.[36]

On or before April 30 in each year, every board of education must give to each nontenured teaching staff member continuously employed by it since the preceding September 30 either:

- A written offer of a contract for employment for the next succeeding year providing for at least the same terms and conditions of employment but with such increases in salary as may be required by law or policies of the board of education; or

- A written notice that such employment will not be offered.

If any board of education fails to give to any nontenured teaching staff member either an offer of contract for employment for the next succeeding year or a notice that such employment will not be offered, the board of education will be deemed to have offered to that teaching staff member continued employment for the next succeeding school year upon the same terms and conditions but with such increases in salary as may be required by law or policies of the board of education. If the teaching staff member desires to accept such employment, he must notify the board of education of such acceptance in writing on or before June 1.[37]

---

[35]N.J.S.A. 18A:27-3.1.

[36]N.J.A.C. 6:3-1.19.

[37]N.J.S.A. 18A:27-10 et seq.

Any teaching staff member receiving notice that a contract for the succeeding school year will not be offered may, within 15 days thereafter, request in writing a statement of the reasons for such non-reemployment. The statement of reasons must be given to the teaching staff member in writing within 30 days after the receipt of such request.[38] Whenever a nontenured teaching staff member has requested in writing and received a statement of reasons for non-reemployment pursuant to *N.J.S.A.* 18A:27-3.2, he may request, in writing, an informal appearance before the district board of education.[39] This request must be submitted within 10 calendar days of receipt of the board's statement of reasons.[40]

RETIREMENT PROVISIONS

New Jersey provides for the retirement of its professional staff employees through the State Teachers' Pension and Annuity Fund (TPAF).

All teachers employed by boards of education in New Jersey are required to become members of the fund. The law defines "teacher" very broadly to cover virtually any member of the professional staff, including nurses. However, substitute teachers are not permitted to join.[41]

Prior to the enactment of the Quality Education Act of 1990, a board of education's share of pension and social security contributions was paid for by the state. Under the new funding law, for 1991-92 and 1992-93 school districts will advance the employer's share of pension and social security costs but they will receive state aid in the exact amount of their payment. Beginning in 1993-94, this state aid will cease. From that point on, foundation aid districts will receive assistance from the state in paying for these costs. The amount will vary, depending on the wealth of the district.[42]

Boards of education are required to deduct from salaries of members of the fund a "contribution rate" based on entrance age. Such deductions must be forwarded to the fund monthly or at such intervals as the trustees of the fund designate. A 6 percent interest charge is levied on any board which delays transmittal of such deductions more than 15 days. Failure to transmit deductions constitutes a default on the part of the board, and the State Department of Education may withhold state aid until the default is made good.[43] A member of the fund receives life insurance coverage

---

[38]*N.J.S.A.* 18A:27-3.2; *Donaldson v. North Wildwood Bd. of Ed.*, 65 N.J. 236 (1974).

[39]*N.J.A.C.* 6:3-1.20; see also *Donaldson, supra.*

[40]Id.

[41]*N.J.S.A.* 18A:66-2; *N.J.A.C.* 17:3-2.1 *et seq.*

[42]*Quality Education Act* Amendments, Ch. 62 Laws of 1991; *N.J.S.A.* 18A:66-33.

[43]*N.J.S.A.* 18A:66-32.

on a noncontributory basis equal to 1.5 times his annual salary.[44] During the first year of employment, a member of the fund is required to belong to a contributory insurance plan. Membership in the contributory insurance plan is optional after the first year of employment.[45]

Members of the fund do not have to make contributions for contributory insurance while on leave without pay for up to two years because of illness.[46]

A member of the fund may elect to retire at any time after age 60 by filing a written request with the board of trustees. According to statute, retirement within one year after age 70 is mandatory.[47]

A member of the fund who has credit for 25 years or more of service may retire on a reduced allowance regardless of age.[48]

A member of the fund under 60 years of age may retire on ordinary disability if he has been a member for 10 years preceding disability.

A member of the fund under 65 years of age may retire on accidental disability if he is permanently and totally disabled as a direct result of a traumatic event that occurred during and resulting from the performance of his duties.[49]

Public school employees other than professional staff are eligible for membership in the Public Employee Retirement System (PERS). Veterans and employees paid $1,500 or more per year who contribute to social security must join the PERS. Provisional or temporary employees with fewer than 12 months of continuous service are ineligible. TPAF and PERS members enjoy similar benefits.[50]

A board, at its discretion, may retire and grant a pension to any employee who is not a member of and was not required by law at the time of his employment, or at any time thereafter, to become a member of a contributory retirement system, under the following conditions:

- The employee is not eligible to receive a pension for the same employment under any law of this state.
- Funds for the payment of the pension must be provided in the board's budget.
- The employee must be at least 65 years of age, or have been employed by the board for at least 40 years, or be permanently and totally disabled.

---

[44]N.J.S.A. 18A:66-38; N.J.A.C. 17:3-3.3.

[45]N.J.S.A. 18A:66-53; N.J.A.C. 17:3-3.1.

[46]N.J.S.A. 18A:66-38.

[47]N.J.S.A. 18A:66-43.

[48]N.J.S.A. 18A:66-37.

[49]N.J.S.A. 18A:66-39.

[50]N.J.S.A. 43:15A-7.

- The amount of the pension must be fixed by the board according to uniform percentages of final average salary applicable generally to all employees, which percentages shall be adopted by resolution, and which shall not exceed:

  a. 30 percent of the employee's final average salary for less than 20 years of employment by the board, or

  b. 50 percent of the employee's final average salary if employed by the board for 20 years or more; provided, however, that an employee having 35 or more years of public employment and being age 65, or having 40 or more years of public employment regardless of age, shall receive not less than 25 percent of such average salary.

- No employee shall be eligible for disability benefits unless she shall have at least 5 years of employment continuously, or in the aggregate, with the board. No employee shall be eligible for other pension benefits unless she shall have at least 15 years of employment continuously, or in the aggregate, with the board.[51]

SICK LEAVE

All school district employees who are steadily employed by the board of education or who are protected by tenure in their position must be granted sick leave with full pay for a minimum of ten school days in any school year.[52] Sick leave is defined by law to mean the absence from his post of duty of any person because of personal disability due to illness or injury or because he has been excluded from school by the school district's medical authority on account of a contagious disease or has been quarantined for such a disease in his household.[53] All days of this minimum sick leave which are not utilized in a particular year are accumulative and may be used for additional sick leave as needed in subsequent years.[54] When all sick leave is exhausted, the board, in its discretion, may pay the difference between the salary of the absent person and that of a substitute.[55]

The board may grant leaves of absence not constituting sick leave or grant sick leave over and above the minimum required by law, except that no person is allowed to increase his total accumulation of sick leave by

---

[51]*N.J.S.A.* 43:8B-2 *et seq.*

[52]*N.J.S.A.* 18A:30-2.

[53]*N.J.S.A.* 18A:30-1.

[54]*N.J.S.A.* 18A:30-3.

[55]*N.J.S.A.* 18A:30-6.

more than 15 days in any one year.[56]

Boards of education may grant partial or full transfer credit for unused sick leave days accumulated in another New Jersey school district. The amount of credit must be fixed by resolution and must be uniformly applicable to all employees.[57]

An employee who is absent because of on-the-job injury is entitled to full pay for up to one year less any worker's compensation pay, without affecting any accumulated sick leave.[58]

The board may require a physician's certificate to be filed with the board secretary in order to validate any sick leave claims.[59]

TEACHING ON HOLIDAYS

No teaching staff member can be required to perform his duties on any day which has been declared by law to be a public holiday, and no deduction can be made from such person's salary by reason of the fact that such a public holiday happens to be a school day. Any term of any contract made with any such teaching staff member which is in violation of these provisions is void.[60] When a board of education has not included a public holiday in its calendar of days off and a teacher independently takes that day off she may be required to work an additional day at some other point in the school year.[61]

The following days are designated by statute as public holidays: New Year's Day, Martin Luther King's Birthday (third Monday in January), Lincoln's Birthday (February 12), Washington's Birthday (third Monday in February), Good Friday, Memorial Day (last Monday in May), Independence Day (July 4), Labor Day (first Monday in September), Columbus Day (second Monday in October), Armistice or Veteran's day (November 11), Thanksgiving Day (fourth Thursday in November), Christmas Day, any general election day, and any day designated by the Governor of New Jersey or the President of the United States as a day of religious observance. Where any of these designated days falls on a Sunday, the following Monday becomes a public holiday.[62]

---

[56]*N.J.S.A.* 18A:30-7.

[57]*N.J.S.A.* 18A:30-3.2.

[58]*N.J.S.A.* 18A:30-2.1.

[59]*N.J.S.A.* 18A:30-4.

[60]*N.J.S.A.* 18A:25-3.

[61]*Dohm v. W. Milford Twp. Bd. of Ed.*, 1983 *S.L.D.* 13.

[62]*N.J.S.A.* 36:1-1.

SUITS AGAINST BOARD EMPLOYEES

Whenever any civil action has been brought against any employee of a board of education, for any act or omission arising out of the performance of his duties, the board must defray all costs of defending such action, including reasonable counsel fees and expenses, together with the cost of appeal, if any, and must save harmless and protect the employee from any financial loss resulting from the suit. Boards of education may maintain appropriate insurance to cover all such damages, losses and expenses.[63]

Should any criminal action be instituted against any employee for any such act or omission and should the proceedings be dismissed or result in a final disposition in favor of the employee, the board must reimburse him for the cost of defending the suit, including reasonable counsel fees and expenses for the original hearing or trial and all appeals.[64]

PHYSICAL EXAMINATIONS REQUIRED OF BOARD EMPLOYEES

The board of education must require a physical examination of every employee annually. The scope of the examination is determined under rules of the state board of education. The board may also require an individual psychiatric or physical examination of an employee whenever in its judgment such employee shows evidence of deviation from normal physical or mental health.[65] When a board requires an employee to undergo such an individual examination, the employee must be provided a written statement of reasons and, if the employee so requests, a hearing before the board. Only those candidates for employment who have already received a job offer may be required to undergo a physical examination upon which employment may be conditioned. The physical examination shall not be used to determine the candidate's disabilities, but rather only to determine whether the applicant is able to perform with reasonable accommodation job-related functions pursuant to the Americans with Disabilities Act of 1990 ("ADA").[66]

Examinations may be conducted by:

- A physician or institution designated by the board, in which case all costs are borne by the board; or
- At the option of the employee by a physician or institution of

---

[63]*N.J.S.A.* 18A:16-6.

[64]*N.J.S.A.* 18A:16-6.1.

[65]*N.J.S.A.* 18A:16-2.

[66]*N.J.A.C.* 6:29-7.4; 42 *U.S.C.* 12112.

his own choice, approved by the board, in which case the expenses are paid by the employee.[67]

COMPENSATION

A board of education may adopt a one, two or three year salary policy, including salary schedules for all full-time teaching staff members. These are binding upon the adopting board and upon all future boards in the same district but shall not prohibit the payment of higher salaries than those required by such policy or schedules nor the subsequent adoption of policies or schedules providing for higher salaries, increments or adjustments.[68] A board of education employing one or more teaching staff members having full-time supervisory or administrative responsibilities shall adopt salary schedules for each school year for all such members, except that the board may adopt a salary schedule for a superintendent of schools. Salary schedules must be filed with the commissioner within 30 days after the adoption or subsequent revision of each schedule.[69]

In 1985, the Legislature determined that competitive starting teaching salaries are necessary in order to retain and attract outstanding teachers. Accordingly, the Teacher Quality Employment Act (TQEA) establishes the minimum salary of a full-time teaching staff member who is not employed as a substitute on a day-to-day basis at $18,500 for an academic year and a proportionate amount for less than an academic year.[70] Teachers receiving more than the minimum salary shall not receive automatic salary increases pursuant to any existing collective bargaining agreement with a salary guide indexed to compute salaries on the basis of a ratio established between the minimum salary and all other ranges, increments, or increases.[71]

Military service credit may be given to teaching staff members. Military service is counted for employment credit as if the employee were employed as a teacher during that time, up to a maximum of 4 years' credit.[72]

No salary schedule adopted by any board of education may provide for lower than the minimum salary.[73] The minimum salary must not include any amounts paid to teaching staff members for duties which are outside of the regular contractual responsibilities, such as remuneration

---

[67]N.J.S.A. 18A:16-3.

[68]N.J.S.A. 18A:29-4.1.

[69]N.J.S.A. 18A:29-4.3.

[70]N.J.S.A. 18A:29-5 ("Teacher Quality Employment Act")

[71]N.J.S.A. 18A:29-5.5.

[72]N.J.S.A. 18A:29-11.

[73]N.J.S.A. 18A:29-5.3.

for coaching, extracurricular activities and summer employment.[74] The TQEA provides a formula by which boards of education shall receive state aid to help fund the minimum required salary during the initial years of the law's enactment.[75]

WITHHOLDING SALARY INCREMENTS

A board of education has the authority to withhold a teacher's employment increment, adjustment increment or both, for inefficiency or other good cause, by a recorded roll call majority vote of the full membership of the board. The board must, within 10 days, give the teacher written notice together with the reasons for the action.[76]

Even though a board of education has the power to withhold an increment, such power must not be wielded in a manner which ignores the basic elements of fair play. A teacher has a basic right to know if and when her superiors are less than satisfied with her performance and the basis for this judgment; without such knowledge, the teacher would have no opportunity either to rectify her deficiencies or to convince her superiors that their judgment is erroneous. However, a full scale plenary hearing or the kind of formal proceedings necessary for dismissal of tenured teachers is not required for the withholding of an increment.[77] A board must pass its resolution to withhold an increment for a 10 month employee by August 31.[78]

The decision to deny an increment lies within the area of a board of education's discretionary powers, and the commissioner will not upset the board's decision unless patently arbitrary, without rational basis or induced by improper motives. The burden of proving unreasonableness is on the teacher. In the absence of clear and convincing proof that the board acted unreasonably or in a cursory manner in withholding the increment, the commissioner will not substitute his judgment for the board's discretion.[79]

The withholding of a teacher's increment in one year will have a continuing effect on the teacher's salary in future years. The teacher's salary will continue to lag behind the salary of other teachers with similar years of experience. The fact that the teacher will always lag behind is not at-

---

[74]N.J.S.A. 18A:29-5.4.

[75]N.J.S.A. 18A:29-5.6.

[76]N.J.S.A. 18A:29-14.

[77]Fitzpatrick v. Bd. of Ed. of Montvale, 1969 S.L.D. 4.

[78]Newark Teachers Union, Local 481, AFT/AFL-CIO and Smith v. Newark Bd. of Ed., 1984 S.L.D. 1045.

[79]Kopera v. West Orange Bd. of Ed., 60 N.J. Super. 288 (App. Div. 1960): Durkin et al. v. Bd. of Ed. of the City of Englewood, 1971 S.L.D. 654, aff'd State Bd. 1972 S.L.D. 669; Longo v. Absecon Bd. of Ed., 1975 S.L.D. 336.

tributable to a new violation each year, but rather to the effect of the board's earlier action.[80]

As a result of the 1990 amendments to the bargaining law, only increments withheld for reasons that relate predominately to the evaluation of a teaching staff member's teaching performance are appealable to the commissioner. Disputes over increments that are withheld for predominately disciplinary reasons must be decided through binding arbitration, where the burden of proof is on the employer. PERC has jurisdiction to determine whether increments were withheld for predominately performance-related or disciplinary reasons.[81]

CERTIFICATION OF TEACHING STAFF MEMBERS

No teaching staff member may be employed in the public schools by any board of education unless he is the holder of an appropriate teacher's certificate. Any contract between the board of education and a teacher is of no effect against the board whenever the board ascertains by notice or otherwise, that the teacher is not in possession of a proper teacher's certificate in full force and effect.[82]

It is the duty of the State Board of Examiners to issue appropriate teacher certificates.[83] The State Board of Examiners consists of the commissioner of education, *ex officio*, one assistant commissioner of education, two presidents of state colleges, one county superintendent, one superintendent of schools of a Type I district, one superintendent of schools of a Type II district, one high school principal, one school business administrator, one elementary school principal, one librarian employed by the state or by one of its political subdivisions, and four teaching staff members other than a superintendent, principal, school business administrator or librarian. The members of the board are appointed by the commissioner of education with the approval of the state board of education.[83]

Any certificate that has been issued by the State Board of Examiners may be revoked or suspended by it for inefficiency, incapacity, conduct unbecoming a teacher, or other just cause including offenses within the terms of the forfeiture or disqualification statutes; but no certificate may be revoked or suspended unless the holder of the certificate has been given the opportunity to be heard.[85]

---

[80]*North Plainfield Ed. Ass'n. v. North Plainfield Bd. of Ed.*, 96 *N.J.* 587 (1984); *Cordasco v. East Orange Bd. of Ed.*, 205 *N.J. Super.* 407 (App. Div. 1985).

[81]*N.J.S.A.* 34:13A-5.3.

[82]*N.J.S.A.* 18A:27-2; *N.J.A.C.* 6:11-3.1.

[83]*N.J.S.A.* 18A:6-38.

[84]*N.J.S.A.* 18A:6-34.

[85]*N.J.A.C.* 6:11-3.4.

Information on the various types of certificates, the methods of certification and the requirements for certification may be found in Title 6 of the New Jersey Administrative Code.[86]

FAMILY LEAVE ACT

When the Family Leave Act is fully phased in, boards of education that employ 50 or more employees must provide eligible employees with 12 weeks of leave in any 24-month period. Leaves of absence under the Family Leave Act are available to care for a newborn or adopted child, at any time within one year after the birth or adoption, and to provide care for a seriously ill child, parent or spouse. An eligible employee may be entitled to leave on a consecutive, intermittent or reduced leave schedule depending on factors including the reason for the leave sought.

The board of education may require advance notice of a leave, and may require that leave be supported by certification issued by a duly licensed health care provider or any other health care provider determined by the Director of the Division on Civil Rights. If the board has reason to doubt the validity of the certification, it may, at its own expense, require that an employee obtain a second opinion. If the second opinion differs from the initial certification, the employer may require, at its own expense, the opinion of a third health care provider jointly approved by the employer and the employee, whose opinion shall be binding.

Upon return from family leave, an employee is entitled to be restored to her previous position or to an equivalent position of like seniority, status, employment benefits, pay and other terms and conditions of employment. During the leave, boards of education must maintain health insurance coverage as if the employee had not taken the leave. All other employment benefits must be maintained pursuant to the employer's policy with regard to benefits for employees on temporary leave from employment. A board may not discriminate or retaliate against employees who avail themselves of family leave, and must inform all employees of their rights and obligations under the Act by conspicuously posting same and through other appropriate means.[87]

BACKGROUND CHECKS

A board of education must not employ or contract for the services of any teaching staff member, substitute teacher, teacher aide, child study

---

[86]*N.J.A.C.* 6:11-3.1 *et seq.*

[87]*N.J.S.A.* 34:11B-1 *et seq.*, Ch. 261, Laws of 1989.

team member, school physician, school nurse, custodian, school maintenance worker, cafeteria worker, school law enforcement officer, school secretary or clerical worker or any other person serving in a position which involves regular contact with pupils unless the board has conducted a criminal history background check. This requirement does not apply to volunteers.[88] Criminal history record checks of bus drivers are required prior to employment and upon application for renewal of a school bus driver's license.[89]

An applicant for employment or service covered by the background checks law must submit to the commissioner his name, address and fingerprints taken on standard fingerprint cards by a state or local law enforcement agency. No criminal records check shall be performed unless the applicant consents to the check in writing. The applicant bears the cost of the background check.[90]

An individual shall be disqualified from employment or service if the criminal history record check reveals a record of conviction for particular crimes and offenses listed in the statutes. A board must not disqualify any person on the basis of any conviction disclosed by a criminal record check if the individual has affirmatively demonstrated to the commissioner clear and convincing evidence of her rehabilitation.[91] An applicant has 30 days from the date of notice of disqualification to petition the commissioner for a hearing on the accuracy of the criminal history record information or to establish his rehabilitation.[92]

A board of education may employ a candidate provisionally for a period not to exceed 6 months, pending completion of a criminal history records check provided that the candidate submits to the commissioner a sworn statement attesting that the candidate has not been convicted of any crime or disorderly persons offense that would disqualify him.[93] Substitute teachers must only undergo criminal history record checks upon initial employment.[94] Any employer who fails to comply with the background check law shall be fined not more than $500.[95]

PROTECTION FROM DISCRIMINATION

No board may make a religious test or inquiry concerning the religion

---

[88]N.J.S.A. 18A:6-7.1.

[89]N.J.S.A. 18A:39-19.1.

[90]N.J.S.A. 18A:6-7.1; N.J.S.A. 18A:39-19.1.

[91]N.J.S.A. 18A:6-7.3; N.J.S.A. 18A:39-19.1.

[92]N.J.S.A. 18A:6-7.1(a); N.J.S.A. 18A:39-20.

[93]N.J.S.A. 18A:6-7.2; N.J.S.A. 18A:39-19.1.

[94]N.J.S.A. 18A:6-7.1b.

[95]N.J.S.A. 18A:6-7.5.

of any candidate for employment.[96] A board may not refuse employment or otherwise discriminate against employees or candidates for employment because of race, creed, color, national origin, ancestry, age, marital status, sex, or atypical hereditary cellular blood trait of any individual or liability for service in the armed forces or nationality.[97] A board must pay female teachers compensation equal to that paid to male teachers holding similar positions and employment with similar training and terms of service.[98]

There must be no discrimination based on sex in scale of wages, compensation, appointment, assignment, promotion, transfer, resignation, dismissal or other matters pertaining to employment.[99]

A board may not deny employment opportunities to an otherwise qualified handicapped, blind or deaf person, solely because of the handicap.[100]

Section 504 of the Rehabilitation Act of 1973 prohibits a school district receiving federal funds from discriminating against qualified handicapped persons seeking employment.[101] Handicapped persons are those who have a physical or mental impairment which substantially limits one or more major life activities, or has a record of such impairment, or is regarded as having such an impairment. Qualified handicapped persons are those who with reasonable accommodation, can perform the essential functions of the job for which they are hired.[102] Furthermore, once such persons are employed, discriminatory terms and conditions of employment may not be imposed upon them. The district must make reasonable accommodation to the physical or mental limitations of an otherwise qualified applicant or employee, unless the district can demonstrate that the accommodation would impose an undue hardship on the operation of its program. Examples of reasonable accommodations include:

- Making facilities used by employees readily accessible to handicapped persons;
- Job-restructuring;
- Modified work schedules;
- Acquisition or modification of equipment; and
- The provision of interpreters.[103]

---

[96]*N.J.S.A.* 18A:6-5.

[97]*N.J.S.A.* 10:5-12.

[98]*N.J.S.A.* 18A:29-2.

[99]*N.J.S.A.* 18A:6-6. See also Title VII of the Civil Rights Act of 1964 as amended, 42 USCA 200(e) *et seq.*

[100]*N.J.S.A.* 10:5-29.1; *N.J.A.C.* 13:13-1.1 *et seq.*

[101]29 *U.S.C.* 794 (Section 504 of the Rehabilitation Act of 1973).

[102]34 *CFR* 104.3(j) and (k).

[103]34 *CFR* 104.12.

In general, a school board may not conduct a preemployment medical examination or make a preemployment inquiry of an applicant as to whether the applicant is a handicapped person or as to the nature of his handicap. However, a board may make a preemployment inquiry into an applicant's ability to perform job-related functions.[104] Additionally, if the board is taking affirmative action to hire handicapped persons pursuant to Section 504 of the Rehabilitation Act of 1973, it may extend the opportunity to applicants for employment to indicate whether and to what extent they are handicapped.[105] The Americans with Disabilities Act (ADA), which takes many of its substantive provisions directly from Section 504, prohibits boards from discriminating against a qualified individual with a disability because of the disability of such individual in regard to job application procedures, the hiring, advancement, or discharge of employees, employee compensation, job training, and other terms, conditions and privileges of employment.[106] Specifically excluded from the ADA's protection are: homosexuality and bisexuality, transvestism; pedophilia, exhibitionism; gender identity disorders not resulting from physical impairments or other sexual behavior disorders, compulsive gambling; kleptomania, pyromania, psychoactive substance use disorders resulting from current illegal use of drugs, or an individual currently engaging in the illegal use of drugs. The ADA does protect a recovering or former user of illegal drugs as well as an individual "erroneously regarded" as using illegal drugs.[107] The most significant difference between the ADA and Section 504 of the Rehabilitation Act is that the ADA covers entities not receiving federal funds. These laws require notice to employees, the ADA specifically requiring posting.

MISCELLANEOUS

- The board may not require teaching staff employees to reside in the school district in which they are employed.[108]
- The Immigration Reform and Control Act of 1986 (IRCA) requires that employers verify the identity and eligibility for employment for all employees. Verification is accomplished by having new employees complete form I-9 no later than three business days following their first day of work; examination of required documents within three business days of employment;

---

[104]34 *CFR* 104.14(a).
[105]34 *CFR* 104.14(b).
[106]42 *USC* 12112.
[107]42 *USC* 12211.
[108]*N.J.S.A.* 18A:26-1.1.

and completion by the board of the attestation part of Form I-9. Employers must keep the form on file for three years or for one year beyond the date that the employee is no longer employed, whichever is later. Boards of education may be assessed civil and criminal penalties for the employment of illegal aliens.[109]

- Under the Conscientious Employee Protection Act, employees are afforded protection against retaliatory action by boards of education taken for the following reasons: the employee has reported or threatened to report to a supervisor or to any public body that a policy, practice or activity of the board violates the law; the employee provides information to, or testifies before any public body conducting an investigation, hearing or inquiry into any violation of law; the employee objects to, or refuses to participate in any activity, policy or practice which the employee reasonably believes will violate the law, is fraudulent, criminal or is incompatible with a clear mandate of public policy concerning the public health, safety or welfare.[110]

  Boards must display conspicuous notice of employees' rights under this act, and use other appropriate means to keep its employees thus informed.[111] An employer violating this law may be assessed compensatory, civil and punitive damages.[112] If an employee brings a baseless action against a board, the board may be entitled to reasonable attorney's fees against the employee.[113]

- By recorded roll call majority vote of the entire board, a board may approve a plan for salary deductions whenever one or more of the persons employed by the board indicate in writing their desire to participate in any plan to purchase U.S. government bonds or stamps.[114]

- A board's disbursing officer shall make payroll deductions from an employee's compensation in such amounts and on behalf of eligible participating charities as the employee may authorize. An employee may withdraw an authorization at any time upon written notice to the board's disbursing officer.[115]

- A board of education may purchase tax sheltered annuities on

---

[109] 8 *USC* 1324(a), (b); 8 *CFR* 274a.
[110] *N.J.S.A.* 34:19-3.
[111] *N.J.S.A.* 34:19-7.
[112] *N.J.S.A.* 34:19-5.
[113] *N.J.S.A.* 34:19-6.
[114] *N.J.S.A.* 18A:16-8.
[115] *N.J.S.A.* 52:14-15.9c9.

behalf of its employees as part of the state administered Supplemental Annuity Collective Trust.[116]

- A board must grant permission to any professional employee to attend the annual convention of the New Jersey Education Association. Such permission may not exceed 2 days per year, and the employee may be required to file with the board secretary a certificate attesting to his attendance at all of the sessions for the dates he actually attended.[117]

- Boards of education are required, when requested by an employee in writing, to pay the amount of her dues to an employee organization and deduct the amount from her salary. Dues means all monies required to be paid by the employee as a condition of membership in an employee organization and any voluntary employee contribution to a committee or fund established by such an organization including welfare funds, political action committees, charity funds, legal defense funds, educational funds, and funds for donations to schools, colleges and universities.[118]

- Upon the request of staff members who are employed for the academic year, the board may adopt a summer payment plan and implement it under rules promulgated by the state board for those employees who wish to participate.[119]

- Contracts between a board of education and teachers must be in writing, in triplicate and signed by the president and secretary of the board and the teaching staff member.[120] Teacher employment contracts must specify:

a. the date the employment is to begin;

b. the kind of certificate held by the teacher and its expiration date;

c. the salary to be paid; and

d. such other matters as may be necessary to a full and complete understanding.[121]

One copy of the contract is filed with the board, one with the employee and one with the superintendent of schools if there

---

[116]N.J.S.A. 52:18A-107 et seq.

[117]N.J.S.A. 18A:31-2.

[118]N.J.S.A. 52:14-15.9e.

[119]N.J.S.A. 18A:29-3.

[120]N.J.S.A. 18A:27-5.

[121]N.J.S.A. 18A:27-6.

is one, and otherwise with the county superintendent.[122]

- The board may designate a person to act in place of any officer or employee who is absent, disabled or disqualified. A person in such an acting capacity does not acquire tenure.[123]

- Any teaching staff member, under tenure of service, who desires to relinquish his position must give the employing board of education at least 60 days' written notice of his intention, unless the board approves of a release on shorter notice; and if he fails to give such notice he will be guilty of unprofessional conduct and the commissioner may suspend his certificate for not more than one year.[124]

- Certified staff who are also members of the New Jersey Senate or General Assembly are entitled to time off from their duties without loss of pay during periods of attendance at regular or special sessions of the Legislature and hearings or meetings of legislative committees.[125] Certificated employees, who are also members of the board of chosen freeholders, are entitled to time off without pay during periods of attendance at regular or special meetings of the board of chosen freeholders or committee thereof, and at such other times as they shall be engaged in performing the necessary functions and duties of their office as a member of such board.[126]

---

[122]*N.J.S.A.* 18A:27-8.

[123]*N.J.S.A.* 18A:16-1.1.

[124]*N.J.S.A.* 18A:28-8.

[125]*N.J.S.A.* 18A:6-8.1.

[126]*N.J.S.A.* 18A:6-8.2.

THE LOCAL BOARD AND THE PUBLIC

9

As public entities charged with important education policy-making responsibilities and the expenditure of public funds, local boards of education must meet a number of statutory requirements designed to insure that the public is kept adequately informed and has access to information concerning the decision-making process and activities of local boards.

THE SUNSHINE LAW

Meetings of Public Bodies

In enacting the Open Public Meetings Act (popularly known as the Sunshine Law) the Legislature declared that secrecy in public affairs undermines the faith of the public in government and the public's effectiveness in fulfilling its role in a democratic society and that the right of the public to witness in full detail all phases of the deliberation, policy formation, and decision-making of public bodies is vital to the enhancement and proper functioning of the democratic process.[1]

In general, the statute requires that the public be given advance notice of and the right to attend meetings of public bodies and that all discussions and official actions, unless specifically exempted, take place in public.

The statute covers every public body organized by law and collectively empowered as a voting body to spend public funds or to perform a public governmental function affecting people's rights, obligations or benefits.[2]

A meeting of the public body is covered if it is open to or attended by all the members of the public body and is held with the intent of discussing or acting on public business. A meeting is excluded from the requirements of the law if it is attended by fewer than an effective majority of the members of the body.[3] An effective majority is defined as that number of members that must be present at the meeting in order for the body to take official action, e.g., five members of a nine member board.[4]

---

[1]N.J.S.A. 10:4-6 et seq.; N.J.S.A. 10:4-7; See also, Polillo v. Deane, 74 N.J. 562, 569-72 (1977).
[2]N.J.S.A. 10:4-8.a.
[3]N.J.S.A. 10:4-8.b.
[4]Guidelines on the Open Public Meetings Law, Department of State, p.4.

A meeting is also exempted if it is attended by or open to all the members of three or more similar public bodies at a convention or similar gathering.[5] However, a court has held that a joint discussion meeting, to which all members of several public bodies are invited for the purpose of discussing public business of mutual concern, is subject to the requirements of the Sunshine Law.[6]

Committee meetings may be subject to the requirements of the Sunshine Law. It is the opinion of the Attorney General that committee meetings are covered by the law if the committee is made up of an effective majority of the public body's members. Where a committee is composed of less than an effective majority of the body, the committee may be covered depending on the nature and extent of the authority delegated to the committee by the public body. According to the Attorney General, the decision turns on whether the committee is merely an advisory body or whether the public body has delegated to the committee the authority, in either a legal or practical sense, to make binding decisions affecting persons' rights or the expenditure of public funds.

It is also the opinion of the Attorney General that some training sessions or workshops are subject to the Sunshine Law. Simply classifying a gathering as a training session or workshop does not exclude it from the statutory definition of a public meeting. If the training session or workshop is attended by, or open to, all members of a local board, and is held to discuss or act on the specific business of that board, it is covered by the statute. It is not subject to the provisions of the Act if it is attended by less than an effective majority of the board or if it is attended by or open to all the members of three or more local boards at a convention or similar gathering.[7]

Notice

For all meetings covered by the statute, advance notice of the meeting must be given to the public. There are two types of notice under the Sunshine Law: annual notice, and adequate or 48-hour notice.

The requirement of annual notice means that at least once each year, within seven days following the annual organization or reorganization meeting, the public body must establish a schedule of its regular meetings to be held during the succeeding year. The schedule must contain the time and date of each meeting and the location of each meeting to the extent it is known. This schedule must be posted and maintained throughout the year in at least one public place reserved for such announcements, mail-

---

[5]*N.J.S.A.* 10:4-8.b.

[6]*Allan-Deane Corp. v. Bedminister Twp.*, 153 *N.J. Super.* 114 (App. Div. 1977), certif. den. 74 *N.J.* 272 (1977).

[7]Atty. Gen. F.O. 1976, No. 19.

ed to two designated newspapers and filed with the appropriate county or municipal office.[8] In addition, all persons requesting that a public body mail them a schedule of meetings must be sent a copy of the annual notice.[9] If the schedule is thereafter revised, the public body, within seven days of the revision, must post, mail and submit the revision in the manner described above.[10]

Adequate or 48-hour notice means written advance notice of at least 48 hours, giving the time, date, location and, to the extent known, the agenda of any regular, special or rescheduled meeting.[11]

The agenda required under this 48-hour notice provision must be somewhat specific as to the matter to be discussed or acted upon. For example, where a public body provided 48-hour notice of a special meeting and the agenda stated only that the purpose was to meet with a certain attorney, a court held that the agenda item was insufficient because the meeting was expressly called by the public body to discuss the settlement of a particular case.[12]

Note that the 48-hour notice provision expressly requires agenda information while the annual notice provision states no such requirement. The statute also states that if the annual notice complies with the statutory requirements, no further notice is required for any meeting contained in the annual notice.[13] Thus, an agenda need not be published for a regular meeting for which annual notice has been provided, and if the public body voluntarily publishes an agenda in this situation, action taken upon matters not included on the agenda will not be voided by a court unless it finds that the omission was intentional or designed to deceive the public.[14]

The adequate or 48-hour notice must be:

- Prominently posted in at least one public place reserved for such announcements;
- Mailed, telephoned, telegrammed or hand-delivered to at least two newspapers, one of which shall be the designated official newspaper;
- Filed with the clerk of the governing body of the political subdivision whose geographic boundaries are coextensive with those of the public body; and

---

[8]*N.J.S.A.* 10:4-18.

[9]*N.J.S.A.* 10:4-19.

[10]*N.J.S.A.* 10:4-18.

[11]*N.J.S.A.* 10:4-8.d.

[12]*In the Matter of the Application of Monmouth Cty. v. To Fix the Compensation to be Paid for the Property of Snyder-Westerlind Corp., 156 N.J. Super. 188 (App. Div. 1978).*

[13]*N.J.S.A.* 10:4-8.d.

[14]*Crifasi v. Governing Body of the Borough of Oakland, 156 N.J. Super. 182 (App. Div. 1978).*

- Sent to those persons requesting that such notice be mailed to them.[15]

The precise wording of this statutory provision would seem to indicate that the public body is not required to publish its notices, only to transmit the notices to the newspapers. The State Department guidelines interpret the provision to require only that the notice be placed in the mail sufficiently in advance of the meetings so as to reasonably expect it to be received by the newspapers at least 48 hours prior to the meeting.[16] However, a court has held that the provision requires that the notice be sent in time to be published, and not simply delivered to the newspapers, 48 hours before the meeting.[17] In another case, mere transmittal did not satisfy the law where the board knew or reasonably could have ascertained that the newspaper's publishing schedule prevented it from printing the notice 48 hours in advance of the meeting.[18] It has also been held that where the notice is provided to the newspapers 48 hours before the meeting, the public body has made every reasonable effort to comply with the law, and its action at the meeting will not be voided simply because the newspaper fails to publish the notice.[19]

At the commencement of every meeting, the presiding person must announce publicly and have entered in the minutes an accurate statement that adequate notice of the meeting has been provided, specifying the time, place and manner in which the notice was provided.[20]

The Legislature recognized the possibility of a need to hold an emergency meeting and statutorily provided for calling one. A public body may hold an emergency meeting without adequate advance written notice if three-fourths of its members present vote in favor of holding the meeting and, as soon as possible following the decision to hold the meeting, notice is posted and given by telephone, telegram or delivery to two newspapers, one of which is the designated official newspaper.[21]

An emergency meeting is defined as one required to be held in order to deal with matters of such urgency and importance that a delay for the purpose of providing adequate notice would be likely to result in substantial harm to the public interest.[22] Even if the public body could have fore-

---

[15]*N.J.S.A.* 10:4-8.d, 19.

[16]*Guidelines, supra* at p.9.

[17]*Jones v. East Windsor Regional Bd. of Ed.*, 143 *N.J. Super.* 182 (Law Div. 1976), appeal dismissed as moot 158 *N.J. Super.* 496 (App. Div. 1977).

[18]*Worts v. Upper Township*, 176 *N.J.Super.* 78 (Ch. Div. 1980).

[19]*Houman v. Mayor and Council of Borough of Pompton Lakes*, 155 *N.J. Super.* 129 (Law Div. 1978).

[20]*N.J.S.A.* 10:4-10.a.

[21]*N.J.S.A.* 10:4-9.

[22]*N.J.S.A.* 10:4-9.b.(1).

seen the need for the meeting and notice could have been given, failure to do so will not void the meeting, if a true emergency exists.[23] Once a meeting is called, it is limited to the matters of importance which necessitated the meeting.[24] At the commencement of an emergency meeting, the presiding person must announce publicly and have entered in the minutes that adequate notice was not provided, the nature of the urgency, the harm to the public in delaying the meeting, the limitation on the matter discussed at the meeting, the time, place and manner in which notice was provided, and the reason why a need for the meeting could not be foreseen or why the adequate notice could not be provided.[25]

Two recent cases interpret what is meant by "substantial harm to the public interest." In *Dunn v. Laurel Springs*, 163 *N.J. Super.* 32 (App. Div. 1978), a town council appointed an individual to fill a vacant council seat at a meeting held without adequate notice. The town argued that substantial harm would result if the meeting were delayed to provide notice in that the council would have missed its statutory deadline for filling the vacancy and the vacancy would have to be filled by a municipal election at a cost of $1,200 in public funds. The court held that the election and its expense did not constitute "substantial harm to the public interest" when balanced against the harm caused by failing to give adequate notice to the public.

In another case, *Jenkins v. Newark Bd. of Ed.* 166 *N.J. Super.* 357 (Law Div. 1978), aff'd 166 *N.J. Super.* 300 (App. Div. 1979), the board held a meeting on three hours' notice, claiming that an emergency existed and that substantial harm to the public interest would result if the meeting was delayed. The board held the meeting to effect program and personnel cutbacks necessitated by a budget deficit and the board asserted that it would have lost some $40,000 per day if 48-hour notice had been given. The court found that the board could have foreseen the need for the meeting in sufficient time to provide the 48-hour notice without this financial loss. The court also found that even if the board *did* have to bear this financial loss in order to give the 48-hour notice, such a loss did *not* constitute substantial harm to the public interest, since the cost when compared to the board's total budget was miniscule and since the public's right to notice of the meeting was more important.

Minutes

Minutes must be kept of all meetings, which at a minimum must include the announcement of the presiding person at the commencement of the meeting, the time and place of the meeting, the names of the

---

[23]*N.J.S.A.* 10:4-9.b.(4).

[24]*N.J.S.A.* 10:4-9.b.(2).

[25]*N.J.S.A.* 10:4-10.b.

members present, the subjects considered, the actions taken and the vote of each member on any items voted upon.[26]

Minutes must be taken of both open and closed session meetings, but the minutes of a closed session may be withheld from disclosure until such time as the reasons for discussing a matter in closed session no longer exist.[27] All others must be made "promptly available" to the public.[28] The meaning of the words "promptly available" is not defined in the statute, but one court, noting the need for an enforceable standard, ruled that a board's minutes must be made available within two weeks after any regular meeting, where the meetings were held two weeks apart. Where the board held successive meetings involving the same subject matter at intervals shorter than two weeks, the minutes of the earlier meeting were to be available in advance of the later meeting.[29] According to the State Department guidelines, if the release of the minutes takes place prior to their formal approval, a statement should be placed at the top of them indicating that the minutes have not been formally approved and are subject to modification at the next meeting.[30]

Members of the public have the right to videotape the open portion of a meeting of a public body. Boards of education may adopt reasonable guidelines concerning the videotaping process. In the absence of board guidelines, boards must follow the Supreme Court's guidelines for camera and audio coverage of court proceedings.[31]

Closed Sessions

All meetings of public bodies must be open to the public at all times, unless the matter under consideration by the public body falls under one of the categories specifically exempted under the statute. Exempt matters may only be discussed in closed session; final action must be taken at an open session.[32] All other matters, regardless of their controversial

---

[26]*N.J.S.A.* 10:4-10, 14; In *Mackenzie v. Princeton Regional Bd. of Ed.*, Superior Court, Law Division (Docket No. L-35698-76 P.W., decided September 23, 1977), the court held that a board may not utilize a secret ballot for the election of board officers at the organization meeting.

[27]*Guidelines, supra* at p. 13-16.

[28]*N.J.S.A.* 10:4-14.

[29]*Matawan Regional Teachers Ass'n v. Matawan-Aberdeen Bd. of Ed., 212 N.J.Super.* 328 (Law Div. 1986)

[30]*Guidelines, supra* at p. 16

[31]*Maurice River Bd. of Ed. v. Maurice River Teachers Ass'n*, 193 *N.J.Super.* 488 (App. Div. 1984).

[32]*Houman v. Mayor and Council of Borough of Pompton Lakes, supra.* However, there may be some exceptional circumstances under which a board may or must vote in closed session. See, e.g., *N.J.S.A.* 18A:6-11, which prohibits boards from considering or acting on tenure charges at a public meeting.

nature, must be discussed and acted upon in public. However, the public body retains the right to permit, regulate or prohibit the active participation of the public at any meeting.[33] There are nine statutory exceptions to the public meeting requirement:

1. Any matter which by express provision of federal law, state statute or court rule is rendered confidential;

2. Any matter in which the release of information would impair a right to receive federal funds;

3. Any matter the disclosure of which would constitute an unwarranted invasion of individual privacy, unless the individual concerned requests in writing that the matter be disclosed publicly;[34]

4. Any collective bargaining agreement, terms and conditions proposed for inclusion in such agreement and the negotiations of terms and conditions with employees or their representatives;

5. Any matter involving purchase, lease or acquisition of real property with public funds, the setting of banking rates or investment of public funds, where the public interest could be adversely affected if discussion were disclosed;

6. Any tactics and techniques utilized in protecting the safety and property of the public, if disclosure could impair such protection, and any investigations of violations or possible violations of the law;

7. Any pending or anticipated litigation or contract negotiation in which the public body is or may become a party and any matters falling within the attorney-client privilege, to the extent that confidentiality is required in order for the attorney to exercise his/her ethical duties as a lawyer. To invoke the litigation exception, the subject under discussion must be the "pending or anticipated litigation" itself, i.e., the board's strategy in the litigation, the position it will take, the strengths and weaknesses of that position, possible settlement or some other facet of the litigation;[35]

---

[33]*N.J.S.A.* 10:4-12.a. Although the Sunshine Law does not limit a board's discretion to prohibit public participation at meetings, the monitoring regulations require that district boards of education provide the opportunity for public comment at their regularly scheduled meetings. *N.J.A.C.* 6:8-4.3(a)2.iii.

[34]*See Jones v. East Windsor Regional Bd. of Ed.*, 143 *N.J. Super.* 182 (Law Div. 1976), appeal dismissed as moot 158 *N.J. Super.* 496 (App. Div. 1977). (Closed session to interview applicants for board vacancy upheld.) Compare with *Gannett Satellite Information Network, Inc. v. Manville Borough Bd. of Ed.*, 201 *N.J. Super.* 65 (Law Div. 1984) (Closed session to interview, deliberate, nominate and vote violated the Sunshine Law).

[35]Atty. Gen. F.O. 1976, No. 30.

8. Any matter involving the employment, appointment, termination of employment, terms and conditions of employment, evaluation of performance, promotion or disciplining of any prospective or current public officer or employee, unless all the individuals whose rights could be adversely affected request in writing that such matters be discussed at a public meeting. It has been held that a closed session to discuss the termination of specific employees in the context of a reduction in force is valid under this exception. However, the public body is required to provide the employees concerned with reasonable notice of its intention to consider in closed session personnel matters related to them in order to allow them to exercise their statutory right to request a public hearing;[36]

9. Any deliberations of a public body occurring after a public hearing that may result in the imposition of a specific civil penalty or suspension or loss of a license or permit belonging to an individual as the result of an act or omission for which the individual is responsible.[37]

A public body may go into a closed session concerning matters included in any of the above exceptions to the public meeting requirement. However, prior to going into closed session, a resolution must be adopted at a public meeting stating the general nature of the subject to be discussed and stating as precisely as possible, the time when and the circumstances under which the discussion can be disclosed to the public.[38] If this resolution is passed at a prior public meeting for which notice has been provided, the public body may hold a meeting limited to the matter to be dealt with in closed session without providing additional notice therefor. In the event a resolution has not been passed by the public body at such prior public meeting, the public body must then provide adequate or 48-hour notice of the meeting and at that meeting pass the required resolution in open session prior to going into closed session.[39]

Sanctions

Any person who knowingly violates any of the provisions of the law is subject to a fine of $100 for the first offense and no less than $100 nor more than $500 for any subsequent offense. If a member of a public body believes a meeting is being held in violation of the law, he should im-

---

[36]*Rice v. Union Cty. Regional High School Bd. of Ed.*, 155 *N.J. Super.* 64 (App. Div. 1977), *certif. den.* 76 *N.J.* 238 (1978).

[37]*N.J.S.A.* 10:4-12.b.

[38]*N.J.S.A.* 10:4-13.

[39]Atty. Gen. F.O. 1976, No. 29.

mediately state this belief and his reasons therefor which must be recorded in the minutes. If the majority of those present overrule his objections, the objecting member may continue to participate without being exposed to personal liability.[40]

Any action taken by a public body at a meeting which did not comply with the provisions of the statute is voidable in a Superior Court proceeding which may be brought by any person within 45 days after the action sought to be voided has been made public. However, a public body may take corrective action by acting *"de novo"* (i.e., anew) at a subsequent public meeting held in conformity with the statute.[41]

Strict adherence to each of the statutory provisions is required by the courts in determining whether a violation of the law has occurred. Substantial but less than perfect compliance with the law is not sufficient. However, once the court has determined that a violation has occurred, it may consider the nature, quality and effect of the violation in fashioning the corrective measures or remedy which it will order.[42]

THE RIGHT TO KNOW LAW

In enacting the Right to Know Law, the Legislature declared it to be the public policy of the state that public records be readily accessible for examination by the citizens of the state, with certain exceptions, for the protection of the public interest.[43] Every citizen is given the right, during regular business hours, to inspect, copy by hand or purchase copies of any public record.[44] This unqualified right to inspection requires no showing of any personal or particular interest in the material.[45] This is not to say that public access is without limitations. The public entity may establish reasonable time and place restrictions on the terms of access.[46] Also, the board is under no obligation to interpret records or meet other unreasonable demands.[47]

Public records are defined in the Right to Know Law as all records which are required by law to be made, maintained or kept on file by any

---

[40]*N.J.S.A.* 10:4-17.

[41]*N.J.S.A.* 10:4-15.a; See also *Houman, supra.*

[42]*Polillo v. Deane,* 74 *N.J.* 562, 577-80 (1977).

[43]*N.J.S.A.* 47:1A-1.

[44]*N.J.S.A.* 47:1A-2.

[45]*Techniscan v. Passaic Valley Water,* 113 N.J. 233 (1988); *Irval Realty v. Bd. of Public Utility Commissioners,* 61 *N.J.* 366, 372-73 (1972).

[46]*Techniscan, supra.* at 237.

[47]*Laufgas v. Barnegat Bd. of Ed.,* oral opinion of Judge Serpentelli, Law Division, N.J. Superior Court (February 10, 1987).

board, body, agency, department, commission or official of the State or any political subdivision thereof or by any public board, body, commission or authority created by the state or any of its political subdivisions.[48] The courts have strictly interpreted the requirement to make and keep documents; thus, any document that is not specifically required by law to be made, maintained or kept on file is not required to be disclosed under the Right to Know Law.[49]

Certain public records are exempted under the statute. A public body may deny access to records of an investigation in progress by such body if the inspection, copying or publication of such records is inimical to the public interest.[50] The statute also provides that records may be exempted by any other statute, resolution of the Legislature, Executive Order of the Governor, rule of court, any federal law, regulation or order, or by any regulation promulgated under the authority of any statute or Executive Order of the Governor.[51] In a case decided under this provision, a court denied a citizen's request under the Right to Know Law to obtain a poll list since another statute required that poll lists be sealed.[52] Another case upheld a board's refusal to disclose the contents of an employee's evaluation on the basis of an Executive Order of the Governor.[53] This Executive Order prohibits a governmental entity from disclosing personnel or pension records of an individual except for an individual's name, title, position, salary, payroll record, length of service, date of separation and the reason therefor and the amount and type of pension she is receiving. The order also allows access to data which discloses conformity with specific experience, education or medical qualifications required for government employment or for receipt of a public pension but prohibits disclosure of detailed medical or psychological information.[54]

In the absence of a specific statute setting a price for a particular record, copies of non-exempted public records must be supplied upon the payment of the following fees:

First page to tenth page . . . . $0.50 per page
Eleventh page to twentieth page . . . . $0.25 per page
All pages over twenty . . . . $0.10 per page[55]

---

[48]N.J.S.A. 47:1A-2.

[49]Nero v. Hyland, 76 N.J. 213 (1978); Collins v. Camden Cty. Health Dept., 200 N.J.Super. 281 (Law Div. 1984).

[50]N.J.S.A. 47:1A-3.

[51]N.J.S.A. 47:1A-2.

[52]Shanahan v. New Jersey State Bd. of Ed., 118 N.J. Super. 212 (App. Div. 1972).

[53]Trenton Times Corp. v. Trenton Bd. of Ed., 138 N.J. Super. 357 (App. Div. 1976).

[54]Executive Order No. 11, November 15, 1974.

[55]N.J.S.A. 47:1A-2.

Any citizen denied the right to inspect, copy or obtain a copy of a public record may apply to the Superior Court for an order requiring the custodian of the record to afford the desired access.[56]

Even if a citizen is not entitled to inspect a public document under the Right to Know Law, the citizen may have the right to examine the document under the common law. The common law right to inspect public records is not absolute, and requires that the citizen's interest in or need for the record be balanced against the public's interest in maintaining the confidentiality of the document.[57]

DESTRUCTION OF PUBLIC RECORDS

No person may destroy or otherwise dispose of public records in his care except as provided for by the Destruction of Public Records Law (1953).[58] The definition of "public records" in the Destruction of Public Records Law (1953) is broader than the definition of "public records" in the Right to Know Law, and includes any record which has been made or is required by law to be received for filing, indexing, or reproducing by any officer, commission, agency or authority of the State or of any political subdivision thereof, or that has been received by any such officer, etc., in connection with the transaction of public business and has been maintained as evidence of its activities or because of the information contained therein.[59]

The Destruction of Public Records Law (1953) and its implementing regulations prohibit the destruction of public records without the written consent of the Division of Archives and Records Management in the Department of State (formerly the Bureau of Archives and History in the Department of Education).[60]

Records retention and disposition schedules designating the length of time particular records should be kept prior to disposal are available to school districts through the Division of Archives and Records.[61] Procedures for requesting authorization for the disposal of public records are contained in regulations, as are detailed instructions for obtaining and preparing the required form requests for records disposal.[62]

The law also contains microfilming standards. A public body must meet

---

[56]*N.J.S.A.* 47:1A-4.

[57]*Techniscan v. Passaic Valley Water, supra.*

[58]*N.J.S.A.* 47:3-15 *et seq.*

[59]*N.J.S.A.* 47:3-16.

[60]*N.J.S.A.* 47:3-17; *N.J.A.C.* 15:3-31 *et seq.*

[61]*N.J.A.C.* 15:3-3.5; *N.J.A.C.* 15:3-3.15 and 3.16

[62]*N.J.S.A.* 47:3-21; *N.J.A.C.* 15:3-3.8.

these standards before the Division of Archives and Management will grant permission to destroy original documents that an agency wishes to convert to microfilm.[63]

PUPIL RECORDS

The specific laws regarding the confidentiality of pupil records remove pupil records from the general category of public records which districts must make available to any person upon request. In 1975, the state board adopted regulations regarding pupil records in order to comply with the federal Family Educational Rights and Privacy Act of 1974, also known as the Buckley Amendment.[64] Pupil records are broadly defined to include any information gathered within or without the school system and maintained within the school system, regardless of the physical form in which it is maintained. Any information maintained for the purpose of second party review is considered a pupil record. Thus, information recorded by school personnel solely as a memory aid, not for the use of a second party, is not considered a pupil record.[65]

A school district may not compile any pupil records, other than the mandated and permitted records defined in state board regulations. Mandated records are those records which districts have been directed to compile by New Jersey statute, regulation, or authorized administrative directive. For example, all records pursuant to rules and regulations regarding the education of educationally handicapped pupils are mandated records. Permitted pupil records are those which a local board of education has authorized the district to collect by resolution adopted at a regular public meeting to promote the educational welfare of the pupil.[66]

Pupil records may contain only such information as is relevant to the education of the pupil, and is objectively based on the personal observations or knowledge of the originator of the record. All permitted records must be reviewed annually by certified school personnel to determine the educational relevance of the material contained therein. Material no longer relevant or descriptive of the pupil is to be deleted, except that prior notice must be given for classified students prior to the deletion of such information.[67]

The rules of the state board on access to pupil records provide that the following persons and organizations shall have the right to view, make

---

[63]*N.J.S.A.* 47:3-26; *N.J.A.C.* 15:3-3.12.

[64]Title V of Public Law 93-380, codified as amended at 20 *U.S.C.* Sec. 1232 g. *et seq.*

[65]*N.J.A.C.* 6:3-2.1.

[66]*N.J.A.C.* 6:3-2.3.

[67]*N.J.A.C.* 6:3-2.2(c) and (i).

notes and/or have a reproduction made of a pupil record:

- A parent, legal guardian, foster parent or parent surrogate of a pupil under the age of 18;
- Pupils under 18 having the written permission of such parent or guardian;
- Pupils at least 16 years of age who are terminating their education by graduating at the end of the term or plan to discontinue their education;
- Adult pupils (18 years of age and older);
- Parents or guardians of adult pupils:

    a. where they have the written permission of the pupil or

    b. where the pupil is financially dependent on them;
- Certified school personnel who have assigned educational responsibility for the pupil;
- A district board of education, through the chief school administrator;
- Secretarial and clerical staff on a limited basis and under the direct supervision of certified personnel;
- Accrediting organizations, the Department of Education and officials of other school districts in which the student is registered or intends to enroll;
- A state agency investigating the need for protective services or supervision and organizations or persons on presentation of a court order;
- Organizations and persons outside the school with the written consent of the parent or adult pupil;
- *Bona fide* researchers under strict conditions of anonymity and confidentiality.[68]

Furthermore, a state statute enacted in 1986 requires the chief school administrator or his designee to request the student records of a new student from the district of last attendance within two weeks from the date the student enrolls. The law is intended to protect against child abuse and abduction by informing public schools of the whereabouts of children in the educational system.[69]

A record may be withheld from an authorized parent or pupil only when the chief school administrator is convinced that disclosure would

---

[68]*N.J.A.C.* 6:3-2.5.

[69]*N.J.S.A.* 18A:36-19a.

create a substantial risk of harm to the pupil or to a person with whom the record is concerned.[70] Pupil records are subject to challenge by parents or adult pupils on grounds of inaccuracy, irrelevancy, impermissive disclosure or denial of access, and appeal may be had to the board of education or to the commissioner.[71]

The chief school administrator or a designee shall be present during inspection to provide interpretation where necessary and to prevent record alteration, damage or loss.[72]

The chief school administrator or his designee is responsible for the security of pupil records and must devise procedures to assure limited access to pupil records. When records are maintained in different locations, the law requires a notation in the central file as to where such other records may be found. When records are stored in a computerized system, the district must provide computer programmed security blocks and maintain a duplicate copy of all records to guard against loss.[73]

Pupil records are considered incomplete and not subject to the Destruction of Public Records Law[74] while the student is enrolled in the district. Upon the permanent departure of a pupil, records may be destroyed in accordance with the Destruction of Public Records Law except that the district of last enrollment shall be required to keep in perpetuity a permanent record of the pupil's name, birth date, sex, address, telephone number, grades, attendance record, classes, grade level, and year completed, name of parent(s) and citizenship status.[75]

The state board regulations on pupil records also contain detailed requirements pertaining to the time period within which requests to see records must be reviewed and procedures by which parents and pupils may challenge the contents of pupil records.[76]

The district board of education shall notify parents and adult pupils annually in writing of their rights under the law.[77] A board shall establish written policies and procedures for pupil records, including a provision for access to student information directories by educational, occupational and military recruiters.[78]

---

[70]N.J.A.C. 6:3-2.6.
[71]N.J.A.C. 6:3-2.7.
[72]N.J.A.C. 6:3-2.6.
[73]N.J.A.C. 6:3-2.4.
[74]N.J.S.A. 47:3-15 et seq.
[75]N.J.A.C. 6:3-2.8.
[76]N.J.A.C. 6:3-2.7.
[77]N.J.A.C. 6:3-2.2(d).
[78]N.J.A.C. 6:3-2.2(g).

DRUG TREATMENT RECORDS

As of January 13, 1988, each local board of education must establish a comprehensive substance abuse intervention, prevention and treatment referral program in the district's elementary and secondary schools.[79] The state board has promulgated standards for the development of policies and procedures to evaluate and treat pupils who have alcohol and other drug-related problems.[80] These state regulations mandate compliance with certain federal regulations pertaining to the confidentiality of alcohol and drug abuse patient records.[81] The federal rules prohibit disclosure by a federally assisted drug program of information concerning its patients without consent, except that the contents of patient records may be disclosed without consent to medical personnel to the extent necessary to meet a medical emergency, to qualified personnel for bona fide research purposes or if authorized by court order.[82]

The federal regulations also impose criminal penalties for violations, provide for the maintenance and disposition of patient records and require notice to patients of the confidentiality provisions.[83]

Compliance with the federal regulations on the confidentiality of drug patient records is also specifically required in the regulations implementing New Jersey's Drug Free School Zone legislation.[84] The Drug Free School Zone Act, part of the Comprehensive Drug Reform Act of 1987, provides enhanced punishment for drug offenders who operate within 1,000 feet of school property.[85] The implementing regulations establish uniform statewide procedures for cooperating with law enforcement drug operations and activities on or near school grounds, and identify circumstances under which school officials shall refer violations to the police.[86] The reporting requirements contained in the regulations are not to be construed to require the transmittal of information in the possession of a substance abuse or counseling program. The principal shall not disclose to law enforcement officials that a pupil or staff member has received or is receiving services from the district's substance abuse program. Also confidential is any information, including the pupil or staff member's identity, or information about illegal activity, where such information was learned in

---

[79]N.J.S.A. 18A:40A-10.

[80]N.J.A.C. 6:29-6.1 et seq.

[81]42 C.F.R. 2. These regulations implement two federal statutory provisions applicable to alcohol abuse patient records, 42 U.S.C. 290 dd-3 and 42 U.S.C. 290 ee-3.

[82]42 C.F.R. 2.1.

[83]42 C.F.R. 2.4; 42 C.F.R. 2.16-2.19; 42 C.F.R. 2.22.

[84]N.J.A.C. 6:3-6.6.

[85]N.J.S.A. 2C:35-7.

[86]N.J.A.C. 6:3-6.1.

the course of or as a result of evaluation or treatment services provided by the district.[87]

The Drug Free School Zone regulations also prohibit the disclosure of the identity of a pupil or staff member believed to possess drugs or drug paraphernalia near school property if the individual has voluntarily sought treatment or counseling for a substance abuse problem if the individual is not implicated in drug distribution activities.[88] Nor shall a principal disclose the identity of any pupil or staff member who voluntarily turns over a controlled dangerous substance or drug paraphernalia for personal use, not distribution activities, provided the individual agrees to participate in an appropriate treatment or counseling program.[89]

HEALTH RECORDS

There are specific statutory and regulatory provisions concerning health records of pupils and staff. The medical inspector shall examine every pupil, and the findings of the examination shall be entered in the health record of each pupil. The record shall be the property of the board of education and shall be forwarded to any public school to which the pupil is transferred.[90] All records of tuberculosis testing conducted by a board of education shall be the property of the board and shall be filed with the medical inspector as confidential information except that such records and reports shall be open for inspection by the state and local boards of health.[91] There is also a specific regulation mandating the confidentiality of all information concerning the identity of a student with an HIV infection, and requiring compliance with the provisions of the regulations relating to pupil records.[92]

Records and reports of physical or psychiatric examinations that a board of education requires of its employees shall be the property of the board and shall be filed with the medical inspector as confidential information but shall be open for inspection by officers of the state and local boards of health.[93] The district's employee medical records shall be stored and maintained separately from other personnel files. Only the employee, the chief school administrator and/or the certified school nurse shall have

---

[87]N.J.A.C. 6:3-6.6.

[88]N.J.A.C. 6:3-6.4. .

[89]N.J.A.C. 6:3-6.5.

[90]N.J.S.A. 18A:40-4; N.J.A.C. 6:29-2.1.

[91]N.J.S.A. 18A:40-19.

[92]N.J.A.C. 6:29-2.4.

[93]N.J.S.A. 18A:16-5.

access to the medical information in an individual's file.[94]

CHILD ABUSE REPORTS

School personnel having reasonable cause to believe that a child has been subjected to child abuse shall report the same immediately to the Division of Youth and Family Services (DYFS). Such reports shall contain the name, age, grade and condition of the child, and any injuries, as well as the name and address of the person having custody or control of the child, and any other information that may be relevant.[95] A person reporting suspected child abuse in good faith will be immune from liability for making that report.[96] A board of education must maintain and secure all confidential information about child abuse cases in accordance with the regulations concerning pupil records.[97] Furthermore, DYFS must keep all reports, as well as all information obtained in investigating reports concerning child abuse, confidential and subject to disclosure only under circumstances expressly authorized by statute.[98] Thus, the Appellate Division has held that a board of education could not use the testimony of a DYFS investigator to substantiate charges at a tenure hearing because the testimony had not been sought "in connection with the provision of care, treatment, or supervision" of the students as required by statute."[99]

---

[94]*N.J.A.C.* 6:29-7.1(e).

[95]*N.J.S.A.* 9:6-8.10; *N.J.A.C.* 6:3-5.2.

[96]*N.J.S.A.* 9:6-8.13.

[97]*N.J.A.C.* 6:3-5.2(a)7 iv.

[98]*N.J.S.A.* 9:6-8.10a.

[99]*Matter of Tenure Hearing of Tyler*, 236 *N.J.Super.* 478 (App. Div. 1989).

SCHOOL BUDGETS 10

Preparing and adopting a budget is one of the most important functions of every board of education. The program of the year and all the dreams envisioned by a board can come true only when they are embodied in the budget; an educational plan expressed in money. Budget procedures, to some extent, vary according to the type of district in which one serves.

Each board of education prepares a budget for the ensuing school year on forms and in the detail prescribed by the commissioner. Attached to those forms is an itemized statement which shows:

- The amounts of money spent for various line items in the preceding school year;
- The amounts appropriated for each item for the current year adjusted as of December 1;
- The amounts estimated to be necessary to be appropriated for each item for the following year;
- The amount of surplus available at the beginning of the preceding school year, the current school year and anticipated to be available for the following school year;
- The amount of revenue, by sources, available for the preceding school year, current school year as of December 1 and anticipated to be available for the following school year.

Should the total expenditure for any line item be $0.00 for the preceding school year, current school year and be anticipated to be $0.00 for the following school year, publication of that line item is not required.[1]

The commissioner is statutorily authorized to provide for a program-oriented budget system.[2] Rules of the state board of education allow boards of education to adopt, by resolution, a program-oriented budget system. This system of program-oriented budgeting utilizes budget categories which reflect different types of instructional and non-instructional programs in order to relate appropriations goals and objectives established

---

[1]N.J.S.A. 18A:22-8.
[2]Id.

153

by the district pursuant to the Public School Education Act of 1975.[3]

The Quality Education Act of 1990 established limits upon the annual growth of school district budgets. For the purpose of calculating foundation aid, the initial QEA limited foundation budget increases to 30 percent over the previous year's foundation budget.[4] The 30 percent foundation budget growth limitation applied to the balance in the current expense and capital outlay budgets after deducting state aid for handicapped pupils, approved transportation and revenue other than local taxation, equalization support, budgeted capital outlay support and State support for bilingual, compensatory and local vocational education.[5]

The March, 1991 amendments to the QEA, P.L. 1991 Ch. 62, established stricter limits on budgetary growth for aid purposes. In 1991-92, non-special needs districts were permitted to increase the aidable portion of their net budget by 7.5 percent to 9 percent. Beginning in the 1993-94 school year, districts may increase the aidable portion of the net budget by up to 20 percent. Districts which have net budget increases that exceed 20 percent will receive no additional foundation aid to support expenditures over these limits. Additionally, the 20 percent net budget growth limitation, unlike its predecessor, includes aid for handicapped pupils and approved transportation. *P.L.* 1991, Ch. 62, Sec. 24.

On or before December 15, the commissioner shall notify each district of the maximum amount of aid payable to the district,[6] and its maximum permissible net budget, should that limitation be applicable. All districts, including special needs districts, face a cap on spending increases. Non-special needs districts are permitted annual net budget increases based on a formula which incorporates the four year average annual percentage increase in state per capita personal income (PCI).[7] For 1991-92, the formula resulted in budget caps of 7.5 percent to 9 percent for non-special needs districts. Special needs districts are subject to an "equity spending cap" which may exceed 9 percent. The equity spending caps are intended to permit special needs districts to spend at a rate which will allow them to achieve spending parity with the more affluent districts of the State by 1995-96.[8]

The commissioner may permit districts to spend above their cap by granting cap waivers in four discrete circumstances:

1. For the two years prior to the prebudget year, the district has

---

[3]*N.J.A.C.* 6:20-2.3(c), (d), (e).

[4]*N.J.S.A.* 18A:7D-29.

[5]*N.J.S.A.* 18A:7D-30.

[6]*N.J.S.A.* 18A:7D-26.

[7]*N.J.S.A.* 18A:7D-3, 28.

[8]*N.J.S.A.* 18A:7D-28.

had an average annual increase in its resident enrollment of greater than two percent;

2. The district has had an increase in special education costs in excess of 5 percent in the preceding year;

3. The district has entered into a lease purchase agreement between July 1, 1990 and April 1, 1991;

4. The district sends pupils and pays tuition to a special needs district.[9]

A district may submit a cap waiver request to the voters or board of school estimate as appropriate. Statutory language indicates that disapproval of such a request shall be deemed final and is not subject to further appeal.[10] The Attorney General has indicated that despite this language the Commissioner has the duty and indeed the obligation to entertain appeals from board of school estimate or voter rejection of cap waiver requests.[11]

The Quality Education Act of 1990 also requires each local board to submit, before February 1 of each year, a copy of its proposed budget to the commissioner for review. The purpose of this review is to determine whether the budget is adequate in light of the local board's annual report on progress made toward the goals and standards it has developed pursuant to the Public School Education Act of 1975.[12]

The board of education of every school district, including school districts having a board of school estimate and regional districts, must prepare a budget for the ensuing year, on or before the first Tuesday in March.[13]

Each board must fix a place, date and time for a public hearing on its budget. The hearing must be held between the first Tuesday in March and March 18 before the board of school estimate in those districts having a board of school estimate and before the board of education in all other cases.[14] The board must publish its budget statement and hearing notice in a newspaper published or circulating in the district no less than seven days prior to the hearing date.[15] The published notice must include the fact that the budget is on file and will be open to examination by the public both prior to and at the public hearing.[16]

---

[9]*Id.*

[10]*Id.*

[11]Atty. Gen. Op. No. 91-0036

[12]*N.J.S.A.* 18A:7D-27.

[13]*N.J.S.A.* 18A:22-7.

[14]*N.J.S.A.* 18A:22-10.

[15]*N.J.S.A.* 18A:22-11.

[16]*N.J.S.A.* 18A:22-12.

TYPE I DISTRICTS AND TYPE II DISTRICTS WITH A BOARD OF SCHOOL ESTIMATE

In each Type I district there exists a board of school estimate consisting of five members; two members of the board of education, appointed by it, two members of the governing body, appointed by it, and the mayor or chief executive officer of the municipality.[17] In those Type II districts which have a board of school estimate, its composition consists of the chief executive officer of the governing body of each municipality and the president of the board of education, ex officio, two members of the governing body of each municipality, chosen by their respective governing bodies, and one member of the board of education, chosen by the board.[18] After the public hearing, but no later than March 18, the board of school estimate fixes the amount of appropriations necessary for the public schools and certifies that amount to the board of education, and to the municipal governing body or bodies.[19] If the board of school estimate is of a Type II district, it must meet within seven days of receipt of the board of education's proposed budget and fix and determine the amounts necessary to be raised for school purposes. It must also send a copy of that certification to the county board of taxation on or before March 25 with a copy to the county superintendent.[20] Within 20 days after receiving the certificate, the board of education must notify the board of school estimate and the governing body or bodies of the district if it intends to appeal the appropriated amount to the commissioner.[21]

The governing body of a Type I district must include the amount certified, up to 1.5 percent of the assessed valuation of the ratables in the community, in its tax ordinance. Any appropriation in excess of 1.5 percent must have the consent of the governing body. Within 20 days after the governing body so appropriates, the board of education must notify the governing body if it intends to appeal the appropriated amount to the commissioner of education.[22] The board has 30 days from the certification of the governing body of the tax levy to file its petition of appeal to the commissioner.[23]

The commissioner of education has the authority, on an appeal based on the failure of the board of school estimate or municipality to certify sufficient money to maintain a thorough and efficient school system, to

---

[17]N.J.S.A. 18A:22-1; N.J.A.C. 6:3-1.2.

[18]N.J.S.A. 18A:22-4.

[19]N.J.S.A. 18A:22-14, 26, 31. N.J.A.C. 6:3-1.2.

[20]N.J.S.A. 18A:22-26, 31.

[21]N.J.S.A. 18A:22-14.

[22]N.J.S.A. 18A:22-17.

[23]N.J.A.C. 6:24-7.4.

order the appropriation of additional funds up to the amount of the budget request.[24]

When a board of education determines that monies must be raised for capital projects, it must deliver a statement of the amount of money needed to the board of school estimate.[25] The board of school estimate then fixes the amount necessary for the capital projects and certifies that amount to the board of education and the governing body.[26] In Type II districts, the board of school estimate is required to hold a public hearing, similar to its budget hearing, between 15 and 30 days after the delivery of the statement to the board of school estimate and prior to fixing the amount.[27] Type II district boards of school estimate must also certify those amounts to the county board of taxation and county superintendent of schools.[28]

When a Type I board of education determines that additional funds are needed in a school year due to emergencies or underestimation of budget requirements, the board must deliver, to each member of the board of school estimate, a statement of the additional money needed.[29] The board of school estimate must then meet within a reasonable time, and determine the amount needed, certifying that amount to the board of education and the governing body.[30] The governing body must appropriate and raise the necessary money in the manner permitted by municipalities in emergencies.[31] The board of education may borrow money, if necessary, between July 1 and January 1, not exceeding one-half of the amount appropriated for current expenses and repairs.[32]

TYPE II DISTRICTS AND REGIONAL DISTRICTS

At or after the public hearing on the budget, but not later than 12 days prior to the annual election, the board of education fixes, by a recorded roll call majority vote of its full membership, the amount of money to be voted upon for the use of the public schools of the district for the ensuing school year.[33] If the budget is approved by the voters, the board

[24]*Board of Education of City of Elizabeth v. City Council of City of Elizabeth*, 55 *N.J.* 501 (1970).
[25]*N.J.S.A.* 18A:22-18, 27.
[26]*N.J.S.A.* 18A:22-19, 30.
[27]*N.J.S.A.* 18A:22-28, 29.
[28]*N.J.S.A.* 18A:22-26, 31.
[29]*N.J.S.A.* 18A:22-21.
[30]*N.J.S.A.* 18A:22-22.
[31]*N.J.S.A.* 18A:22-23.
[32]*N.J.S.A.* 18A:22-25.
[33]*N.J.S.A.* 18A:13-1, 7; 22-32.

secretary must certify that amount plus the sums needed for interest and debt redemption charges to the county board of taxation within two days following the date of the election.[34]

If the voters reject any item at the annual election, the board of education must deliver the proposed school budget to the governing body or bodies within two days of the election. The governing body of the municipality or municipalities, after consultation with the board of education and by April 28, must certify the amounts it determines to be necessary to provide a thorough and efficient system of schools in the district to the county board of taxation.[35]. In the case of a regional district, the governing bodies must also cause the respective municipal clerks to certify the amount appropriated to the regional board of education.[36]

A statement of reasons for the governing body's budget cuts must be given to the board of education at the time those cuts are made.[37] Failure to so submit will create a heavy presumption against the educational validity for those cuts.[38]

Within 15 days after the governing body or bodies has made its certification, the board of education must notify the governing body or bodies if it intends to appeal the amount appropriated to the commissioner. The board has 30 days to file a petition of appeal to the commissioner after the governing body has certified the tax levy to the county board of taxation.[39]

Should the governing body or bodies fail to make such certification, or if the constituent governing bodies of the regional district fail to agree, or if the amount certified is less than required, the commissioner certifies the amount he feels is necessary to provide a thorough and efficient system of schools to the county board of taxation and, in the case of a regional district, to the regional board of education.[40]

When a board determines that additional monies must be raised, over and above that included in the annual budget, by special district tax for capital projects, current expenses, vocational evening schools, classes for foreign born residents or appropriations to the capital reserve fund,[41] it must seek voter approval at a special school election.[42] If the special district

---

[34]N.J.S.A. 18A:13-1; 22-33.

[35]N.J.S.A. 18A:22-37.

[36]N.J.S.A. 18A:13-19.

[37]N.J.A.C. 6:24-7.4.

[38]Deptford Township Board of Education v. Mayor and Council of the Township of Deptford, 116 N.J. 305 (1989).

[39]N.J.S.A. 18A:22-37; N.J.A.C. 6:24-7.4.

[40]N.J.S.A. 18A:13-20; 22-38.

[41]N.J.S.A. 18A:21-1; 22-40.

[42]N.J.S.A. 18A:22-41.

tax is authorized, the board may borrow upon notes in anticipation of taxes to be raised.[43]

The annual or special appropriations for regional districts, including the redemption of and interest paid upon bonds, are to be apportioned among the constituent districts included within the regional district based upon each district's portion of the regional's equalized valuation.[44] The regional's equalized valuation is allocated among the regional and constituent districts in proportion to the number of pupils in each of them.[45]

---

[43]*N.J.S.A.* 18A:22-42.

[44]*N.J.S.A.* 18A:13-23.

[45]*N.J.S.A.* 18A:7D-3.

SCHOOL ELECTIONS

11

DATES AND NOTICES

The annual school elections in Type II districts, including regional districts, are held on the first Tuesday in April.[1] If the Tuesday falls on a legal holiday, the election is held the following day.[2] The Commissioner has the authority to make any changes in the school budget or election calendar which may be necessary should the date of the election coincide with a period of religious observance. The Commissioner must notify local school boards of any such adjustment by the first working day in January of the election year.[3]

The board secretary must post at least seven notices not less than ten days before the election, one on each schoolhouse and the others at public places designated by the board. The notices must specify the date, time and place of the election, the offices to be filled, if any, the substance of any public question to be submitted to the voters, the boundaries or numbers of the polling districts and the location of the polling place for each district as well as such other information as may be required by law. The election notice must be published in at least one newspaper published in the municipality or, if there be none or if such a newspaper will not be published in time, in a newspaper published in the county or State and circulating in the municipality.[4]

CANDIDATES

Each candidate for election, including incumbents seeking reelection, must be nominated directly by petition, signed by at least 10 persons, none of whom may be the candidate. The signatures need not all appear on a

---

[1]*N.J.S.A.* 18A:13-10; 14-2.
[2]*N.J.S.A.* 18A:14-2.
[3]*N.J.S.A.* 18A:14-2.1.
[4]*N.J.S.A.* 18A:14-19.

single petition as multiple petitions for a single candidate are permitted.[5] Each nominating petition, addressed to the secretary of the board, must set forth:

- That the signers are qualified voters;
- The name, residence and post office address of the candidate and the office for which he is endorsed;
- That the signers endorse the candidate and request that his name be printed on the ballot;
- That the candidate is legally qualified to be a board member.

A certificate must accompany the nominating petition, signed by the candidate, stating that he is qualified to be a board member, that he is not disqualified as a voter, that he consents to be a candidate, and that, if elected, he will accept the office. A candidate who falsely declares that he is not disqualified as a voter is guilty of a crime of false swearing, a crime of the fourth degree.[6] Each nominating petition must be sworn to by one of the signers, stating that the petition is signed in the handwriting of the named persons, that the signers are legally qualified to vote at the ensuing election, and that the petition is prepared and filed in good faith to nominate the candidate and secure his election.[7] A person falsely signing a nominating petition shall be guilty of a misdemeanor.[8]

Nominating petitions must be filed with the secretary on or before 4:00 p.m. of the 54th day preceding the date of election.[9] Except for an inadequate number of signatures, if the board secretary, on or before the 49th day preceding the date of the election, finds a nominating petition to be defective, the secretary must notify the candidate of the defect and the opportunity to remedy the defect not later than the 49th day preceding the date of the election. Under no circumstances may signatures be added. Nominating petitions not found to be defective as of the 48th day preceding the election are deemed conclusively valid.[10]

A candidate for a board of education may withdraw his name as a candidate by filing a signed notice in writing of his withdrawal with the secretary of the board, on or before 4:00 p.m. of the 46th day before the date of the election or before the ballot is printed, whichever is later. The name of the candidate is then withdrawn from the ballot. The board secretary shall also remove from the ballot any candidate who has not

---

[5]*N.J.S.A.* 18A:14-9.

[6]*N.J.S.A.* 18A:14-10, 10.1.

[7]*N.J.S.A.* 18A:14-11.

[8]*N.J.S.A.* 2C:43-16; *N.J.S.A.* 18A:14-68.

[9]*N.J.S.A.* 18A:14-9.

[10]*N.J.S.A.* 18A:14-12.

remedied a nominating petition defect. The other names on the ballot listed below the withdrawn name(s) are advanced one place respectively.[11]

CAMPAIGNING

School elections are subject to the New Jersey Campaign Contributions and Expenditures Reporting Act.[12] This statute requires every school election candidate who intends to spend over $2,000 to file a detailed report on campaign contributions and expenditures with the Election Law Enforcement Commission. If expenditures do not exceed $2,000, any contribution of more than $100 from any one source must still be reported and the source identified.[13]

School election campaign materials must be properly identified. The name and address of the printer must appear on the face of campaign materials. Materials must also contain the name and address of either:

- The person causing the material to be printed, copied or published or
- The person who is paying for the materials.[14]

The material can be printed or paid for by an organization, and the name and address of the organization may be used, provided that the name of at least one person in authority and acting for the group is also given.[15]

These requirements apply to any circular, statement, advertisement or other printed matter but do not apply to any *bona fide* news item or editorial comment published in a newspaper. Any person violating the requirements concerning campaign materials shall be deemed a disorderly person.[16]

School funds may not be used to support a particular candidate or to advocate adoption or rejection of a bond issue or budget; campaign materials may not be produced or distributed through the use of school equipment or facilities.[17] Public school pupils cannot be used to distribute any type of literature that favors or opposes any candidate, bond issue, or public question.[18]

---

[11]*N.J.S.A.* 18A:14-12.1.

[12]*N.J.S.A.* 19:44A-1 *et seq.*; *N.J.A.C.* 19:25-1.1 *et seq.*

[13]*N.J.S.A.* 19:44A-16(c).

[14]*N.J.S.A.* 18A:14-97.

[15]*N.J.S.A.* 18A:14-97.2.

[16]*N.J.S.A.* 18A:14-97.3, 104.

[17]*Citizens to Protect Public Funds v. Parsippany-Troy Hills Board of Education*, 13 N.J. 172, 179-82 (1953), *Robert Morris Ed. Assoc. et al. v. Bd. of Ed. of the Borough of South Bound Brook, et al.* (U. S. Dist. Ct., D.M.J., DN 83-2365, decided November 23, 1983).

[18]*N.J.S.A.* 18A:42-4.

VOTERS

The board secretary must make written request for the necessary signature copy registers at least 10 days before any school election. The registers list all persons entitled to vote in the election. The signature copy registers will be given to the secretary on the day preceding or the day of the election. They must be returned to the commissioner of registration by 3:00 p.m. of the day after the election.[19]

Persons who may vote at the election are: every citizen of the United States age 18 years, or older, who shall have been a resident of the State of New Jersey and who has been permanently registered in the county in which he/she will vote for at least 29 days prior to the date of the election.[20]

On or about 54 days prior to the date of the election, the board secretary shall have published, in at least one newspaper, notice of the availability of absentee ballots and the method by which they may be obtained.[21]

Civilian absentee ballots may be applied for and cast by qualified registered voters who will be unable to vote at the poll because:

- Of absence from the state;
- Of illness or physical disability;
- Of observance of a religious holiday;
- Of resident attendance at a school, college or university; or
- Of the nature and hours of the voter's employment.[22]

Military absentee ballots may be applied for and cast by a voter who is unable to cast his ballot at the polls because he is:

- Absent on military service, provided he has resided in New Jersey at least 30 days and in the county at least 30 days;
- A resident of a military station within this state, and who claims his/her vote in the municipality wherein the residence is located.[23]

A person who claims he is registered, despite the fact that his name does not appear in the register, may vote if he signs a prepared affidavit form prescribed by the commissioner. A person registered in another district of the county, who claims he has filed a change of address notice at the proper time before the election may also vote through this affidavit process. Any school election officer can take such affidavit.[24] A person

---

[19]*N.J.S.A.* 18A:14-42.

[20]*N.J.S.A.* Const. art. 2 par. 3; *N.J.S.A.* 18A:14-44; *N.J.S.A.* 19:4-1.

[21]*N.J.S.A.* 18A:14-25.

[22]*N.J.S.A.* 19:57-3.

[23]*Id.*

[24]*N.J.S.A.* 18A:14-52.

falsely signing such an affidavit shall be guilty of a misdemeanor.[25]

POLLING PLACES

At least one suitable polling place must be provided in a schoolhouse or other convenient public place within the school district.[26] The board may provide additional temporary polling places whenever it anticipates an unusually heavy vote in a particular election or whenever 100 or more registered voters so petition at least 20 days before the election.[27] Whenever, at two consecutive annual elections, more than 500 votes are cast in a polling district, the board shall establish an additional polling place for each 500 votes or part thereof, and shall divide the district approximately equally.[28]

Each polling place must be suitably equipped with booths, chairs, tables, lights, and other proper equipment.[29] At least two booths must be installed at each polling place, and, where paper ballots are used, at least one booth for each 100 votes or major fraction thereof cast at the preceding annual school election in the polling district.[30] The ballot box shall be at least one foot in depth, width, and length and constructed of wood, metal, or glass with a properly slitted hinged top, which must be kept locked while the polls are open.[31]

BALLOTS

Paper ballots, if used, must conform to specific requirements set forth in the law, including:

- Instructions to the voter to use crosses (x), plus signs (+) or checks (✔) as the valid marks;
- Directions to not vote for more candidates than are to be elected;
- Designation of the terms for which candidates are to be elected;
- Blank spaces in which the names of unlisted candidates may be written or pasted.[32]

---

[25]*N.J.S.A.* 2C:43-1(b); *N.J.S.A.* 18A:14-66.

[26]*N.J.S.A.* 18A:14-4.

[27]*N.J.S.A.* 18A:14-4.1.

[28]*N.J.S.A.* 18A:14-5.

[29]*N.J.S.A.* 18A:14-20.

[30]*N.J.S.A.* 18A:14-21.

[31]*N.J.S.A.* 18A:14-23.

[32]*N.J.S.A.* 18A:14-35, 36.

Should the supply of paper ballots be exhausted, unofficial ballots, made as neatly as possible in the form of the official ballot and approved by the election officials, may be used.[33]

The position in which the name of the candidate appears on the ballot is determined by the drawing conducted by the board secretary within 48 hours subsequent to 4:00 p.m. of the last day for filing nominating petitions. Should that day fall on a Sunday or on the day of, or the day immediately preceding, a public holiday, the drawing is held on the next succeeding day which is not a public holiday.[34] The grouping of two or more candidates or political party designations is expressly prohibited.[35] Questions to be voted on are placed immediately following the names of the candidates.[36] Ballots must be printed on plain uniform white paper of such thickness that printing cannot be distinguished from the back of the paper.[37]

Each board of education must appoint a judge of elections, an inspector of elections, and two clerks of elections for each polling place and may appoint additional clerks not to exceed one for every two signature copy registers. The election officers must be qualified voters of the district who are not members or employees of the board or candidates for board membership. If qualified voters of the district are not available, qualified voters of the state may be utilized. The appointments are made at the January meeting of the board if paper ballots are to be used or at the last regular meeting not less than 40 days prior to the election if voting machines are used.[38] The board shall pay each election official 1/13 of the daily compensation payable to district board of elections members for each hour actually worked.[39]

VOTING MACHINES

Boards may, by resolution, determine to use voting machines in annual or special school elections if machines are used in their districts in the general or municipal elections.[40] To use voting machines, boards must notify the superintendent of elections or the county board of elections, in writing, not less than 40 days before the election date. The machines

---

[33]N.J.S.A. 18A:14-38.

[34]N.J.S.A. 18A:14-13.

[35]N.J.S.A. 18A:14-42.

[36]N.J.S.A. 18A:14-37.

[37]N.J.S.A. 18A:14-33.

[38]N.J.S.A. 18A:14-6.

[39]N.J.S.A. 18A:14-8; N.J.S.A. 19:45-6.

[40]N.J.S.A. 18A:14-39.

will be delivered at such polling places and at such time as the board of education shall designate.[41] Elections with voting machines are conducted in essentially the same manner as general and municipal elections.[42] The superintendent of elections and the county board of elections perform the same duties as they perform in general and municipal elections, except that they shall not be required to prepare, challenge or strike out lists for use at school elections.[43] The board of education must appoint, at a regular meeting at least 40 days prior to the election, such election officers as are necessary, including a judge of elections, an inspector of elections and at least two clerks of elections for each polling district. They must be chosen from the qualified voters of the district who are not members or employees of the board and who do not intend to be candidates for board membership. If qualified voters of the district are not available, qualified voters of the state may be utilized.[44] The secretary must furnish to the officers having control and custody of the voting machines, at least seven days before the election, official ballots for use in voting machines.[45] Written notice of the time and place when the prepared voting machines may be examined must be mailed to each candidate.[46] The board of freeholders may charge a rental fee of $5.00 per machine plus the cost of any damages or it may waive the fee. The board of education may also be required to pay the expenses of transporting the machines or other reasonable costs.[47]

CONDUCT OF ELECTIONS

Polls must be open between the hours of 5 and 9 p.m. and during any additional time which the board may designate between the hours of 7 a.m. and 9 p.m. The polls shall remain open as long as is necessary to permit those present to cast ballots.[48] A board member, or in his absence the judge of the election, or in the absence of both, the secretary of the board shall declare the polls opened at each polling place at the time fixed by the board. Voting continues without recess from then until the time the polls close.[49]

---

[41]*N.J.S.A.* 18A:14-40.

[42]*N.J.S.A.* 18A:14-42.

[43]*Id.*

[44]*N.J.S.A.* 18A:14-6.

[45]*N.J.S.A.* 18A:14-41.

[46]*N.J.S.A.* 18A:14-42.

[47]*N.J.S.A.* 18A:14-43.

[48]*N.J.S.A.* 18A:14-45.

[49]*N.J.S.A.* 18A:14-46.

Each candidate may act as a challenger and may also appoint one challenger for each municipal election district included in each polling district. Names of challengers and their assigned polling places shall be filed with the board secretary not later than five days before the election. All challengers must be legal voters in the district. The secretary shall give each challenger a certificate which shall be submitted by the challenger to the election officer at the designated polling place.[50] Each challenger shall wear identification as a challenger, furnished to him by the board secretary.[51] In any election in which a public question is submitted, the appointment of one challenger favoring and one challenger opposing the question is permitted for each polling place within the district.[52] Petitions for the appointment of such challengers must contain the signatures of at least 10 qualified voters and must be filed with the secretary of the board at least five days before the election.[53] If the polls will be open for more than four hours, alternate challengers may be appointed to permit periodic relief of challengers not more often than every two hours.[54]

The board must provide, and one of the election officials must keep, a poll list at each polling place.[55] Each voter must sign his/her name and state his/her address prior to receiving an official ballot. The number of each voter's ballot must be recorded opposite his/her name.[56] The voter's signature in the poll list must be compared with the signature found in the signature copy register before he/she is given a ballot.[57] Procedures are provided for those unable to write.[58] If a voter is challenged, it is the duty of the election officials to determine his/her right to vote.[59] The election official shall instruct voters how to fold the ballots and shall see that the requirements of a secret ballot are met.[60]

Immediately after the close of the polls the election officers shall count the votes for each candidate and for and against each public question. The counting must be open and public. The election officials must keep tally sheets of the votes as counted which are to be signed by the judge and clerks of the election.[61]

---

[50]N.J.S.A. 18A:14-15, 16.

[51]N.J.S.A. 18A:14-17

[52]N.J.S.A. 18A:14-18.1.

[53]N.J.S.A. 18A:14-18.2.

[54]N.J.S.A. 18A:14-15, 18.1.

[55]N.J.S.A. 18A:14-48.

[56]N.J.S.A. 18A:14-50.

[57]N.J.S.A. 18A:14-51.

[58]N.J.S.A. 18A:14-51.1.

[59]N.J.S.A. 18A:14-51.2.

[60]N.J.S.A. 18A:14-53.

[61]N.J.S.A. 18A:14-57.

A plurality of the votes cast is sufficient to elect a candidate. Any proposal, resolution or question shall be deemed approved if the number of votes in favor of the adoption exceeds the number of votes cast in opposition.[62] The judge of the election must announce the result publicly.[63] A candidate may secure a certified statement of the count upon request made in writing to the members of the election board, which certificate shall be issued before the closing of the polling place.[64] Any person destroying, falsifying, or altering records of elections shall be guilty of a misdemeanor.[65]

The tally sheets, poll list and ballots for each polling place are placed in a package and sealed by the inspector of the election. The judge of the election delivers the sealed package to the secretary of the board accompanied by a statement of the result of the election signed by the election officers. The secretary adds to the tally the canvass of the absentee ballots as certified to him by the county board of elections. The secretary then combines the reports from all polling places and announces the result of the election.[66]

The board secretary must forward to the county superintendent, within five days of the election, a statement of the results of the election, the ballots, poll lists and tally sheets. The county superintendent must preserve these records and make the poll lists available for public inspection for one year.[67]

SPECIAL ELECTIONS

Special elections may be called whenever in the judgment of the board the interests of the schools require it.[68] No more than two special elections for the same purpose may be held within any period of six months without approval of the commissioner. Special elections are conducted in the same manner as the annual school election.[69]

When an election is called to vote on a bond issue, the same form of ballot as is required for submission of public questions at annual school elections shall be used.[70] No action to contest the validity of any election

---

[62]N.J.S.A. 18A:14-58.

[63]N.J.S.A. 18A:14-59.

[64]N.J.S.A. 18A:14-60.

[65]N.J.S.A. 18A:14-65.

[66]N.J.S.A. 18A:14-61.

[67]N.J.S.A. 18A:14-62.

[68]N.J.S.A. 18A:14-3.

[69]N.J.S.A. 18A:14-3.2.

[70]Id.

ordering the issuance of bonds shall be commenced after the expiration of 15 days from the date of such election.[71]

RECOUNTS

If voting machines are used, their counter compartments must be locked by the election officials as soon as the count of the vote is completed. The compartments shall remain locked for a period of 15 days or for a maximum of 30 days if the commissioner so orders.[72] When any defeated candidate has reason to believe that an error was made in counting the vote, he may apply within 10 days of the announcement of the results to the commissioner for a recount.[73] Similarly, any 10 voters having reason to believe that an error was made in counting the votes on any question, proposition or referendum may apply to the commissioner for a recount.[74]

Any recount shall be made under the supervision of an authorized representative of the commissioner with the cooperation of county election officials and the parties at interest or their representatives, within 30 days after the date of the election or the announcement of the result of the voting.[75] If the recount reveals errors which alter the result of the election, the commissioner shall order the expenses of the recount to be paid by the school district.[76] If no error shall appear sufficient to alter the result of the election, the expenses of the recount must be paid from the security deposit required to be made by the party or parties making the application.[77]

Where the commissioner finds as a result of a recount that an error has occurred which alters the result of the election, he shall order such relief as is appropriate.[78]

OFFENSES AND PENALTIES

Particular school election law offenses and penalties have been set forth in this chapter. Additional disorderly persons offenses include any person

---

[71]*N.J.S.A.* 18A:24-65.

[72]*N.J.S.A.* 18A:14-63.1.

[73]*N.J.S.A.* 18A:14-63.2; *N.J.A.C.* 6:24-6.1(b).

[74]*N.J.S.A.* 18A:14-63.3; *N.J.A.C.* 6:24-6.1(c).

[75]*N.J.S.A.* 18A:14-63.5.

[76]*N.J.S.A.* 18A:14-63.8; *N.J.A.C.* 6:24-6.2(c).

[77]*N.J.S.A.* 18A:14-63.6, 63.7, 63.9; *N.J.A.C.* 6:24-6.2(d).

[78]*N.J.S.A.* 18A:14-63.13; *N.J.A.C.* 6:24-6.5

who obstructs or interferes with any voter, polling booth or entrance to a polling place;[79] any person who distributes or displays any circular or printed material or who solicits support for any candidate or public question within 100 feet of the polls;[80] and any person who displays, sells, gives or provides political badges, buttons or insignia to be worn within 100 feet of the polls.[81] Election offenses rising to the level of a misdemeanor include disclosing how a person voted,[82] fraudulent conduct as to voting;[83] robbing or plundering the ballot box;[84] soliciting illegal voter registration or multiple voting;[85] gifts for votes[86] or to election officers[87] and receipt of gifts for votes.[88] Any person who violates a school election law provision for which no penalty is provided shall be guilty of a misdemeanor.[89]

---

[79]N.J.S.A. 18A:14-72.

[80]N.J.S.A. 18A:14-72, 81.

[81]N.J.S.A. 18A:14-85.

[82]N.J.S.A. 18A:14-80.

[83]N.J.S.A. 18A:14-77.

[84]N.J.S.A. 18A:14-83.

[85]N.J.S.A. 18A:14-86.

[86]N.J.S.A. 18A:14-88, 91, 93, 94, 95.

[87]N.J.S.A. 18A:14-89.

[88]N.J.S.A. 18A:14-92, 96.

[89]N.J.S.A. 18A:14-104.

SCHOOL DISTRICT BUSINESS PRACTICES

12

In discharging their responsibilities, boards of education expend public moneys appropriated to them. The expenditures of such funds are controlled by law to insure that taxpayers' interests are safeguarded. Statutes pertaining to the control of school district business practices were, at one time, found in both Title 18A and in Chapter 11 of Title 40A, the Local Public Contracts Law. On March 3, 1976, however, an amendment became effective removing school districts from those governmental units subject to the provisions of the Local Public Contracts Law. School districts later received their own statutory coverage with the passage of the Public School Contracts Law (hereafter referred to as "the statute") on June 2, 1977. This law purported to unify those statutes dealing with school district business practices which were formerly found in both Title 18A and Title 40A. At the same time, it repealed Chapter 18 of Title 18A and all amendments and supplements thereto.

REQUIREMENTS OF THE PUBLIC SCHOOL CONTRACTS LAW

Purchases, Contracts and Agreements Requiring Advertising

As a general statement, public advertising for bids and a competitive bidding process must precede every contract for the performance of work or the furnishing or hiring of any materials or supplies to be paid out of school funds. Contracts requiring public advertising for bids and competitive bidding may be awarded and made only by the board of education.[1]

The requirement of public advertising for bids does not apply to a purchase, contract or agreement where the school funds expended, or foreseeably to be expended for similar work or materials, during the fiscal year do not exceed the threshold amount. The threshold amount is currently $10,700.[2] In the case of purchases that are not annually recurring, public advertising is not required as long as the school funds foreseeably

---

[1]*N.J.S.A.* 18A:18A-4.

[2]*N.J.S.A.* 18A:18A-3.

to be expended do not exceed the threshold amount in any one year period.[3] Boards of education are thus required to estimate purchases of a similar nature over the course of a year and are specifically prohibited from dividing contracts or purchases, which are single in character and have a value equal to or exceeding the threshold amount, into smaller parts in order to avoid the requirements of public advertising and bidding.[4] When contracts involve less than the threshold, they may be made, negotiated and awarded by the board's contracting agent (secretary, business administrator or business manager) when so authorized by a resolution of the board.[5]

Commencing January 1, 1983, and every two years thereafter, the Governor in consultation with the Department of Treasury, shall adjust the threshold amount which was set forth in 1983 as $7,500, in direct proportion to the rise or fall of the consumer price index for all urban consumers in the New York City and the Philadelphia areas as reported by the United States Department of Labor. The Governor is to notify all school districts of the adjustment, which shall become effective July 1st of the year in which it is reported.[6]

The statute lists 16 subject matter areas where advertising for bids is not required. These purchases or contracts may be made and awarded by the board by resolution at a public meeting without public advertising for bids or bidding even where the purchase or contract exceeds the threshold amount.[7]

1. Professional services—Such services are defined as those rendered by a person authorized by law to practice a recognized profession, the performance of which requires knowledge derived from specialized instruction. Professional services also include those rendered in the performance of work that is original and creative in character in a recognized field of artistic endeavor.[8]

2. Extraordinary unspecifiable services—Such services are defined as those which are specialized and qualitative in nature requiring expertise, extensive training and proven reputation in the field of endeavor.[9] The statute specifically mandates that these services are excepted from the bidding requirement on-

---

[3]*Id.*

[4]*N.J.S.A.* 18A:18A-8.

[5]*N.J.S.A.* 18A:18A-3.

[6]*N.J.S.A.* 18A:18A-3.a., 3.b.

[7]*N.J.S.A.* 18A:18A-5.

[8]*N.J.S.A.* 18A:18A-2(h).

[9]*N.J.S.A.* 18A:18A-2(g).

ly when they cannot reasonably be described by written specifications. The legislative preference is for open competitive bidding in this area.[10]

3. Work done by employees of the contracting unit—This exception to the requirement of advertising for bids is curious, as the statute contains no definition of the term "contracting unit." Early drafts of the statute defined "contracting unit" as "any board of education or district." The final version, however, deleted this definition. In the body of the statute, numerous uses of the term "contracting unit" were deleted; "contracting unit" was consistently replaced by "board of education." It would, thus, seem safe to assume that the legislative intent was to remove work done by employees of the board of education from the requirement of advertising for bidding.

4. The printing of all legal notices and legal briefs to be used in any legal proceeding in which the board of education is a party.

5. Textbooks, copyrighted materials, kindergarten supplies, and student produced publications and services incidental thereto.

6. Food services and supplies, including food supplies for home economics classes when purchased pursuant to rules of the state board and in accordance with the provisions of *N.J.S.A.* 18A:18A-6. (This latter provision requires a vendor of fresh milk to agree to purchase an amount from New Jersey producers or associations at least equal to the amount he proposes to furnish to the school district.)[11]

7. Any products or services of a public utility which is subject to the jurisdiction of the Board of Public Utilities.

8. The printing of bonds, and documents necessary to the issuance and sale thereof, by a board of education.

9. Equipment repair service when such is in the nature of an "extraordinary unspecifiable service" (see above definition).

10. Insurance, including the purchase of insurance coverage and consultant services.

11. The publishing of legal notices in newspapers as required by law.

12. The acquisition of artifacts or other items of unique, intrinsic, artistic or historic character.

13. Election expenses, including advertising expenses incidental thereto.

---

[10]*N.J.S.A.* 18A:18A-5(a)(2); *N.J.A.C.* 6:20-8.1.
[11]*N.J.A.C.* 6:3-1.7.

14. Electronic data processing service obtained from another board of education.

15. Driver education courses provided by licensed driver education schools.

16. Work or services, or the furnishing of materials, supplies or equipment for the purpose of conserving energy in buildings owned by any board of education, the entire price of which shall be established as a percentage of the resultant savings in energy costs.

Without public advertisement for bids, a board may also enter into any purchase, contract or agreement with the United States, the State of New Jersey, a county or municipality or any board, body, officer, agency or authority of this State, or any other state.[12] The board may make use of a further exception when it has advertised for bids on two occasions and has received no response. If the board determines after reasonable inquiry that no other governmental body or agency is able to meet its specifications, it may then negotiate a contract or agreement. Such a contract must be authorized by the affirmative vote of two-thirds of the full membership of the board.[13]

Another exception to the requirement of advertising for bids occurs when the board has previously advertised on two occasions and has rejected all bids received. Such bids may be rejected on two grounds:

1. When the board has determined that they are not reasonable as to price on the basis of cost estimates prepared for the board; or

2. When the board has determined that they were not independently arrived at in open competition.

After such rejection of bids, the board may then negotiate and award a contract as long as it meets the following conditions:

- The board must provide both notice of its intention to negotiate and a reasonable opportunity to negotiate to each responsible bidder;

- The negotiated price is lower than the lowest rejected bid price of a responsible bidder who bid thereon, and is the lowest negotiated price offered by any responsible supplier;

- Any change in the terms, conditions and specifications in the original advertisement for bids must be stated in the board resolution awarding the contract; and

- The negotiated price must be lower than the price of the same

---

[12]*N.J.S.A.* 18A:18A-5(b).
[13]*N.J.S.A.* 18A:18A-5(c).

or equivalent materials or supplies available from the state, county or municipality in which the board is located.

The board's contract must, once again, be authorized by a resolution adopted by the affirmative vote of two-thirds of the full membership of the board.[14]

The final exception to the requirement of advertising for bids arises in emergency circumstances when the health or safety of occupants of school property requires the immediate delivery of articles or the immediate performance of services. Such articles or services may be ordered by the contract agent (the board secretary, business administrator or business manager) after she has received a written requisition describing the nature of the emergency, certified by the employee in charge of the building where the emergency occurred. After the articles or services are furnished, the board becomes obligated for payment and must take action to pay the vendor. The statute directs the state board of education to prescribe rules and procedures to implement the section dealing with emergency purchases and contracts.[15]

Solicitation of Quotations

Although the statute does not require public advertisement for bids in all cases, it requires that the board's contracting agent solicit quotations, whenever practicable, when the estimated cost of a contract or purchase is 20 percent or more of the threshold amount set forth in or calculated by the Governor pursuant to *N.J.S.A.* 18A:18A-3. Contracts for professional services are specifically excepted from this requirement.[16]

After quotations have been solicited, the award of the contract shall be made on the basis of the lowest responsible quotation received, which quotation is most advantageous to the board of education, taking other factors into consideration. The statute, however, requires the contracting agent to file a statement of explanation of the reason or reasons why she did not award a particular contract or purchase on the basis of the lowest quotation received. When she deems it "impractical", the contracting agent is not required to solicit quotations in the case of an extraordinary unspecifiable service. She must, however, file a statement explaining why such solicitation would have been impractical.[17]

Joint Purchasing Agreements

The statute authorizes two or more boards of education to enter into

---

[14]*N.J.S.A.* 18A:18A-5(d).

[15]*N.J.S.A.* 18A:18A-7; *N.J.A.C.* 6:20-8.5

[16]*N.J.S.A.* 18A:18A-37.

[17]*Id.*

agreements for the purchase of supplies, materials or work. A board of education may also enter into such agreements with the governing body of the municipality or county wherein it is located.[18] These joint agreements must set forth the categories of work, materials and supplies to be purchased, the manner of advertising for bids and of awarding of contracts, and the method of payment by each participating board of education, municipality or county.[19]

Any board of education may contract or lease to another school board, electronic data processing services, and together they may undertake the joint operation of electronic data processing of their several official records and other information. The records and other information originating with any participating school board in such a contract or lease may be combined, compiled or conjoined with the records and information of all other participating units; however, where the law requires such records to be kept confidential or to be retained by any school board or offices thereof, those records shall be considered to be isolated.[20] These contracts or leases must set forth the charge for all services provided, and in the case of a joint agreement, the proportion of the cost that each party will assume, specifying all the details of the joint management, and any other matters that are considered necessary to be included.[21]

If a controversy arises among the parties (assuming they are all school districts within the same county), the matter shall be referred to the county superintendent for a determination. His decision may be appealed to the commissioner and state board. If the parties are school districts in different counties, the dispute shall be referred to the county superintendents of the counties for joint determination. If they are unable to agree, the matter shall be referred to the commissioner for determination.[22]

Specifications and Plans

Any specifications drawn for purposes of bidding must be drafted in a manner to encourage free, open and competitive bidding. No specifications may require any standard, restriction, condition or limitation not directly related to the purpose, function or activity for which the purchase or contract is made. Nor may specifications require that a bidder be a resident of, or have her place of business located in, the county or school district where the contract is to be performed. Such a residency requirement may be imposed, however, where the physical proximity of the bid-

---

[18]N.J.S.A. 18A:18A-11.

[19]N.J.S.A. 18A:18A-12.

[20]N.J.S.A. 18A:18A-14.2.

[21]N.J.S.A. 18A:18A-14.3

[22]N.J.S.A. 18A:18A-14.

der is necessary for the efficient and economical purchase or performance of the contract.[23]

Specifications drawn for purposes of competitive bidding may not discriminate on the basis of race, religion, or national origin. Specifications may not require the furnishing of "brand name" goods or materials but may require "brand name or equivalent." When the materials to be supplied or purchased are patented or copyrighted, such materials may be purchased by specification when the board resolution authorizing their purchase so indicates. Furthermore, the special need for such patented or copyrighted materials must be directly related to the performance, completion or undertaking of the purpose for which the purchase or contract is made. [24] Three further requirements of specifications for bids are:

1. They must include any option for renewal, extension or release which the board may intend to exercise or require;

2. They must include any terms and conditions necessary for the performance of any extra work; and

3. They must disclose any matter necessary to the substantial performance of the contract.[25]

The purpose of these requirements is to alert all potential bidders to all information which may impact upon their decision to bid and the price that they bid.

Any specification which the board knows will exclude the possibility of performance, bidding or qualification by all bidders but one shall be null and void. Such contract shall be set aside and readvertised.[26]

Public schools are not subject to height, yard, bulk and other municipal zoning requirements, except use restrictions. Proposals for construction or addition of public schools are not subject to final approval by the local planning board.[27] No construction permit shall be issued to a board of education unless the final plans and specifications have been first approved by either the Bureau of Facility Planning Services in the Department of Education or by an appropriately licensed code official employed by any municipality with the written consent of that municipality. Subsequent changes in such specifications must be approved by whichever of those entities originally approved the plans.[28] Additional approval by the Bureau of Facility Planning Services in the Department of Education is required

---

[23]N.J.S.A. 18A:18A-15.

[24]Id.

[25]Id.

[26]Id.

[27]Murnick v. Asbury Park Bd. of Ed., 235 N.J. Super. 225 (App. Div. 1989); certif. den. 118 N.J. 201 (1989).

[28]N.J.S.A. 18A:18A-16, 49; N.J.S.A. 52:27D-130; N.J.A.C. 6:22-1.1 et seq.

when a review for educational adequacy is necessary.

The types of building construction work requiring a review by the Department of Education for educational adequacy are new school buildings including pre-fabricated facilities, additions to existing school buildings, any change involving the total number of instructional spaces or the number of any one kind of instructional space, any change in the dimensions of any instructional space, a change of use that would require physical, mechanical or electrical changes, the utilization of pre-manufactured trailers or vans, and any site or building change for the purpose of making it free and accessible to handicapped persons.[29]

Although a board of education does not need municipal approval for its buildings plans and qualifications, it must refer the proposed capital project for review and recommendation to the local planning board whenever the planning board has adopted any portion of a master plan. If a municipal planning board recommends against the approval of plans and specifications, and files notice with the Bureau of Facility Planning Services for consideration during the plan review process, the Bureau shall not approve the preliminary plans and specifications for educational adequacy until the objections of the planning board have been considered.[30]

A board of education is exempt from paying the municipal fee charged to secure a construction permit. However, the Department of Education or municipality may impose a fee for its review of final plans and specifications.[31]

Public school construction must be done in accordance with the State Uniform Construction Code (U.C.C.), which mandates access for the physically handicapped.[32] The education statutes require that all specifications for bids for the construction, remodeling or renovation of any public building shall provide facilities for physically handicapped persons. The state board has authority to promulgate rules prescribing the kinds, types and quality of such facilities.[33] Additionally, all new construction, and alterations occurring after January 26, 1992 must comply with standards prescribed by the Americans With Disabilities Act.

When the entire cost of the construction, alteration or repair of a building will exceed the amount set forth in or calculated by the commissioner pursuant to *N.J.S.A.* 18A:18A-3, separate plans and specifications must be prepared for each of the following:

- The plumbing and gas fitting work;

---

[29]*N.J.S.A.* 52:27D-130; *N.J.A.C.* 5:23-3.11A(c); *N.J.A.C.* 6:22-1.1.

[30]*N.J.S.A.* 18A:18A-16; *Murnick v. Asbury Park Bd. of Ed.*, *supra*, 235 *N.J. Super.* 225, at 229-230.

[31]*N.J.S.A.* 52:27D-130.

[32]*N.J.A.C.* 6:22-5.1; *N.J.A.C.* 5:23-7.1 *et seq.*

[33]*N.J.S.A.* 18A:18A-17; *N.J.A.C.* 6:22-1.1 *et seq.*

- The heating and ventilating systems and equipment;
- The electrical work, including any electrical power plant;
- The structural steel and ornamental iron work; and
- All other work and materials required for the completion of the project.

The board shall advertise for and receive separate bids for each of these five categories and also bids for all the work and materials required to complete the building to be included in a single overall contract. In the event that the sum total of the amounts bid by the lowest responsible bidder for each category is less than the amount bid by the lowest responsible bidder for all the work and materials, the board shall award separate contracts for each of the categories to the lowest responsible bidder therefor.[34]

Two final requirements for specifications are:

1. They must fix the date before which the work shall be completed, or the number of working days to be allowed for its completion; and

2. They must specify that only products manufactured or grown in the United States be used, wherever available.[35]

Bidding

Except as provided for set-aside contracts permitted by *N.J.S.A.* 18A:18A-55, all advertisements for bids must be published in a newspaper sufficiently in advance of the date fixed for receiving the bids to promote competitive bidding, but in no event less than 10 days prior to such date. The advertisement must designate the manner of submitting the bids and the time and place at which the bids will be received. If bids are received by mail, they shall be sealed and not opened until such time as all bids are unsealed. At that time, the board's contracting agent (secretary, business administrator or business manager) shall publicly unseal all bids and announce the contents. All bidders have the right to be present at this occasion.[36]

No bid shall be accepted which does not conform to the specifications previously announced by the board. The board, furthermore, retains the right to reject *all* bids.[37]

The board may require from any bidder a certificate showing that she owns, leases or controls all the necessary equipment required by the

---

[34]*N.J.S.A.* 18A:18A-18

[35]*N.J.S.A.* 18A:18A-19, 20; see also *K.S.B. Technical Corp. et al. v. North Jersey District Water Supply Commission et al.*, 75 *N.J.*272 (1977).

[36]*N.J.S.A.* 18A:18A-21.

[37]*N.J.S.A.* 18A:18A-22.

specifications. If the bidder is not the owner of such equipment, her certificate should state the source from which the equipment shall be obtained, and shall be accompanied by a certificate from the owner granting the bidder control of the equipment during such time as may be necessary to complete the work.[38]

The board may also require that a bid be accompanied by a guarantee in the amount of 10 percent of the bid, but not in excess of $20,000. The purpose of this guarantee is to insure that, if the contract is awarded to the bidder, she will enter into said contract and will furnish any performance bond (defined in *N.J.A.C.* 6:20-8.4(a)(3)) or other security required. If in connection with a financial grant, any federal law imposes a condition other than the 10 percent—$20,000 guarantee, the federal law prevails.[39] The guarantee may be given by certified check, cashier's check, or by bid bond (defined in *N.J.A.C.* 6:20-8.4(a)(1)).

When a performance bond is required by the advertisement or specifications in a contract, the board shall require from every bidder a certificate from a surety company stating that it will provide the contractor with a bond in such sum as is required. A bidder may offer the bond of an individual, instead of that of a surety company, by submitting with his bid a certificate signed by such individual. The board of education may reject any such bid if it is not satisfied with the sufficiency of the individual surety offered.[40]

Qualifications of Bidders

All persons desiring to bid on any contract requiring public advertisement for bids, the entire cost whereof will exceed $20,000, must first be classified as to the character and amount of public work on which they are qualified to submit bids. The board shall accept bids only from persons qualified in accordance with such classification, who have submitted a statement under oath as required by *N.J.S.A.* 18A:18A-28 within one year preceding the date of the opening of bids for the contract.[41] The statute authorizes the state board to adopt regulations which establish the qualifications of bidders. Such qualifications shall be fixed according to the financial ability and experience of the bidders and the capital and equipment available to them. All qualification regulations must, however, be written in a manner which:

• Will not unnecessarily discourage full, free and open competition;

---

[38]*N.J.S.A.* 18A:18A-23.

[39]*N.J.S.A.* 18A:18A-24.

[40]*N.J.S.A.* 18A:18A-25.

[41]*N.J.S.A.* 18A:18A-32.

- Will not unnecessarily restrict the participation of small business in the bidding process;
- Will not create undue preferences; and
- Will not violate any other provisions of law.

The statute permits the state board to delegate to the Department of the Treasury, or other appropriate state agency, the authority to qualify bidders.[42]

Upon the completion of every contract for public work, the entire cost of which exceeds $20,000, the board of education shall report as to the contractor's performance to the department responsible for qualifying bidders.[43] The board shall also furnish such a report if the contractor is in default. The department responsible for qualifying bidders is then required to consider such reports as a basis for denial of a favorable classification to prospective bidders.[44]

Awarding Contracts

The board of education must award the contract or reject all bids within such time as it has specified in its advertisement for bids, but in no case can it take more than 60 days to reach that decision. The board may, however, hold any bids for consideration for a longer period with the consent of the bidders.

After 10 days from the opening of the bids (Sundays and holidays excepted), all bid security except the security of the 3 apparent lowest responsible bidders shall, if requested, be returned. Within 3 days (Sundays and holidays excepted) after the awarding of the contract and the approval of the contractor's performance bond, the bid security of the remaining unsuccessful bidders shall be returned to them.[45]

The statute mandates that all purchases, contracts or agreements which require public advertisement for bids shall be awarded to the lowest responsible bidder.[46] However, because the board retains the right to reject all bids, only when the board decides to award a contract must it make such an award to the lowest responsible bidder. The term "lowest responsible bidder," as used in the Public School Contracts Law, has not yet received a definitive judicial interpretation. However, the same term was used in the now repealed Section 18-20 of Title 18A. That section contained a clause stating that "all contracts shall be awarded to the lowest responsible bidder." This clause was given a definitive interpretation by

---

[42]N.J.S.A. 18A:18A-27; N.J.A.C. 6:20-7.1 et seq.

[43]N.J.S.A. 18A:18A-15(e).

[44]N.J.S.A. 18A:18A-29; N.J.A.C. 6:20-7.1 et seq.

[45]N.J.S.A. 18A:18A-36.

[46]N.J.S.A. 18A:18A-37.

the New Jersey Supreme Court in the early case of *Schwitzer v. Board of Education*.[47] The Court held that the question of whether the "lowest" bidder was also the "lowest responsible" bidder should be determined by the board of education. However, before disqualifying the lowest bidder, the board should conduct an investigation upon notice and hearing. The lowest bidder is thus entitled to a hearing before the board at which time he can present evidence as to his "responsibility." If the board then decides to reject the lowest bidder as being "irresponsible," such action is final and will not be disturbed by the court unless it appears that it was taken in bad faith or the proofs were of such character as to satisfy reasonable persons of the company's responsibility.[48]

Form of Contracts and Bonds

The Public School Contracts Law requires all contracts for the performance of work or the furnishing of materials, supplies or services to be in writing. The state board is given authority to prescribe the form and manner in which such contracts shall be made and executed, and the form and manner of execution and approval of all guarantee, indemnity, fidelity and other bonds.[49]

A contract for which the total price exceeds $100,000 which involves construction, alteration, repair or maintenance or improvement to buildings may require the withholding of payment from contractors until the satisfactory completion of the job. The contractor may agree to withholding of such payments in the manner prescribed in the contract, or may deposit negotiable bearer bonds with the board of education in an amount equal to that which otherwise would be withheld. These bonds shall be deposited in an interest bearing account, until such time as the contractor fulfills the contract, whereupon the board shall return the bonds plus interest. Any interest accruing on cash payments withheld shall be credited to the board of education.[50]

Such a contract exceeding $100,000 must provide for partial payments to be made at least once each month as the work progresses, unless the contractor shall agree to deposit negotiable bearer bonds as described above.[51] If the contractor does not deposit negotiable bearer bonds and the contract requires the withholding of payments, two percent of the amount due on each partial payment shall be withheld by the board of

---

[47]79 *N.J.L.* 342, 344 (1910).

[48]*Id.* at 344; see also *Rose v. Bd. of Ed. of East Orange*, 39 *N.J. Super.* 565 (Law Div. 1956); *Case Box Lunch, Inc. v. Bd. of Ed. of the City of Trenton*, 72 *S.L.D.* 479.

[49]*N.J.S.A.* 18A:18A-40.

[50]*N.J.S.A.* 18A:18A-40.2.

[51]*N.J.S.A.* 18A:18A-40.1.

education pending completion of the contract.[52]

The statute further authorizes contracts to include liquidated damage clauses. Such damages are those which the parties themselves agree in advance are reasonable in the event of violation of the terms and conditions of the contract.[53]

Contracts Extending Beyond the Fiscal Year

Boards of education are authorized by *N.J.S.A.* 18A:18A-42 to enter into contracts exceeding the fiscal year in the following areas:

- The supplying of:
  a. fuel for heating purposes, for any term not exceeding in the aggregate three years; or
  b. fuel or oil for use of automobiles, auto-buses, motor vehicles or equipment for any term not exceeding in the aggregate, three years.
  c. Thermal energy produced by a cogeneration facility, for use for heating or air conditioning, for any term not exceeding 20 years.
- The plowing and removal of snow and ice for any term not exceeding in the aggregate, three years.
- The collection and disposal of garbage and refuse, for any term not exceeding in the aggregate, three years.
- Data processing service, for any term of not more than five years.
- Insurance, for any term of not more than three years.
- Leasing or servicing of automobiles, motor vehicles, electronic communications equipment, machinery and equipment of every nature and kind, for any term not exceeding in the aggregate, five years, provided, however, that such contracts shall be entered into subject to rules and regulations promulgated by the state board of education.[54]
- The supplying of any product or the rendering of any service by a telephone company which is subject to the jurisdiction of the Board of Public Utilities for a term not exceeding five years.
- Materials, supplies or services that are requested on a recurring basis from year to year, for any term not exceeding in the aggregate two years; however, the contract may be renewed

---

[52]*N.J.S.A.* 18A:18A-40.3.

[53]*N.J.S.A.* 18A:18A-41.

[54]*N.J.A.C.* 6:20-8.2.

yearly for three additional years without further solicitation of bids where the board finds that services are being performed in an effective and efficient manner, or that the materials and supplies continue to meet the original specifications. If a board elects to renew an existing contract, the terms shall remain substantially unchanged; any increase in contract cost over the three year period may not exceed a total of 20 percent over the initial cost.

- Driver education instruction conducted by private, licensed driver education schools, for any term not exceeding an aggregate of three years.

- The performance of work or services or the furnishing of materials, supplies or equipment for the purpose of conserving energy in buildings owned by a board of education, the entire price of which shall be established as a percentage of the resultant savings in energy costs, for a term not to exceed 10 years.

All of these multiyear leases and contracts, except contracts for services rendered by a telephone company, shall contain a clause making them subject to the availability and appropriation annually of sufficient funds as may be required to meet the extended obligation, or contain an annual cancellation clause. However, the following contracts are excepted from this requirement: insurance coverages, insurance consultant or administrative services, participation or membership in a joint self insurance fund, risk management programs or related services of a school board insurance group, participation in an insurance fund established by a county pursuant to *N.J.S.A.* 40A:10-6, contracts for thermal energy, and contracts for the performance of work or services or the furnishing of materials, supplies or equipment to promote energy conservation.

Supervision, Inspection, Condemnation, Rejection

Repairs of all school buildings shall be supervised by the business manager of the district. If the district does not have a business manager, the board of education may delegate such power to any appropriate officer of the board.[55]

The business manager (or if none exists, an appropriate officer employed by the board) shall also have authority to inspect all work, materials or supplies that are furnished to the district under contract. In the event that any of the work, materials or supplies do not conform to the specifications of the contract, they shall be rejected.[56]

---

[55]*N.J.S.A.* 18A:18A-43.
[56]*N.J.S.A.* 18A:18A-44.

Sale of Personal Property

A board of education may, by resolution, authorize the sale of its personal property not needed for school purposes. If the estimated fair value of the property exceeds the amount set forth in or calculated by the commissioner pursuant to *N.J.S.A.* 18A:18A-3 in any one sale, and it is neither livestock nor perishable goods, it shall be sold at public sale (auction) to the highest bidder. Notice of the date, time and place of the public sale, together with a description of the items to be sold and the conditions of sale, shall be published once in a newspaper. Such sale shall be held not less than seven nor more than 14 days after the publication of the notice thereof.[57]

The board may reject all bids at a public sale if it determines that such rejection is in the public interest. In any case where the board has rejected all bids, it may readvertise the personal property for subsequent public sale. If, at the second sale, it elects to reject all bids again, it may then sell such personal property at a private sale without additional public notice. However, the negotiated price at such private sale cannot be less than the highest price of any bid rejected at the preceding two public sales.[58]

Personal property may be sold to the United States, the State of New Jersey, another board of education or to any body politic by private sale without advertising for bids. Furthermore, if no bids are received at a public sale, the property may then be sold at a private sale without further publication or notice thereof. In no event, however, may it be sold at less than its estimated fair value. Estimated fair value means the market value less the cost to the board of education of continued storage or maintenance of the property.[59]

The board is also authorized to sell personal property at private sale without advertising for bids if its estimated fair value does not exceed the amount set forth in or calculated by the commissioner pursuant to *N.J.S.A.* 18A:18A-3, or if it is either livestock or perishable goods.[60]

Miscellaneous Provisions

No board of education shall be subject to any legal action for damages for actions taken by virtue of the provisions of the Public School Contracts Law.[61]

The provisions of the Public School Contracts Law do not apply to contracts for the transportation of pupils to and from schools. Pupil transportation contracts continue to be regulated by Chapter 39 of Title 18A.[62]

---

[57]*N.J.S.A.* 18A:18A-45.

[58]*Id.*

[59]*Id.*

[60]*Id.*

[61]*N.J.S.A.* 18A:18A-46.

[62]*N.J.S.A.* 18A:18A-49.1; *N.J.A.C.* 6:21-1 *et seq.*

A board of education may, by resolution, establish a minority business enterprise set-aside program, a women's business enterprise set-aside program and/or a small business enterprise set-aside program. In authorizing any one of these programs, the board must establish a goal of setting aside a certain percentage of the dollar value of total procurements to be awarded as set-aside contracts to the particular enterprise.[63] The terms "minority business enterprise", "women's business enterprise", "small business enterprise", and "set-aside contract", are defined by statute along with other terms pertinent to set-aside programs.[64] The Public School Contracts Law applies to set-aside contracts except where it is superseded by the particular provisions of the statutes governing set-aside programs.[65]

A board which establishes a set-aside program shall designate that the contract or other means of procurement of goods, services, equipment or construction shall be awarded to the particular type of enterprise, if the board is likely to receive bids from at least two of the appropriate enterprises at a fair and reasonable price. All advertisements for bids must be published in at least one newspaper which will best provide notice of the advertisement to the appropriate category of enterprise sufficiently in advance of the date fixed for receiving the bids to promote competitive bidding, but not less than 10 days prior to that date.[66] If the board determines that two bids cannot be obtained, the board may withdraw the designation of the set-aside contract and solicit bids on an unrestricted basis. If the board determines that the acceptance of the lowest responsible bid will result in the payment of an unreasonable price, the board must reject all bids and withdraw the designation of the set-aside contract, with notice to the appropriate enterprises.[67] Any board of education which has established a set-aside program must prepare an annual report by January 31 describing the board's efforts in attaining its set-aside goals.[68]

Other Statutory Provisions

Although for the most part, the Public School Contracts Law governs school district business practices, school board members should also be aware of several other important statutes.

- The Law Against Discrimination applies to all contracts for the construction, alteration or repair of any building or public work

---

[63]N.J.S.A. 18A:18A-52
[64]N.J.S.A. 18A:18A-51
[65]N.J.S.A. 18A:18A-54
[66]N.J.S.A. 18A:18A-55
[67]N.J.S.A. 18A:18A-56
[68]N.J.S.A. 18A:18A-57

or for the acquisition of materials, equipment, supplies or services. The board must include verbatim, in its bid specifications and contracts, three paragraphs which are set out in the statute. These paragraphs require that:

1. The contractor will not discriminate against any employee or applicant for employment because of age, race, creed, color, national origin, ancestry, marital status or sex, and the contractor must take affirmative action to ensure that such applicants are recruited and employed without regard to these characteristics;

2. The contractor, in all advertisements for employees, must state that all qualified applicants will receive consideration for employment without regard to age, race, creed, color, national origin, ancestry, marital status or sex; and

3. The contractor will send to each labor union with which she has a collective bargaining agreement a notice advising the union of the contractor's commitments under the Law Against Discrimination.[68]

- A corporate bidder for public school contracts must submit with its bid a list of the names and addresses of all stockholders owning 10 percent or more of its stock. If the bidder is a partnership, it must submit a similar list of those owning a 10 percent or greater interest in the partnership. Since a board may not award a contract to any corporation or partnership failing to comply with this requirement, it should be included in the bid specifications.[70]

- The New Jersey Prevailing Wage Act requires the board to ascertain from the Commissioner of Labor and Industry the prevailing wage rate in the locality for each craft or trade needed to perform the contract and to specify in the contract that workers employed by the contractor shall be paid not less than the prevailing wage rate.[71]

- Boards are required to make sure that bills are paid properly and that no bill is paid unless it is authorized by law and the rules of the board, is fully itemized and verified, has been duly audited as required by law, has been presented to and approved by the board at a meeting, or presented to, and approved by a person designated by the board for that purpose, and that the amount required is available for the purpose.[72] Every bill ex-

---

[69]N.J.S.A. 10:5-33; N.J.A.C. 17:27-1.1 et seq.

[70]N.J.S.A. 52:25-24.2.

[71]N.J.S.A. 34:11-56.25 et seq.

[72]N.J.S.A. 18A:19-2.

ceeding $150, except for payrolls and debt service, must be verified by affidavit or a signed declaration that the bill is correct, that the articles have been furnished or services rendered, and that no bonus has been received or given.[73]

- It is the board's responsibility to designate the depository of school funds.[74]

- Every local board of education, by means of a report of the board secretary, must make a detailed report to the county superintendent of its financial transactions and of any other matters in such manner and form as are prescribed by the commissioner.[75] The state board shall prescribe a uniform system of double entry bookkeeping consistent with generally accepted accounting principles and financial accounting terminology and classifications. By July 1 of 1995, all districts must conform to the prescribed system of bookkeeping.[76]

- The board may publish an annual report of the conditions of the schools and the finances of the district.[77] The board may also establish and operate petty cash funds pursuant to state board rules.[78] All funds derived from athletic events or other activities of pupil organizations must be administered, expended and accounted for pursuant to state board rules.[79]

- Finally, the school board must cause an annual audit of its accounts and financial transactions to be made by its accountant. This audit must be completed not later than four months after the end of the school fiscal year.[80] Within five days of the submission of this report of the audit to the board, the accountant must file two duplicate copies in the office of the commissioner. The commissioner must then publish annually a summary of the recommendations made by the accountant for each school district and the steps which have been taken in each district for their implementation.[81]

---

[73]*N.J.S.A.* 18A:19-3.

[74]*N.J.S.A.* 18A:17-34.

[75]*N.J.S.A.* 18A:17-10.

[76]*N.J.S.A.* 18A:4-14, 14.1; *N.J.A.C.* 6:20-2.1 *et seq.*

[77]*N.J.S.A.* 18A:11-2.

[78]*N.J.S.A.* 18A:19-13; *N.J.A.C.* 6:20-2.10.

[79]*N.J.S.A.* 18A:19-14.

[80]*N.J.S.A.* 18A:23-1; *N.J.A.C.* 6:20-2.1 *et seq.*; 6:20-2A-1 *et seq.*

[81]*N.J.S.A.* 18A:23-3.

The New Jersey Court System

SUPREME COURT

Final Appeal In:

Chief Justice and 6 Associate Justices. Initial term of 7 years with tenure on reappointment. Mandatory retirement at 70.

1. Constitutional questions
2. Issues where dissent in Appellate Division
3. Capital causes
4. Certification
5. In such cases as provided by law

SUPERIOR COURT

402 Judges authorized. Term, tenure, and retirement same as Supreme Court.

359 appointed. The Court's 15 vicinages, each administered by an Assignment Judge, carry out the court functions in the State's 21 counties

APPELLATE DIVISION

During the 1988-89 court year, there were 28 judges in the Appellate Division, each chosen by the Chief Justice from one of the Superior Court's trial divisions.

Appeals From:

1. Law and Chancery Division
2. Tax Court
3. State Administrative Agencies
4. As provided by law

LAW

CRIMINAL DIVISION

1. General jurisdiction in all criminal cases

CIVIL DIVISION

1. General jurisdiction in all civil cases
2. Appeals from Municipal Courts
3. Probate

SPECIAL CIVIL PART

1. Contract, penalty, and tort actions up to $5,000
2. Landlord and tenant actions
3. Small Claims up to $1,000

CHANCERY

GENERAL EQUITY DIVISION

1. General jurisdiction in equity cases
2. Probate

FAMILY DIVISION

1. Juvenile delinquency
2. Dissolution (Matrimonial)
3. Non-Dissolution (Domestic Relations)
4. Adoptions
5. Juvenile and family in crisis

MUNICIPAL COURTS

365 Judges. Term 3 years

1. Traffic and motor vehicle violations
2. Ordinance violations
3. Disorderly persons offenses
4. Fish, game, and navigation violations
5. Other specified crimes
6. Probable cause hearings on indictable offenses

SURROGATES' OFFICE

21 Surrogates. Elected. Term 5 years.

1. Uncontested probate matters
2. Deputy clerk of the Superior Court for probate matters

TAX COURT

9 Judges authorized. Term same as Superior Court except for the 1979 appointments. Tenure and retirement same as Supreme Court. The Tax Court reviews the determinations of agencies and officials charged with administration of:

1. Local property tax assessments
2. State tax assessments
3. Equalization tables promulgated by the director of the Division of Taxation or the County Board of Taxation

The United States Court System

U.S. Supreme Court

Chief Justice and 8 Associate Justices.

Any six constitute a quorum.

Reviews Courts of Appeals cases in certain circumstances.

13 U.S. Courts of Appeals

Number of judges ranges from 6 to 28.

Chief judge is the circuit judge who is senior in active service and under 70 years of age.

Hears appeals from U.S. District Courts.

94 U.S. District Courts

Conducts trials where:

Matter arises under U.S. law or U.S. Constitution.

Parties are citizens of different states and amount exceeds $50,000.

APPENDIX

An Overview of the New Jersey and Federal Judicial Systems

The usual process of resolving school law disputes by appeal to the commissioner, the state board, and the appellate courts is outlined in Chapter 1. Local boards of education, however, are often involved in litigation which arises through other court process. They are also involved in disputes which fall under the jurisdiction of state administrative agencies other than the Department of Education. For this reason, a basic knowledge of these agencies and of the state and federal court systems will prove beneficial.

Boards of education are frequently involved in proceedings before the Public Employment Relations Commission. PERC's quasi-judicial jurisdiction extends to unit determination and recognition questions, unfair practice charges, and scope of negotiations determinations.[1]

Boards of education may also become involved in disputes over the eligibility of former employees for unemployment benefits under the Unemployment Compensation Law.[2] Local appeal tribunals initially hear cases involving unemployment benefit disputes; appeals from these tribunals may be taken to the Board of Review.[3] Similarly, the state Division of Workers' Compensation contains the administrative machinery to hear cases involving job-related injuries.[4]

Cases involving boards of education also may arise in the state Division on Civil Rights. This agency is empowered to hear cases involving allegations of discrimination based on race, creed, color, national origin, ancestry, age, marital status, sex, liability for service in the Armed Forces of the United States, and disability.[5] At the federal level, the Equal Employment Oppor-

---

[1]For a complete discussion of PERC and the Public Employment Relations Law, see Volume 6 of the *School Board Library* series, Wary, Strassman and Vogt, *The Public Employment Relations Law*, (NJSBA, 1991).

[2]*N.J.S.A.* 43:21-1 *et seq.*

[3]*N.J.S.A.* 43:21-6, 10.

[4]*N.J.S.A.* 34:1A-5.1, 12.

[5]*N.J.S.A.* 10:5-6, 4.1.

tunities Commission exists to hear similar claims of discrimination in employment practices.[6]

Appeals from the decisions of all New Jersey administrative agencies may be taken to the Appellate Division of Superior Court. (Refer to the diagram of the New Jersey court system on page 189). The Appellate Division also hears appeals from the major trial-level courts in the state. The most important trial-level courts, for school board purposes, are the Law Division of Superior Court, and the Chancery Division of Superior Court. The Law Division of Superior Court has jurisdiction in civil and criminal cases arising in the county; where to file such a suit is largely a tactical consideration for the plaintiff's attorney. Examples of civil cases that may be heard by the Law Division of Superior Court are the following:

- Personal injury suits against boards of education;
- Litigation arising from construction and commercial contracts entered into by boards; and
- Litigation arising from the interpretation of collective bargaining agreements.

The Chancery Division of Superior Court is also a trial-level court, but its jurisdiction lies mainly in general equity matters. The term "equity" is best understood by referring to the type of relief the plaintiff is seeking. If the plaintiff seeks an order compelling the defendant to perform some action or refrain from performing some action (as opposed to an order compelling the defendant to pay a sum of money), the plaintiff is seeking a remedy in equity. For example, a suit seeking an injunction compelling striking employees to return to work would constitute an action in equity and would, therefore, be filed in the Chancery Division of Superior Court. Another example of an action in equity would be a suit seeking a court order compelling a defaulting contractor to finish construction of a building. (A suit against the same contractor for the payment of monetary damages would constitute an "action at law.") The Chancery Division of Superior Court also has jurisdiction of trials where the plaintiff seeks to enjoin arbitration proceedings under a collective bargaining agreement, or where the plaintiff desires to have the arbitrator's decision overruled.

Board members should also be aware of the jurisdiction of the municipal courts (cases involving traffic offenses, minor crimes, and ordinance violations).

Although the litigation involving New Jersey school districts arises primarily in the state court system, there are instances when actions are initiated in the federal courts. The United States Constitution states: "The

---

[6]Title VII of Civil Rights Act of 1964, as amended, 42 *U.S.C.A.* 200(e) *et seq.*

judicial power of the United States shall be vested in one supreme Court, and in such inferior Courts as the Congress may from time to time ordain and establish."[7] Under this constitutional grant of authority, Congress has seen fit to create 94 federal judicial districts in the United States.[8] A United States District Court sits in each of the 94 federal judicial districts. The United States District Courts are the trial-level courts within the federal system.

The boundaries of one of the federal judicial districts are the same as those of the State of New Jersey; thus, there exists a United States District Court for the District of New Jersey. Congress has mandated that the President shall appoint 17 district judges for the federal judicial district of New Jersey.[9] Court sessions are held in Camden, Newark and Trenton.[10]

The federal district courts have original jurisdiction of civil cases arising under the federal Constitution or federal statutes including cases arising under the Civil Rights Acts and the Bankruptcy Act.[11] Also, the federal district courts hear cases when the parties are citizens of different states, and the amount in controversy exceeds $50,000.[12]

An appeal of a United States District Court decision may be taken to the United States Court of Appeals for the circuit in which the district court is located. Congress has created 13 circuits, most of which comprise several states, and the District of Columbia. New Jersey, Pennsylvania, Delaware and the Virgin Islands constitute the Third Circuit.[13] The Court of Appeals for the Third Circuit sits in Philadelphia. The President is required to appoint 14 judges to sit on the Third Circuit.[14]

The federal court system's highest court is, of course, the United States Supreme Court. Appeals of the decisions of the Courts of Appeals may be taken to the Supreme Court on a limited basis.[15]

---

[7] U. S. Const., art. 3, sec. 1.

[8] 28 *U.S.C.A.* 81 *et seq.*

[9] 28 *U.S.C.A.* 133.

[10] 28 *U.S.C.A.* 110.

[11] 28 *U.S.C.A.* 1331, 28 *U.S.C.A.* 1343; 28 *U.S.C.A.* 1334.

[12] 28 *U.S.C.A.* 1332.

[13] 28 *U.S.C.A.* 41.

[14] 28 *U.S.C.A.* 44

[15] 28 *U.S.C.A.* 1254.

INDEX
References are to Pages

For Civil Actions, 31, 125
Life Insurance (Employee), 121-122
Property Loss and Damage, 50

INTEREST RATES
In General, 157-159

**INTERSTATE COMPACT
FOR EDUCATION**
In General, 14-15

JANITORS
Reduction in Staff, 117
Tenure, 117

JOINTURE COMMISSION
Children with Disabilities, 27, 67-69

JUDGES
In General, 189-190

LABOR
Compliance with N.J. Prevailing Wage
   Act, 187

LAW ENFORCEMENT OFFICERS
Employment, 61

LEAVE OF ABSENCE
In General, 123-124, 129
Attendance at Legislative Sessions, 135
Attendance at Meetings of Chosen
   Freeholders, 135
Family Leave Act, 129

LECTURES
In General, 28

LIABILITY (SCHOOL BOARD)
For Actions of Board Members, 26, 31, 185
For Actions of Employees, 61, 125
For Dangerous Conditions on School
   Property, 51, 61
For Discrimination, 53
For Pupil Injury, 61
For Safety Patrols, 60-61

LIBRARIES
County Superintendent's Duties, 11
Use of School Property, 51

LOCAL EDUCATIONAL INSTITUTIONS
Establishment of by Legislature, 13-15

MINUTES (BOARD MEETING)
In General, 31-32, 106, 140-141

MUNICIPAL TAX COLLECTOR
In General, 111

MUSEUMS
Board Maintenance of, 28, 63

NARCOTICS AND ALCOHOL (USE)
Mandated Instruction, 62

NEGLECTED CHILDREN
In General, 52, 152

**NEW JERSEY SCHOOL BOARDS
ASSOCIATION**
Dues, 13
Statute Establishing, 13

NIGHT SCHOOLS
(see Evening Schools)

NOMINATIONS (SCHOOL BOARD)
(see also Chapter 11, School Elections)
In General, 107-108, 160, 161
Petitions, 107-108, 160, 161
Procedures, 107-108, 160-161

NON-PUBLIC SCHOOLS
Auxilliary Service for Pupils, 70
Contracts With Private Vocational Schools, 28
Remedial Services for Pupils, 70
Transfer of Pupils, 53
Transportation of Pupils, 37, 55, 69, 70
Tuition for Sending of Children With
   Disabilities, 67-70

NOTICE
(see Advertising)

NURSERY (SCHOOL)
(see also Health and Safety)
Board Authority to Establish, 27

OATHS AND PLEDGES
Before Local Board, 15
Before State Board of Education, 8
Pledge to U.S. Flag, 101
Secretary's Duties, 107

ORGANIZATION (SCHOOL DISTRICT)
*(see Chapter 2, The Legal Structure of Local
   School Districts)*
(see also Chapter 10, School Budgets)

PARENTAL LIABILITY
For Correction of Health Defects of Child, 58
For Truancy of Child, 53

PARENTAL RIGHTS
(see Children with Disabilities)

PARKS AND PLAYGROUNDS
In General, 50

PENALTIES AGAINST BOARDS
(see also Liability (School Board))
In General, 51, 53, 56

PENSIONS
Granted by Board, 122-123
Rights of Employees In Dissolved
   Districts, 116
State Teachers' Pension and Annuity Fund,
   37, 40, 41, 42, 45, 122-123
Tax-sheltered Annuities, 133-134

PERC
*(see Public Employment Relations
   Commission)*